Advance Praise

"*Relatable* is a brilliant, encouraging, revealing, informative and fascinating look at the history up to current times of relationships between men and women in church. I love Vicky's humour, which brings a lightness to what can be a very intense subject. I will be referring back to it, as on a first read there is simply too much to take it all in. Very excited to see this book out there and cannot recommend it strongly enough!"

Katharine Welby-Roberts, speaker and author of *I Thought There Would be Cake*

"Through wit, candour, and fresh research, Vicky Walker gives us not another how-to-get-hitched book, but a snapshot of varied opinions on modern day love, partnering and matrimony. The results are enlightening, sometimes concerning, and always educational, providing a necessary critique of much relationship advice and the distortions they can carry. *Relatable* will be a helpful resource for church leaders wanting to really know the lived experience of the single, newly coupled, and the rest of us navigating modern relationships."

Sheridan Voysey, writer, speaker, broadcaster, and author of *The Making of Us: Who We Can Become When Life Doesn't Go as Planned*

"Of all of the confusing things I experienced growing up 'on fire for Jesus,' the way faith leaders talked about love and relationships was among the blurriest. Sexual purity seemed to be oddly conjoined with 'real' faith, and this led, for me, to all kinds of shame and fear and unkindness. *Relatable* offers a way through all of the misinformation and slanted theology about love, sex, and marriage present in Christian culture. Drawing from a deep well of resources, including church history, cultural constructs, and a broad range of interviews, Vicky Walker helps readers think through the complexities of relationships in a way that leads to wholeness."

Addie Zierman, writer and author of *When We Were On Fire*

"So many books about Christian dating paint a simplistic, narrow and formulaic fairy tale of what love and life are supposed to be. But *Relatable* does the opposite – and that's what makes this book so remarkably refreshing. In portraying the messiness of people's vast and varied stories and experiences of singleness, dating, marriage and beyond, Vicky shows that there is no one-size-fits-all approach. This is a story the Church needs to be telling, and in so doing, liberating people from the pain that can often arise from unrealistic relationship expectations. This is more than a dating manual, but a deep dive into the history, sociology and story of real-life love."

Chine McDonald, writer, broadcaster and speaker

"If you're a Christian woman like me, chances are you'll find Vicky Walker's new book aptly named. *Relatable*, an inside-look at how Christians in the UK and beyond navigate sex, relationships, singleness, having children, not having children, and much more had me "mm-hmm"ing and "that's right"ing the whole way through."

Linda Kay Klein, author of *Pure: Inside the Evangelical Movement that Shamed a Generation of Young Women and How I Broke Free,* and founder of Break Free Together

"I can't stop telling people about this book! I think it is brilliant. For too long Christian culture's neat and tidy answers to relationships and dating have left women and men ill-equipped to deal with the reality, particularly as the waters are muddied further by technology and social media. Vicky's wisdom, insight and humour make this book a must read for Christians struggling with dating and relationships, for Christians who haven't struggled, and for church leaders. Giving practical advice and honestly grappling with the challenges, this book is incredibly well researched, with a survey of nearly 1500 Christians forming the basis of Vicky's analysis. I cannot recommend it highly enough!"

Natalie Collins, feminist activist and author of *Out of Control: Couples, Conflict and the Capacity for Change*

"Finding a mate in the age of textlationships and Tinder can be confusing, and if you're also bringing a religious faith to the party, the crossed wires and complications can just multiply. Vicky Walker's thoughtful, evidence-based and frequently funny tour of singleness and relationships isn't just a brilliant guide for people seeking love, but also for churches wanting to connect with the real lives of single people."

Simon Jenkins, *Ship of Fools*

"Debunking our assumptions about the biblical and historical basis for much Christian teaching on sex, Vicky Walker offers a brave and exciting alternative. *Relatable* is grounded in what the Bible really does and doesn't say, the realities of the world which we actually inhabit now, and the lived experience of faithful twenty-first century Christians. The result is a profoundly holy and highly practical steer through the dilemmas of male-female relating. It reads like great advice from a wise friend with a very cheeky sense of humour. Intelligent, refreshing and searingly honest, unlike many offerings on the same theme this book will do more good than harm."

The Revd Rosemary Lain-Priestley, author and Researcher and Adviser to the Bishop of London on Policy and Strategy

"Vicky has dealt with a tricky topic – relationships – gently and with humour, drawing upon a wide range of Christian relationship texts, challenging some of the more damaging ones. Vicky's book draws together insights for all kinds of male-female relationships. For churches seeking to promote healthy relationships, including for singletons (going beyond 'finding a partner' which seems to be the mission of most churches). Vicky emphasises the need to develop healthy adult relationships, emotional health, and good boundaries, in all situations, including within the digital environment. She thankfully challenges the notion that technology is the cause of all relational ills, providing guidance on how to enjoy the best, and, as with any form of communication, avoid the worst."

Dr Bex Lewis, Senior Lecturer in Digital Marketing and author of *Raising Children in a Digital Age*

Relatable

Exploring God,
love & connection
in the age of choice

Vicky Walker

malcolm down

PUBLISHING

'For all those who kept on, and for all those who couldn't.'

23 22 21 20 19   7 6 5 4 3 2 1

First published 2019 by Malcolm Down Publishing Ltd.
www.malcolmdown.co.uk

British Library Cataloguing in Publication Data
A catalogue record for this book is available from the British Library.

ISBN 978-1-912863-12-9

Cover design by Micah Purnell
Art direction by Sarah Grace

Printed in the UK

Contents

Welcome to Relatable

Christians, love, sex, marriage, and relationships: has anything ever been more straightforward? From Adam, Eve, and all that patriarchal polygamy to contemporary dilemmas over swiping right, 'headship', dating outside the faith, and sexting, opinions on 'what God wants' vary wildly. Whether single, dating, married, or anywhere in between, how Christians talk about men and women, and how real-life relationships unfold can be worlds – or heavens – apart.

Relatable looks at what Christians believe about relationships between women and men across the spectrum of faith, and how expectations have changed – or not. Little things like:

- Where ideas about women and men come from.
- The role of science, history and sociology in shaping modern faith, and what's influencing the future.
- How technology is bringing us closer than ever before to creating our own realities and introducing new moral dilemmas.
- What people *really* think, and how they live and love.

Powering the book are the stats and stories of the exclusive Real Life Love survey, a collection of nearly 1,500 people's experiences of relationships and Christian culture I developed to understand what's really happening. Only one-in-five who responded said they agree with Christian culture's predominant messages about relationships, so there's lots to discuss. (You can read more about the who, what and why of the survey at the end of the book in the 'Relatable Resources' section). Bless all of you beautiful people who shared your lives and stories. With questions covering the influence of faith on relationship decisions, to non-negotiables in seeking a partner, to sex, dysfunction, singleness, marriage and boundaries, to advice that helped and advice that definitely didn't, responses were frank, honest, and often wise.

And then there are the practicalities: How dating has changed, and what marriage is like after 'I do'. How to develop discernment while navigating a way through centuries of belief. How ideals might not transfer to real life, or whether there is such a thing as 'Christian marriage'. Why you might have been told you're 'called to singleness' or that God will provide the perfect partner if you just keep waiting. Who's having sex and who has vowed they never will. And why all of this is still such a big deal.

If you're new to the strange world of Christians and relationships, don't panic. Feel free to peer in cautiously, marvel at the strangeness of it all, and stop for a nap/strong drink whenever it gets too much. (The same advice applies to all readers. And most definitely to the author.) I come to the project with my own stories, experiences and filters, of course. I am working out life and love along with everyone else and have been writing about, studying and speaking about the mystifications of Christianity and relationships for several years. This has generally prompted more mystification, questions and wonderings. By taking a trip through the varied landscape of Christian relationships between women and men, sharing thoughts and learning from real experiences, together we should find an honest and hopeful take on real-life love. Thanks for jumping in.

Chapter One
Modern Love:
How Did We Get Here?

Way back in the simpler times of 1983 all David Bowie could sing about was getting to the church on time, and *Modern Love* was his transport of choice. He only just made it. Traditional Christian weddings in England and Wales were falling out of favour but still holding on. The puff-sleeved perfection of a certain royal wedding a couple of years earlier hadn't hurt their appeal (back when Charles and Diana looked set for happy ever after . . .). It was the same year when little-known Denzel Washington, Vladimir Putin, and Hulk Hogan all married for the first time (this would be a different book, and probably a reality series, had that been the same ceremony). Times were changing, as the pressure to marry in church and have an – at least superficially – Christian wedding was dropping off. Civil ceremonies had first edged ahead in popularity in the UK in 1976,[1] and after some vying for the top spot, by 1992 finally outnumbered faith-based ones without looking back (1983 was a tightly-run but ultimately winning year for the Lord.[2] Praise be). If you were getting married from the early nineties onwards, you were statistically more likely to have a civil ceremony than plighting your troth 'according to God's holy law'.[3] By 2014 religious weddings accounted for just over a quarter of the marriages performed that year in England and Wales.[4] 2016 research indicates a decline in faith ceremonies in the US too, dropping from four-in-ten in 2009 to just one-in-four.[5] Getting divine approval on your love life was officially going out of fashion.

Bowie's take on modern love was pre-internet too. The first .com domain was registered in 1985, though the concept was slow to take off.[6] By the time religious weddings fell behind civil ones in 1992 fewer than 15,000 .com websites had been created.[7] Clicking to meet the person of your dreams was pure science fiction, although curious computer scientists had started testing automated matchmaking possibilities as far back as the late 1950s[8] (Mr Putin was not thought to have been involved). The first text was sent in 1992; it was another 20 years before couples began proudly declaring they'd met their soulmates via their smartphones. Stories of 'Tinder weddings' began hitting the news a couple of years after the invention of the app in 2012. Of the close to 300 million domain names now registered globally, over a thousand are dating websites registered in the UK, with estimates of 2,500 in the US, and up to 8,000 globally.[9]

The spiritual climate has shifted too. Church attendance is no longer a necessity to avoid social ostracism (rather, the opposite could be true), and it has slipped persistently down the list of likely places to meet a life partner. Back in the 1940s more than one-in-ten Americans first encountered their significant other in their place of worship; in the early 1990s, just before online dating became a thing, it was 7%, and by 2010 it was just 2%.[10] (It's unclear whether the introduction of smoke machines in worship services was a factor in the decline but it certainly didn't help visibility.)

There are social as well as technological changes to consider too. Despite one or two tiny cultural differences between the

UK and the USA – just one-in-five Americans has no religion[11] compared to over half of the UK[12] – there are many similar social trends. The dwindling influence of family in the 20th century is a factor – the 1940 figure of almost a quarter of Americans meeting a partner directly through their family was down to 7% by 2010.[13] Changes in work and education have had an impact too; the practice of barring women from employment once they married continued into the 1970s in some places, forcing women to choose between employment and matrimony (though it often wasn't a choice). More women now pursue further education. Before 1920 women weren't allowed to join or graduate from Oxford University, yet by 2017 50% of Oxford students were female.[14] (In a gender split closely mirroring the church, recent data showed 66% of students at King's College in London were female.)[15] All of these trends affected how people met, how their aspirations were shaped, and what options were available to them.

In the 20th century people generally married someone close to them – from school, church, or their neighbourhood. Sometimes the actual boy or girl next door. Falling under the catchy name of residential propinquity, research showed the closer people were physically over time, the more chance there was of them forming friendships or romantic relationships (which is why I wrote this all down and didn't come around to your house to explain in person). This proved largely reliable until the internet arrived and changed what proximity could look like. How marriage was viewed and understood has changed frequently, having evolved from a survival necessity in ancient times to a still-debated romantic partnership today. It has often represented the influence of God via the church, and was a life stage that was assumed and expected for anyone entering adulthood. People married younger, too (obviously not younger than in Bible times, but we'll come to that later). The average age of marriage in England and Wales in 1973 was 26 for women and 28 for men; by 2013 it was 34 for women and 36 for men.[16] In 1950s America, women were marrying at the age of 20; by 2017 the average age was 27.[17] Over centuries life expectancy increased as social conditions, nutrition and medicine improved. A 2012 UK Government report noted that most causes of death recorded even less than a century earlier would now be classed as preventable[18] (which is probably why you don't hear many stories of typhoid ruining promising dates in Stockport McDonald's these days).

The average length of a marriage has varied throughout history, affected by factors like life expectancy (you'd be lucky to see your mid-30s in Tudor times, even more so if married to a king; around 950 years if you were in the Methuselah clan).[19] Marriages in Colonial America have been calculated at under 12 years because of the life-shortening conditions,[20] though it's worth noting the average length of marriages that ended in divorce in England and Wales in 2014 was 11.7 years.[21] The same studies showed divorce – first legalised in UK courts in 1857, though with all advantages tipped towards the husband, and reaching a peak in the 1970s after laws were liberalised and equalised between spouses – declining for the first time in 2009.[22] This downturn has been attributed to factors ranging from cohabitation replacing marriage, couples marrying after 'testing' their relationship for longer (including through living together), and marriage becoming the choice for couples more likely to stay together anyway.[23] Organisations promoting marriage bemoaned cohabitation as a worrying precursor of future breakdowns as couples would lose the skills or will to maintain marriages indefinitely. Traditional Christians, who have generally steered away from pre-marital sex, cohabitation, adultery and divorce throughout the centuries – at least, officially – have seen their influence on society dwindle.

We Are Gathered Here Together...

Which takes us to church, metaphorically at least. News reports regularly suggest the decline of the western church in varying degrees and for all kinds of reasons, not least the on-going discussions of broadening marriage to same-sex couples. The gender ratio in the UK church is often discussed with concern, with current estimates averaging out at approximately two women to every man.[24] (No official allocation system exists. Thus far.) Around the world, the religiosity of men compared to women is much debated, but an evenly matched, gender balanced church remains elusive. The statistics point to a church shifting in shape, size and age. A 2017 report suggested just 7% of London residents were regular Sunday churchgoers.[25] In 2010, the Church of England reported the average age of churchgoers in the UK was 61, with the young cool kids in London (average age 54) balancing out some of the rural congregations with an average age of 65 (for perspective, the average age of a British person at the same date was 48).[26] Research on singleness and the UK church published in 2015 suggested between a quarter and a third of regular congregations, varying by denomination, were single (though the research also highlighted different categories of singleness, including 'never married' and 'previously married').[27] The research also recorded the tendency of churchgoers to most notice people like them – theoretically suitable matches - or their absence. A particularly interesting development has been the increasing departure of women from churches, part of a group researchers from the Barna Group call people who 'love Jesus but not the church'.[28] Of the one-in-ten of the population the group includes, over 60% are women. They often maintain a strong personal faith, with orthodox views about God and Christianity; women who still pray and practise their faith but outside of traditional structures.

Times are changing. Bewildered western Christians find themselves at the mercy of the fluctuations of society, the changing roles and nature of marriage, and the shifting influence of the church, wondering if they can pick up an ancient Middle Eastern text and find everything they need to know about how to meet a partner they like, live a rewarding single life, or something, *anything*, in between in the 21st century. So, let's look at how personal relationships have changed over time, starting with a brief history of how love, sex and marriage interacted with the church.

Two Become One. Or More.

The popular perception of Christian marriage is a form and practice barely changed since times BC, morphing neatly from Adam and Eve to the nuclear family of the 1950s (ignoring the awkward polygamy-of-the-patriarchs phase) until recent decades of change and uncertainty. This is understandable, but apparently wishful thinking. According to social historian Stephanie Coontz, marriage has always been in flux. There has never been a 'golden age' of marriage, she claims, but rather, every era has adapted the institution - and complained about its demise or corruption in some form.[29] Additionally, most permutations of personal relationships regarded as modern have some precedent: babies born out of wedlock, the prevalence of stepfamilies, and the frequency of divorce have all fluctuated in popularity and practice since ancient times. They are not a sign of changing moral standards in modernity. In different societies, even now, what is perceived as a 'marriage crisis' varies. Both low birth rates and overpopulation, and delayed marriage and child marriage have all been recent concerns around the world, and illustrate how localised and contrary worries can be. Some of these have involved Christian communities or at least occurred in traditionally Christian countries.

There have been cultural mismatches between the UK and US. Programmes like the abstinence-based 'True Love Waits' were originated (let's not say conceived) by conservative Christian groups in America to persuade teenagers to avoid all sexual contact outside of marriage, and received federal funding to expand into schools. The UK equivalent, the Silver Ring Thing (the ring symbolic of a pledge to remain abstinent until marriage) was considerably more niche. It resulted in a lost court case for the organisers when their daughter was refused permission to wear her ring at school, and received negative publicity when their media consultant was identified in the press as an ex-lingerie model and TV extra of fluctuating age, with a criminal conviction, a hard-to-control passion for Michael Jackson and connections to far right groups[30] (note for readers who aren't Christians: this is rare, and only happens in about... maybe 30% of churches. Kidding. At least I hope I am).

(Kind of) Like a Virgin

For Christians in times past, virginity was a deadly serious matter. Old Testament rules about girls (funnily no mention of boys) have informed centuries of expectation about parentally managed chastity, forbidden sexual activity (sex, it seems, was only ever done to female virgins), and community-regulated female bodies. Have a look at Deuteronomy 22's laws concerning sexual purity to see just what you'd have to do to deserve stoning as an unmarried woman (clue: have sex). Standards for men related much more to not impinging on another man's territory: 'No man is to disgrace his father by having intercourse with any of his father's wives'. Any of them. No wiggle room on that one.

Trace back Christian thinkers' views on sex in the early and Middle Ages, and they range from disgust to grudging acceptance for the sake of procreation. St Augustine, who before conversion to Christianity wrote he 'ran wild in the jungle of erotic adventures'[31] (no direct reference exists, but it can be assumed on this basis he visited Stockport McDonald's at least once), imagined how Adam and Eve might have had sex without desire: 'In Eden, it would have been possible to beget offspring without foul lust. The sexual organs would have been stimulated into necessary activity by will-power alone, just as the will controls other organs.'[32] Augustine and the other church fathers had a huge influence on how sex and women were perceived in the Middle Ages and beyond. Little of it appears cheering or supportive.

The current popularity of a more sex-positive view of what was written in the Bible still lies squarely within heterosexual marriage. If the theme of Song of Songs is full-on sexy times, as many pastors like to claim, then modern day popular Christian relationship advice portrays it as part of the 'big sell' when encouraging people to wait until their wedding day (night, actually, unless the guests are provided with cake and a string quartet by way of distraction). Waiting = mind-and-every-other-bit-blowing amazing sex is the new story. It's far removed from the prevalent Christian view of sex popular since Augustine, Jerome, and all those who thought women should be 'filled with shame at the thought she is a woman',[33] and any man 'who is too ardent a lover of his own wife is an adulterer'.[34] Along with the new, passion-embracing take on the Bible and marriage is the implicit guarantee that anyone who wants to marry someone with whom to have amazing sex will have opportunity to do so. But only if they cross their legs and wait.

Love Wins?

Despite this, the historical role of love in marriage is debatable. Yes, really. As Stephanie Coontz notes, 'The system of marrying for political and economic advancement was practically universal across the globe for many millennia.'[35] From the earliest recorded times, women had few rights, and what mattered most was property, its protection and passing on to an equally invested party: a legitimate child. This is demonstrably true in the Old Testament, as well as in wider culture. The word matrimony derives from the Latin word for mother, suggestive of the taking of a woman in order to produce children.

Love as a basis for marriage was regarded as an inconvenience, even a risk. In the first half of the 20th century, where partners chose to marry (compared to earlier centuries where parental involvement was significant, and social status dictated potential matches), couples often married quickly after 'going steady' or courting. Marriages were tied more strongly to specific roles for each party, based on what was expected by society. Stephanie Coontz says, 'The average couple wed after just six months – a pretty good sign that love was still filtered through strong gender stereotypes rather than being based on deep knowledge of the other partner as an individual.[36] The only difference between this and the kind of marriages described in the Old Testament is that the couple themselves may have made the choice to be together. And fewer wives. Usually.

In 2017, the US-based Council on Contemporary Families reported that younger people in America – specifically that mysterious group known as Millennials – were wavering on what they thought relationships should be in the future: equal in theory but somehow old fashioned and traditional as well.[37] Given the choice, they reported, young people believed men and women would naturally veer towards stereotyped roles even if all options were open to them (structural barriers limiting maternity leave and pay for American women have ensured all options never have been). Young men were more convinced of this likelihood and benefit than young women. European research hadn't shown a similar slide in the same period, but the political climate in the west is unpredictable with views that could be described as regressive, traditional and progressive fighting over the public sphere, marriage and gender, so shifts in any or multiple directions are possible.

Despite the long-term prevalence of patriarchal society (a social system where men have authority over women in law or in practice), history reveals some interesting alternatives. Stories of tribes not exposed to Christian doctrine or traditional models of arranging domestic communities are a fascinating contrast. Studies of very early agrarian societies suggest shared roles and group parenting in ways that seem completely removed from most known models. Historians indicate that only the invention of weapons, the hoarding of resources, and the creation of property drove a need to divide and assert ownership – and therefore guarantee the passing of the bloodline (and property) through legitimate offspring (for Christians this would be evidence of the 'postlapsarian' world following Adam and Eve's fall and departure from Eden). Examples include North Alaska Inuit who married and then co-married – both men and women[38] – and small societies in South America, such as the Bari in Venezuela, where a pregnant woman expected shared fathering (food and resources) from as many men as she had sexual contact with during a pregnancy – often with her husband's knowledge – to improve her child's chances of good care throughout life.[39] Another South Pacific tribe believed sexual activity was not regarded as a definitive commitment between a couple but eating a meal together away from the rest of the tribe was[40] (there are present day churches like this, but without the sex part).

The banning of polygamy, adultery, and other relationships outside of marriage occurred near to the end of the Roman Empire and were intended in part to signal the restraint and sophistication of the society compared to less civilised groups. Women were still without most rights, but were necessary for childbirth and ensuring lineage. Romans gave engagement rings as a symbol of contractual agreement (the old romantics). Iron rings for the lower classes, gold for the upper (a sign also that a future wife could be trusted with valuable property). The tradition of the 'ring finger' emerged from the belief / poetic fantasy that a vein - the *vena amoris* – ran from that finger directly to the heart, although it transpired all fingers had a similar structure.[41]

Early Christians evolved in a world where marriage was a

largely practical matter. The New Testament church's focus on Jesus' imminent return changed the focus from marriage, tribe building and extending family lines. The new family models extolled by Jesus were a radical departure from the property and lineage focused ones of the day. Paul's exhortation to stay single if possible, but to marry if at risk of being overcome by lust, changed what would have been the standard expectation. With the end of the world believed to be imminent, and the example of Jesus and his commission to go and make disciples of all people, Paul urged early churches to look to their eternal destiny rather than immediate circumstances. Widowed women were advised to stay single if possible, and the church was instructed to care for them. The shift to the relationship between the individual and God first, and the outworking of love and family within the community of believers was unique and counter-cultural. There was nothing resembling what we would recognise as a 'church wedding'. In fact, the origins of the modern-day church service and vows are found in the 1500s, in the post-Reformation Book of Common Prayer after England had split from Rome and the Pope thanks to Henry VIII.

Don't Joke About 'I do'

Marriages themselves hadn't always been church sanctioned or 'traditional'. In pre-Christian ancient Rome cohabitation and legal marriage were only determined by the intentions of the couple (and often their families' wishes). This belief was also held by the Catholic Church for several centuries (if you said *I do*, no matter where or when, you were stuck with each other) and by many other non-Christian societies. In England and Wales, the church relied on people's own statements for over a thousand years. The 'verbum' promise was made just between the couple with no need for a cleric or witnesses.[42] People may have requested the involvement of a priest, or a blessing to aid fertility, but at their own discretion. Hand-fasting, a centuries-old betrothal tradition requiring couples to consent to each other, was regarded as valid in Scotland until a change in the law at the start of the Second World War (and recognised again as a legitimate neo-Pagan marriage in Scotland in 2004. Scotland seems to be steering a course away from traditional religious ceremonies;[43] by 2017 humanist weddings outnumbered those conducted by the Church of Scotland).[44] In the Middle Ages churches were available to register marriages, but couples were under no obligation. Henry VIII's shenanigans ripped up church norms, at least for himself, and set up a whole new way of formalising marital relationships. Archbishop Thomas Cranmer's wording of 'love and cherish' became the minimum requirement for marrying couples from that time onwards, rather than from biblical times.

There is no direct line from the Bible to the modern institution, no matter how many times mid-ceremony readings of 1 Corinthians 13 might suggest otherwise. Marriage as a concept – the joining of two people, symbolic of God and humanity – is clearly laid out and runs throughout the text of the Bible but isn't formalised. The input of the early church fathers, like Augustine and Jerome, did much to shape attitudes toward sex and relationships for the following centuries, and their influence is still felt. A popular belief in the early church that sex and marriage had only become necessary because of Adam and Eve's 'original sin', and therefore all sexual activity was connected to sin, has been hard to shake. Origen, an early scholar of the Coptic Church, believed sex was necessary post-Eden to provide fallen souls with bodies but should never be enjoyed. He insisted the marital bedroom should not be used for prayer, and the Holy Spirit could not be present during sex.[45] (I feel some relief none of these chaps are around in the time of YouTube. Imagine the comments.)

Present day marriage is more about personal fulfilment than ever before. For some Christians this can result in spiritualising very human desires: the expectation of finding God-delivered physical perfection, emotional fulfilment and a version of sanctification through their romantic relationships. Recent philosophical thought has picked up a parallel thread: people of no faith projecting their yearning for transcendence onto romantic love, as widely- and long-held belief in God has fallen away in mainstream society. Love of God and neighbour was held up as the standard for human interaction in the Torah – literally laid out in the verses 'You shall love the Lord your God with all your heart, and with all your soul, and with all your might' and 'You shall love your neighbour as yourself'. Philosopher Simon May explores this shift in *Love, A History*, digging into the intense sacrificial depths of loving God as laid out in the book Christians call the Old Testament, a love that requires God to be put first wholeheartedly, and fellow humans, especially strangers and the struggling, to be cared for.[46] Romantic love, lust and passion feature as facets of humanity, but as May identifies, the all-consuming nature of loving God has led humans to raise their expectations of the power of feelings in their own romantic relationships. If God loves people unconditionally and eternally, should people not be able to do the same with each other? As belief in God has diminished, this heightened passion and expectation has focused solely in this direction: human to human, in pursuit of a totally fulfilling, transcendent love. Stephanie Coontz notes that many early Christian texts used the word love to refer to God or neighbours, rather than towards a spouse.[47] Almost none mentioned a #smokinghotwife.

Horrible Histories

History has also intervened in the institution many times. When the Black Death halved the population of medieval London, new legal freedoms followed for widows who didn't remarry and continued their husband's businesses, and for girls to become apprentices and learn trades (they may have been expected to marry later but at least they knew how to make a barrel, something most modern teenagers can only dream about).[48] Following the mass casualties of the First World War, women outnumbered men of marriageable age for a generation. Two million women whom society had expected and equipped to only become wives found themselves labelled 'surplus women' (there are fascinating parallels here with perceptions of the gender split in current church numbers, which we'll come to later).[49] Royal behaviour has also had a profound influence, none more than Queen Victoria's romance with Prince Arthur. Despite a planned strategic marriage, passionate love blossomed, which coincided with the burgeoning industrial revolution.

A growing monied middle class aspired to private family lives as an indicator of elevated social position. Weddings were the only significant occasion to be made more public as a statement of social standing. Centuries of community celebrations of high days and holidays mostly fell away as the middle classes now kept to themselves in private homes.[50] Christian marriage (at least for those who could afford it) took on new values: that it was more virtuous to focus on the home and immediate family than on wider society. In the USA, in what could have been the birth of the prosperity gospel, preachers encouraged middle class husbands to pursue wealth and spend their money on their immediate families, through which they would model good lives and influence society. For the poor and working class, life continued as before. Women who could not afford to be 'kept' by their husbands and needed to earn money risked the perception of impurity, failing to reach required standards of good womanhood, no matter what their personal faith might be.[51] By 1900 marriages were estimated to be lasting around 35 years due to longer life expectancy, a significant increase on previous centuries.[52] Till death do us part, indeed.

To Love, Honour and..?

Modern Christian debate around marriage between men and women has centred around two main areas: longevity (how to maintain a marriage), and the roles of men and women (who should do what, and what did God say about it). There is an additional on-going conversation around marriage versus celibacy, singleness and abstinence, but it receives significantly less attention. Jesus' own unmarried state, and the exhortations of Paul to remain unmarried if possible are often overlooked, and consequently, the majority of Christian interpersonal advice is not about how to flourish as a single person but rather how to meet, marry and maintain a significant other – and then reproduce.

Some basic tenets of 'Christian marriage' seem to be set. There is little debate now about polygamy in wider society, for example. No mainstream western Christian group practises it, and it was outlawed as far back as ancient Rome (though concubines and prostitution were still tolerated) despite featuring significantly in the Old Testament. The New Testament verse about a deacon being a 'husband of one wife' confirms that monogamous marriage was expected (although this verse has also been used to insist only married men can be in positions of spiritual leadership). St Augustine was hesitant to condemn it overall. He wrote in *Of the Good of Marriage* that polygamy 'was lawful among the ancient fathers; whether it be lawful now also, I would not hastily pronounce.'[53] It was not directly forbidden in the Bible – indeed it was widely practised in the Old Testament – and even Martin Luther and puritan John Milton were twitchy about speaking about it negatively as they did not wish to suggest the biblical patriarchs who had multiple wives had sinned by doing so, even though neither wanted to encourage anyone down that path.[54] Adultery was most definitely forbidden by God (although with the option of numerous wives, the implications and effect on society would have been very different to a monogamous marriage) and is still widely disapproved of.

So, what has shaped Christian marriage, singleness, dating, courtship, relationships and community into their popular forms today? How did we arrive at an odd combination of Old Testament patriarchy, New Testament urgency, Tudor machinations, Victorian purity, the 1950s model of respectable breadwinner-led family (more about that later), a sometimes-panicked amalgamation of post-sexual revolution prurience and reaction, and paradigm-shifting developments in technology, filtered through varying theologies interpreting the Bible in different ways and a rapidly changing society? Simple, really. Christians settled for the ideal of one-man-one-woman, abstinence-then-wild-passion lifelong union with taken-for-granted fertility and a cosy living set up, with an overlooked side order of singleness for those who 'felt called', from an array of sources (often failing to acknowledge those whose sexuality fell outside of these parameters) and we're going to look at just some of them. This holy hybrid is now the predominant theme and message of mainstream Christian relationship advice.

But there are still questions. Why is marriage such a goal? Is 'singleness' a state only Christians worry about? What about those who followed the rules, 'saved themselves', and found it hasn't been straightforward? What do the Christians for whom it all seems to have worked out well make of the debates about damaging relationship advice? Are men and women really so different that they require different roles? It seemed the best way to try and discover answers to these questions and more was to ask.

Chapter Two
Christian Relationships Are Really Easy and Straightforward

Ask around (or ask a thousand or so people, as I found myself doing) and a standard template for Christian relationships looms into focus. It should be:

- Between Christians (assumed to be a man and woman).
- Virginity is the ideal state.
- That means NO SEX.
- Did you get that? NO SEX. At all.
- Focused on getting to marriage.
- Which will happen if you pray enough.
- The One exists. God will bring them to you. Wait it out.
- But don't wait too long.
- Or get too old.
- Men should initiate and choose.
- Women should work on themselves and prepare to be chosen.
- Sex drives are masculine: boys get carried away; girls should be on guard.
- 'Don't touch what you haven't got.' (Actually, don't touch what you have got, either. In fact, just don't touch anything, OK?)
- Make sure they're The One. You'll probably *just know*. Finish immediately with anyone who isn't. It's what God would want.

- Have marriage on the horizon and gallop towards it. Prayerfully.
- NO. SEX.

If you clambered successfully over this emotional obstacle course, marriage was your reward. The three-legged race, an event for winners. Tethering yourself to another forever and living happily ever after, with no stumbles, a nice certificate, enhanced social standing, and cake. This was what marriage apparently should look like, and it was perceived to be stepping into another, better, version of yourself. Prepare yourself for the following, Christian soldier:

- A lifelong commitment (barring disaster) to another Christian.
- SEX! And lots of it. Really, really good sex.
- The clearest indicator of adulthood and maturity yet known to humanity.
- Problems, but only to be referred to euphemistically, and entirely surmountable through private prayer and public smiles.
- It would be 'HARD! But so worth it…'
- Children. Almost inevitable. And desired.
- Living out the best metaphor for God's relationship with the church.
- Creating social media posts about 'date night' and being / referring to a 'hot wife' which is code for…SEX (and sanctified lust / objectification).
- Unlimited use of #blessed in social media posts.
- The instant, permanent eradication of all external temptations.

- Being looked up to by single people.
- Realising you've made it! Marriage is the goal and the pinnacle. You have gone to the next level, emotionally and spiritually, and are now going to be extra holy.

Where to start unpacking this teetering pile of emotional baggage? All aboard the fast train to abstinence central...

DON'T LOOK, DON'T TOUCH

I know, all caps. It's a very big deal. The dominant message given to young people in the Christian faith about personal relationships is: *save yourself*. Stay pure ('impurity' equalling anything sexual, from a thought to any sort of touch). The softer version of the message is transactional: stay pure and the sexual payoff *when* – not if - you get married will be amazing. This is a more recent development. The harder version of the message, also transactional, was and is directed predominantly at girls: stay pure or you'll be damaged goods and nobody will want to marry you (the *super*-hardcore version is even more fun: stay pure or go to hell). Girls found themselves compared to chewing gum (used and thrown away), roses (crushed by being passed around many hands), a glass of water that had been spat in, and given pearls as symbols of sexual value ('we were told our virginity was a precious gift to give away,' wrote one Real Life Love survey respondent), a balloon ('once it's popped it's gone'), and, er, dental products ('once the toothpaste is out you can't put it back in.') Anything to warn off wide-eyed teenagers from touching each other (specifically to warn girls not to let boys touch them).

Sex outside of marriage would create unhealthy bonds or 'soul ties' ('a spiritual tie between two people,' one respondent

23

called it, that needed to be renounced). Boys were told they had stronger and harder to control sex drives while little was said about what girls wanted. 'The Church's avoidance of discussing physical attraction was particularly unhelpful, especially because when it was discussed it was presented as if men wanted sex all the time and women didn't even have a sex drive,' said one survey respondent. The girls were told their job was to cover up, be demure, not cause their brothers to 'stumble' through a flash of shoulder or midriff. 'So many teachings when I was a kid in church swayed towards teaching me my body is dangerous, that it can ignite sin like a spark falling on gun powder can ignite a fire, causing me to bundle up shame and confusion for this part of me,' wrote another. The message rarely changed. Survey respondents talked about what they had been told:

'Don't be alone with someone of the opposite sex that you date - always have a chaperone.'

'Teaching that you should only date/kiss someone you're sure of marrying wasn't helpful (I even taught stuff like this myself).'

'Save kissing until your wedding day.'

'I was always told I was a flower and each sexual encounter was like a petal being plucked from me until I was nothing (you've guessed it – another story for girls only).'

'I have vivid memories of purity being equated to a glass of water with sex being orange squash, once you add the squash no matter how much water you add you will never dilute the orange enough. This has stuck with me ever since and made the pain of my "first time" not being perfect even worse.'

And the impact:

'I think a huge part of this was the idea that those bad boys were going to pressure us girls into situations we didn't want. There was very little honesty about the fact that girls and women had their own sexuality to contend with.'

'I was taught that sexual sin was dirtier than other sin and that even if God forgave you, you were still a changed person.'

'I found a lot of teaching focused only on the sexual aspect of dating relationships (i.e. don't do it until you are married). I got far too involved and emotionally dependent in a relationship which broke down and I was badly hurt; no one had talked about boundaries and healthy dating relationships in terms of the non-sexual stuff.'

Whether or not people had remained abstinent until marriage – or were single and still trying to be – there were hundreds of responses about how unhelpful this kind of teaching was, and these were the dominant messages received. In a pre-internet world there had been few sources for alternative views, or even kindred spirits. Did other people have questions? Until recently there was no way to tell, and the rapid increase in technology available to younger people has created a whole new set of issues as well as offering connection. Sadly, many of the responses to the question of what advice had been helpful also emphasised how little had been, especially for younger people. Although no statistics exist about the age of Christians marrying compared to those of no faith, anecdotally there exists a sense that Christians who have grown up in the culture and are 'doing it right' will marry young. In interviews I conducted in 2012 women in their early 20s expressed fear and sadness that it was already 'too late' for them. There was no equivalent view in the men interviewed, at any age.

How Was It for You?

How did Real Life Love participants describe their relationship history? Selecting from: straightforward and happy; up and down but overall happy; little bit bumpy; complicated; unhappy, with an option for 'Haven't had any significant relationships'; and the brace-yourself option of 'How long have you got . . . ?' over 1,400 people responded. A very small minority of Real Life Love-rs ticked the 'straightforward and happy' romantic lives box. That's a lot of not-straightforward and potentially a lot of not-happy. Almost a third (30%) of responses were of experiences that had been 'up and down but overall happy', the most popular answer. There was some crossover between 'complicated' and 'unhappy'. Almost a fifth of responses related to no significant relationships, which didn't preclude a sense of unhappiness or complication. Overall, only 13% of answers fell into the heady category of romantic lives that had been 'straightforward and happy'. 13%! That hadn't been predicted in youth group teaching. In another question, just 17% said their lives had followed their own expectations for relationships (and there were no guarantees their expectations had been positive). Nearly nine-in-ten (85%) respondents said their faith had influenced their relationship decisions, and over half of those said how had changed over time; an evolving understanding rather than a fixed stance.

Normalising the Exceptions

So why were all these other stories not being told? What about the 87% who had something more than a simple 'happy from the start and ever after'? Somewhere along the way the exceptions had become the expectation. Rather than accepting or even expecting that life was going to throw emotional curve balls at most Christians, along with every other human, most relationship advice started from a spiritualised ideal and exhorted, encouraged and insisted it was an achievable standard for the majority, if not everyone. Much of the teaching came from men who were happily married (or gave the appearance of being so) and had married young, with stable, settled lives modelling the modern Christian dream. Single women sometimes heard from long-term single women. For younger people, advice often came from people not much older or experienced than them (which may account for some of the scaremongering). There was little space for questions, concerns or helping people make good choices and develop healthy relationships. When people explored the paths their lives had taken, and how different they'd been to their expectations, the reflections were honest, varied and empathetic. Considering that almost half (46%) of respondents said that although their faith had influenced their relationship decisions, their view on how had changed over time, it's not surprising they were philosophical about where life had taken them:

'My expectations have changed – I thought I'd be married and have a family by now, but I don't feel disappointed with the path my life has taken and my current singleness.'

'I married and had children young like I expected. But I did not expect to get pregnant while engaged. I did not expect to only date long-distance or to "give in" and have sex before marriage. I did not expect to have such differences with my spouse concerning sex drive and frequency.'

'My expectation – because it's what I had seen modelled – was that I would get to the end of university and get married to the person I had met there. I would be married by 24, tops. And then when I wasn't, I had to do some recalibration. Actually, none of my close friends were . . . In my twenties, I learned so much about myself and what I wanted in a relationship, and I dread to think what I'd be like now had those early expectations been met.'

'When I was single and having bad experiences of relationships - I felt very confused about what God thought of it all. I am very blessed to have a happy marriage and in many ways it has met my expectations. It's definitely not always easy but I feel very privileged and I don't take it for granted. I think things are a lot more complicated for single Christians and having been one for a long time I still feel a lot of pain and confusion for those in that situation.'

'I never, ever expected to be single at 28, let alone not having had a date by then. I assumed I'd meet someone at university or perhaps at church in my early twenties and be married by now.'

'I really believed I'd meet a Christian guy in some conference at home or abroad and we'll have a nice family. Never expected that at almost 35 I'll still be unmarried.'

'Growing up I probably had too simplistic a view of relationships and thought marriage would solve all my problems. But that view has matured and become a bit more realistic!'

'I thought I'd get married earlier. I thought it'd be simpler, I thought God would be more directive.'

This last comment encapsulates one of the main themes in the survey: the expectation that marriage was inevitable and would be reached quickly and straightforwardly with God's direct intervention. For many people, their relationships and feelings about being straight and single orbited around this assumption. If it had happened that way – and clearly this was the case only for a small number – respondents reflected on what had followed. Happiness and contentment for some; abuse, divorce, widowhood or other unexpected sadnesses for others, and for some a more philosophical view on marriage overall.

Singleness as a valid and rewarding possibility for life had not been modelled or spoken about in positive ways for most respondents, who nevertheless declared strongly it was a great way to live – just not for them. Only 2% said they felt called to singleness, compared to the 39% who concurred with 'I do not feel called to singleness but am single'. Considering this, it is surprising that nearly nine out of ten respondents (88%) agreed with the statement 'Singleness is a valid and respected calling', and concerning that less than a third of respondents believed that mainstream Christian culture felt the same way. The apostles would surely be tutting.

Stepping Out

Once people began to contemplate dating or even started relationships, they met with more advice: being told 'everything would be a fairy tale if we waited', said one respondent. 'Mostly people telling me as a single person that I just had to be content and then I'd suddenly magically get a boyfriend. Also, once I did date someone, being asked "if I felt more whole"', said another. 'I felt my church growing up had very little trust of individuals in relationships and got overly involved when they didn't need to, which was painful for many people', wrote one respondent, who also related several stories of heavy-handed intervention in young adult relationships.

Where did that leave the large majority who hadn't had the heavenly fairy tale? Often frustrated, ashamed, struggling with not living up to expectations – their own and others' – and with few places to turn. Churches, which were the centre of many respondents' spiritual lives, with over 45% describing their churchgoing as 'regular and committed' and nearly 39% as 'enthusiastic and involved' (these were not mutually exclusive responses), were often not places of help or comfort, even if good intentions were there. It was hard for those who wanted support and community, whatever their relationship status, to feel they would find it in their spiritual communities, regardless of denomination or theology. Over two-thirds (68%) of respondents agreed with the statement 'couples are more respected than single people in the church / Christian life'. Just over half of all who responded believed 'church is a safe place for me'.

'As a child I went to a charismatic church where we were taught through meetings, youth groups and books, we had to wait for the right "one" – this isn't biblical and is also promotes anxiety, fear and oppression – funny that . . . things Christianity are meant to set you free of.'

'We singles are often left to navigate the landscape alone! The whole thing of dating as an adult needs to be talked about more, especially as there are many in our churches who are single, whether never-married, or divorced or widowed.'

'I worked for a church for five years, and as a single woman, some of the men there could not work out whose authority I was under, since I wasn't married and I didn't live with my parents/dad any more. If I'd have been married that would have been so much easier for them, because any issue they had, they could have taken to him to complain about, rather than addressing it to me. Dealing with the fact that I was responsible for myself and accountable to God just didn't fit into their worldview.'

But the Bible Says...

A significant amount of survey responses related to biblical interpretations, with most focusing on complementarian and egalitarian theologies. Complementarian theology was prevalent across much of the church experience discussed, though it seemed for some it was 'the water they swam in' – simply true Christianity and not just one possible interpretation, a realisation many had come to later. Put simply, complementarian theology views men and women as 'equal but different' with defined roles.

Based on the creation order in Genesis, with Adam created first and Eve as 'helper', and later as a reflection of the Trinity, this is interpreted to mean men should 'lead' relationships, being initiators and decision makers, with women submitting and supporting. It was crystallised in The Danvers Statement of 1987 created by the Council for Biblical Manhood and Womanhood, a predominantly white American Southern Baptist organisation,[1] and has continued to evolve. It stated that women 'are of equal value and dignity' but that certain leadership and teaching roles should be men-only, and men should maintain 'headship' at home with women taking a 'subordinate' role.[2]

Egalitarian theology believes men and women partner and submit to each other in marriage, without pre-determined gender roles. There is room for discussion about the spectrum of beliefs that fall along this scale, and we'll look at some of these as we go. One response expressed frustration with theological clashes: 'While my relationship would probably be best described as egalitarian, I'm so tired of my complementarian friends with good, mutually enjoyable marriages getting demonised in the current climate.' Though some had good, mutually enjoyable marriages, other respondents described different experiences. Many had experienced teaching that insisted marriage could only be as God intended if both parties lived up to certain roles. 'I have read or started reading things in the past that were very dogmatic about the roles of men and women throughout life, both in relationships and outside of them. Definitely not helpful . . . some to the point of being very unhelpful and making me actually feel worse about life', wrote one person. 'I remember reading a book that advised that in a marriage, the man should always drive the car as a way of showing their children what headship looked like', said another.

A key area was sex drive and sexual expression – or lack of. The majority of respondents wrote about the emphasis on natural male desire, and lack of female. Wrote one respondent:

'I think the most unhelpful bit of advice is that women are mostly interested in and attracted to the emotional dimensions of a relationship and are much less interested in physical intimacy than men. I think this makes it harder than it should be as a woman to talk about the challenges of not acting on strong desires for physical intimacy.'

Said another:

'I had to unlearn unhealthy and unnecessary ideas about my body, which I had been taught to see as a trap for men. I had to learn that it was okay (and good!) for my partner to be attracted to me. I had to learn that I was capable of making my own decisions about my life and that any mistakes I made could be my own, and that hiding behind someone else's spiritual authority was unhealthy.'

Unity on the Surface

One of the most startling findings from the survey was how many respondents were happy to call themselves Christians, be active in churches, and yet not believe they shared views and values with their church (to some extent) and mainstream Christianity (to a much greater extent). Either through what was explicitly taught or through what was modelled, people were convinced they were at odds with the cultural expressions of the faith with which they identified, and yet they persisted.

We'll be examining the impact of this disconnect or cognitive dissonance as we proceed. These views, and more that emerged throughout the survey, influence churches, faith communities, mainstream Christianity, and the individual journeys of many people, single, married and all the other stages of life. Many relate to how men and women interact, how they differ, and what sex and marriage should be. Some examples are startling.

'**A woman's role is to support / prioritise her husband and family**' - less than a quarter (23%) of respondents agreed personally, yet 74% believed this was mainstream Christianity's view, and four-in-ten believed it was their church's stance.

Almost 88% of respondents agreed with the statement '**Marriage should be about mutual submission**' but only 32% believed this view was shared by mainstream Christianity, and 59% thought this was their church's stance.

Just 26% thought '**Marrying young is a good thing**' but 69% believed this was a mainstream Christian view.

Internalised polarity seemed to be normalised. There was uncertainty about the role of dating and courtship, with a leaning towards suspicion that any contact that was not guaranteed to lead to marriage was less than ideal in the wider world of Christianity.

22% of respondents personally believed '**Only date someone you're very sure you could marry**' but three-quarters believed this was the mainstream Christian view.

While 89% agreed with the statement 'It's OK to date someone to see if you could have a long-term future' less than half (47%) believed this was acceptable to mainstream Christianity. The hangover of the courtship movement dating back to the 1990s may be more powerful than many realise.

In relation to so-called modesty teaching, only 15% agreed with the statement 'Men are wired to lust, women should help them by covering up', but more than 80% believed this was the mainstream Christian view.

This perception continued into responses about pornography.

Nine-out-of-ten respondents believed the statement 'Pornography is a problem because it encourages objectification of women/others' was correct but under half – 44% – thought this was the mainstream Christian view. Just over half (54%) thought this was their church's view.

42% agreed with the statement 'Pornography is a problem mostly because it affects Christians' personal purity' but over three-quarters (76%) thought this was reflective of mainstream Christian culture.

Interestingly, respondents were in line with one key area of what they believed mainstream Christianity and their own churches taught: that 'humans are designed for lifetime monogamy or commitment'. In this area 80% believed this was the mainstream faith view, 76% that this was their church's view, and 72% held this view themselves. Where there was common ground – and this finding may be influenced by the number of already married people who completed the survey – it was unclear how this was influencing interactions within communities. Some of the key themes to emerge include the following.

Safe Places

When asked where they would turn for advice with a relationship problem, only a quarter (24%) of respondents named a church leader, around the same number who would go online for help. The majority, 83%, preferred to speak to friends. Family, partners and external experts, including doctors, counsellors and Samaritans (the non-biblical version, presumably) were also important, but church groups were a choice for only 14%. Maybe it's a tad awkward to respond to 'And does anyone have any prayer requests?' with a monologue about an ambiguous situation with a 'friend' who only texts after midnight. For many people, there was an absence of anything that represented their relationship situations. Only 19% of respondents responded 'very well' to the question 'How well does your church or faith community understand modern relationship challenges?' and 45% of respondents believed 'Church leaders are often out of touch with what's happening romantically in their congregations'. 39% said yes to the statement 'Christian leaders' relationships are used as an example of success' and 30% assume 'spiritual leaders have healthy romantic lives' (no pressure).

Single. Don't Mingle.

Singleness seemed to go through several seasons. It was seen as a precarious state of purity to be protected in the young, an inevitably short season for young adults before marriage, an under-resourced and under-discussed subject for older single people (older could mean anyone over 25), and a source of awkwardness the longer it continued ('As I turned 40, suddenly being single became taboo particularly within church circles. No one would talk to me about it – they avoided the subject which made me feel something was wrong with "me" I just wish people had been open about discussing it with me – it wasn't an issue for me but clearly a very uncomfortable issue for others', wrote one respondent). People sought support where they could, turning to their own peer groups first and their official spiritual networks much later, if at all. With nearly two-thirds (64%) believing 'Pressure to get married is strong in church or Christian culture', it is not hard to understand why people who didn't fit neatly into this bracket may have struggled to know where to go for support or advice, or even positive role models.

Sex

Sex was a strong theme of the Real Life Love survey. Big surprise. The church's teaching about sex over centuries and the norms of biblical patriarchy have had a profound impact, to the present day, leaving many Christians confused about what is right for them. It was often a practical issue: what was allowed? One respondent described being taught sex was 'a special, precious, awkward, funny, literally messy thing worth saving for marriage.' Where did sex fit into relationships overall – was it a no-go area until the wedding night and orgasmic fireworks every day after or were there natural progressions in physical intimacy as relationships developed? Did God care if Christians had one night stands? Did the same standards apply – indeed, were the same ethics appropriate – for teenagers lectured by youth leaders fearful of pregnancies and STDs, and unmarried people in their 40s? (Sadly, no research exists on how many youth leaders are fearful of unmarried fortysomethings; that could be another book.) What if choices were taken away? 'I was educated with the facts about sex within marriage but I experienced sexual abuse which didn't match the facts so it was hard to overcome the difference', wrote one respondent. If people weren't holding to a traditional view on sex (abstinence and then sexy marriage) what was driving their ethics and morality? Just over a third – 36% – of survey respondents agreed with the statement 'Sex before marriage is always wrong' with only 2% believing 'Sexual activity is the primary indicator of a Christian's personal purity', yet many resources existed supporting those messages. Half of the survey respondents (49.8%) agreed with the statement 'Christian culture emphasises abstinence over teaching about healthy relationships', indicating a strong likelihood many emotional needs were going unmet and questions unasked. Was pragmatism a bigger driver than strategy or principles for people in terms of how physical relationships evolved? What was the impact of adhering to church teachings about abstinence over time, particularly if the 'heavenly timeline' of chastity then early, blissful marriage did not occur? A few thoughts from survey respondents:

> 'Even though I had a softly evangelical background and not a hard-line one, the background still gave me unhelpful assumptions and behavioural habits as regards romantic relationships and left me ill-equipped to navigate such relationships in a normal and healthy way in the real world (by which I mean the world outside the evangelical subculture).'

'I feel betrayed by Christian culture. I was completely unequipped to deal with a relationship in a physical sense once I started one. Maybe the teaching works if you get married at 22 – which is after all when you're supposed to get married! – though I suspect it's not great then either, but when you're 30 or whatever, it's no use at all. Because you're in this relationship and you're no longer fresh faced, you have life behind you, and baggage, and experience . . . Our young people get married straight out of university because it's the only way they can get any! Marriage is more important than we make it – because it isn't just a vehicle for being able to have sex.'

'Ideally Christians should wait until marriage, however sadly for some, through prolonged abstinence, sex becomes an idol and being an older virgin seems to turn people a funny shape with regard to developing normal relationships. I would rather have had sex before marriage and view it in a healthy light, than have waited and put it on a pedestal and have had an unhealthy fixation with it. In terms of emotional health, it's the lesser of two evils I think.'

'The first person I had sex with was my husband but we weren't married at the time. Christian culture tells me I should regret this but in all honesty I was glad, when it came to our wedding night, that I didn't have to worry about it. I think I might have felt differently if I hadn't married the first person I had sex with but that is just speculation.'

'OK I'm not single any more, but was for a long time and my problem was always – what the heck was I supposed to do with sexual desire?? Because that's swept under the carpet, as if single people don't experience desire.'

Abstinence teaching, or at least the emphasis on sex within marriage, was the dominant message. And it had upsides – some unexpected – for some people:

'I benefitted hugely from Christian teaching on sex and relationships, and am particularly grateful to my youth group for emphasising abstinence before marriage – but grace and forgiveness and NO SHAME for anyone who didn't do this…I know that many others are telling their stories now of damage from purity culture, or feeling that the church's teaching has failed them. I feel the church's teaching protected me and helped me.'

'Being taught to avoid sex by the church was helpful in that I think without it I would have been fully promiscuous and probably never committed to anyone.'

'All the "save yourself/don't touch each other" stuff was useful as a justification for not having drunk sex. Secular teaching didn't really impart the message that I, as a man, could not want sex on an occasion and that that was fine.'

Under Pressure

Perfectionism also emerged as a theme, with a sense that church communities could easily become places where it was easier to hide problems than face or discuss them. Said one respondent:

'I think there's a huge amount of pressure on Christian people (men too, but particularly women) to get married young. I also think there's a huge pressure in the church to put on a good face within relationships, to pretend that Christian marriages are perfect. I think that is really harmful in stopping people from getting the help they need and making them feel like failures when things are tough.'

Another commented, 'Growing up in church the teaching was always very black & white and made to sound so simple. When real life hit, I found it difficult to draw help or comfort from this. I don't think people were particularly honest with me, this meant I didn't feel able to share truthfully with them.'

Christian relationship advice provoked strong feelings, especially the advice that came in neat book form. Without naming names, here are just a few of the responses to some well-known titles:

'Extremely offensive cutting short what I believe God's intention for love.'

'Throw it all in the bin.'

'I threw one book across the room.'

'The worst book I've ever read about anything ever.'

It can be tricky to share these less-than-positive feelings about what seem to be mainstream and largely unchallenged views and ways of doing things. Christianity is meant to have all the answers. Stick to the book, or books, and it will all fall into place. Church structures and unity depend on everyone obeying the rules. Except the rules – if indeed there are any – don't fit many of the situations people find themselves in. Society has evolved and continues to, though some suggest Christians should not be influenced by this in any way. The Big Book has many stories of patriarchs taking several wives and, of course, none of dating apps and hook ups. And many ideas about what men and women are have made it barely altered from the Old Testament to the present day. Dare we examine just how accurate they are? Onwards, brave soldiers...

Chapter Three
Girls and Boys and Women and Men and God

Where do Christians learn what it means to be a man or woman? The answers are woven throughout what could be loosely termed Christian Culture, a heady brew of all things God-and-Jesus-related ('Christianity has always placed a strong emphasis on hygiene', reports the Wikipedia page for 'Christian Culture', which is reassuring). Amid that winning combination of – *deep breath* - churches, conferences, student Christian Unions and campus ministries, small groups, youth camps, books, devotionals, possible home-schooling, Christian festivals, family homes, and increasingly, Christian TV, radio, podcasts, webinars, social media, blogs, vlogs and magazines – and the various translations, interpretations and misinterpretations of the Bible – lie the answers. Marriage is presented as an important goal for Christians – often the sole purpose for women, and a natural step for a man upon reaching maturity, when he takes on the mantle of leader of his home and family. Despite the New Testament emphasis on the value of singleness, the modern church *loves* marriage (probably enough to marry it). As of the end of 2018, Amazon offered over 20,000 Christian marriage books but only 281 for Christian singleness[1] – although singleness was often a temporary burden, with titles like *Not Yet Married*, the subtle *God, Send Me My Husband!* and books offering *Wisdom for*

Wives in Waiting.[2] As one woman recalled: 'I was given the impression that I would get married at some point in my future, and that it would be the most important thing about my life.'

Christian Culture can reinforce roles and purpose in myriad ways, such as: who speaks from the front of church (and about what), the line-up of Christian conferences, activities at men's breakfasts and women's groups, the language used to describe the sexes, who looks after the children, and, of course, the resources. 'Men and women are fundamentally wired differently', wrote one survey respondent, 'we were told this with "scientific" evidence over fifty years old in our premarital counselling.' Most often, messages about what it means to be a Christian man or woman are picked up through everyday life, just as they are in wider society.

For Better or For Worse

Christian marriage resources mostly steer safely towards the warm-watered shores of mainstream, conservative, God-made-us-different-whatcha-gonna-do eye-rolling, light complementarian Christianity where the rules are clear and defined differences set the tone. Women are often valued as homemakers above all else. Often books themselves are a giveaway about men and women's roles. The blurb for Mark and Grace Driscoll's *Real Marriage*[3] – an apparently best selling Christian book we'll come to later – describes Grace as a Public Relations graduate who now 'delights in being a stay-at-home mom.' Bible teacher Derek Prince's 1978 book *The Marriage Covenant: The Biblical Secret for a Love that Lasts*[4] is introduced by his new wife Ruth, who writes of Lydia, Prince's deceased first wife, giving up her ministry when they met:

'When Derek married her she was a respected spiritual leader with an established work of her own. However, she willingly accepted the behind-the-scenes role of intercessor, homemaker, and supporter – that of a true wife.' *Uh-huh.*

And God Made Them Pink and Blue?

Many books, resources and messages about God-designed differences between men and women often originate in mainstream American Christianity – a tranquil and uncontroversial place, particularly since the era of Trump began – which has a significant influence on American politics and therefore around the world. Some Christians seek to distance themselves from others, like a dysfunctional extended family at an awkward reunion. Liberal or progressive vs conservative. White Evangelicals, a large American voting bloc, significantly backed Donald Trump – some lauding him as God's choice – and they lead the charge for a return to 'traditional' values, including gender roles. Significant here is Dr James Dobson, who founded interdenominational conservative Christian organisation Focus on the Family in the 1970s. The organisation campaigns for traditional gender roles, among other things, and in 2016 was reclassified as a church, exempting its multi-million-dollar income from tax.[5] Dobson's book *Bringing Up Boys* lists a dizzying array of male-specific traits: assertive, audacious, risking life and limb for no reason, hazardous, daring, sporty, and uninterested in writing (maybe he got a girl to pen his books for him).[6] In his equivalent title on raising girls, he emphasises that parents must work to instil, among other things, 'self-discipline, self-control, generosity, and sweetness of spirit' and 'modesty, morality, and manners'.[7] He even mentions the necessity of working to overcome girls' propensity towards violence and aggressiveness (which I confess I have experienced while reading some Christian relationship advice), and talks about 'teaching girls to become ladies', and have 'moral purity'.

Oddly, many of the things described as innate in girls seem not to occur naturally, but girls who don't have these qualities bred in them will be damaged beyond measure in later years. They are expected to become supportive wives to the grown-up versions of wild and unpredictable boys, and much will hinge on their ability to absorb the untameable manliness, and be sweet, gentle and emotionally generous because boys and men can't be expected to do this for themselves. It is firm belief in this essentialism that provokes rage and threats of boycott when department stores decide to display toys by category and not by gender, thus upsetting the divine order of toy shops, as specified in the Bible (at least in some translations). Boys' strength and robustness and girls' nurturing sweetness are promoted as God-given, despite any evidence children may not be made that way.

A 2017 BBC show – *No More Boys and Girls: Can Our Kids Go Gender Free?* – explored what might occur if children weren't treated as two distinct types.[8] The show explored stereotypes, and how these affect children's views of themselves and each other. In one experiment, adults who believed themselves free of prejudice were asked to play with babies whose clothes had been swapped. Unprompted, they offered dolls and soft toys to girl babies dressed in pink and flowery patterns (who were actually boys), and robots and activity toys to boy babies in blue (who were, of course, girls), only learning later about the clothes swap and expressing shock at their own behaviour. Anyone who has ever bought a new birth card, a toy for a child, or shopped for clothes knows gendering – and pink and blue - is almost impossible to avoid. Campaigns like Let Clothes Be Clothes (and an equivalent group for toys)[9] highlight ongoing divisions of children's products to reinforce imagined difference.[10]

Despite boys and girls being similar in size and shape until puberty, clothes, toys and homewares designed for them suggest very different lives. In 2018 Marks & Spencer, the UK's biggest clothing retailer, offered boys grey, blue and red with images of bears, sharks, gorillas and dinosaurs and activities like football and surfing. Trains, cars and superheroes feature too.[11] For girls, the options are teddy bears not grizzlies, along with bunnies and puppies, fantasy creations like unicorns and mermaids, and Disney princesses. Flowers, tropical islands and rainbows, and pyjamas with tutus make an appearance too. The language also differs. Striker, explorer, warrior for boys; dream, heart, love for girls (with a concession that 'Girls can run the world' on one t-shirt). Children – and, to be fair, most adults – don't want to stand out as different. If boys and girls are told there's a way to be a good boy or girl, most will adopt it, and society will tell them almost nothing else. A six-year global study published in the *Journal of Adolescent Health* in 2017 indicated children believe stereotypes about their sex by the age of 10 – most notably that girls are vulnerable and suited to indoor, domestic life, and boys are robust and suited to adventures and exploring the wider world (sound familiar?).[12] Girls learn early to be concerned about their body and appearance, perceived by society as both their biggest asset and biggest risk. Boys believe they gain social status from taking part in active, even dangerous behaviours. While this plays out differently in different countries, researchers found the messages absorbed were very similar whether societies were conservative or more liberal. For girls and young women, body image and self-esteem are significant factors affecting mental health and wellbeing. A 2017 study by *Girlguiding* of 1,900 girls and women, found two-thirds of 11-16 year olds and 83% of 17-21 year olds surveyed identified toys and clothes as a factor reinforcing limiting gender stereotypes, along with media representations, gendered language and expectations of adults.[13] Throw in what Christianity might offer, and these roles are often reinforced further.

Please Turn to the Book of . . .

Popular Bible stories promote male 'heroes' more than female, and often overlook the character flaws that drove their actions. Female 'heroines' will have their sexual behaviour highlighted and questioned, even joked about, in contemporary sermons with the context of their lives often overlooked: Rahab, the woman at the well, Mary Magdalene, Bathsheba and Tamar, for starters. Children growing up Christian will hear about more men to emulate than women, and churches often reinforce stereotypes along with the more conservative elements of society. Devotional books for girls and boys may contain the same readings (at least in the early years) but are packaged to emphasise difference: action and sports motifs for boys; pastels, pinks and flowers for girls.

For teen girls, glitter, delicate images of nature and homewares, and references to being beautiful (or 'Beautifully Brave') abound. Older boys are offered manga cartoons, activities and exhortations to Stand Strong or have Bold Brave Faith.[14] Mirroring, and only slightly subverting the messages of wider society, girls are encouraged to look inwards and understand themselves as beautiful in some way, not the worldly physical way, but the kind of internally, spiritually beautiful God made and endorses. 'Girl groups in church would often revolve around being "beautiful on the inside"', said one survey respondent. Boys, instead, must reckon with becoming the kind of heroes God made them to be. Self-made, strong, resilient, natural leaders. Reality is clearly not so straightforward.

There is pressure in different ways on boys and men too. They are much less likely to be the victims of sexual violence, forced marriage, domestic abuse, genital cutting, sex-selective abortion, and body image issues, but are more likely to be the victims of violence from other men. According to the Office for National Statistics (ONS) statistics for 2016 in the UK, while women were far more likely to be killed by partners or ex-partners – accounting for 44% of all female victims aged 16 and above compared to 7% of male victims of the same age – men were more likely to be killed by men they knew as friends or acquaintances.[15] They are more likely to end their own lives too. The ONS also recorded 5,965 suicides in the UK, of which around three-quarters were men.[16]

There are also signs that men are internalising issues girls and women have struggled with for decades. In the UK, men are currently being admitted to hospital for eating disorders at the same rates as women for the first time, the increase in part due to changing expectations around men's appearance but also longer-term sufferers coming forward for help as society begins to allow men to admit infallibility. Overcoming the stereotype of male strength may mean more men are willing to seek help, but elsewhere men are absorbing messages proliferating online that their physical appearance matters.

Though in 2015 globally men spent on average just $6.50 on personal grooming for the year, compared to $58.50 spent on average by women,[17] there has been a four-fold rise in body-changing steroid use by young men in the UK, attributed to changing ideas about masculinity and the ever-watchful eye of social media with unforgiving, often unrealistic notions of body image.[18]

Teenage Kicks

Social media has also allowed a new generation of Christian influencers to spread old messages about masculinity and femininity with a sheen of cool. In 2013 vlogger Jon Jorgenson uploaded 'Who You Are', a spoken word poem addressed to no fewer than all women (it's subtitled 'A Message To All Women' in case there was any doubt).[19] Straight to camera, he announces 'you are beautiful' before going on to list funny, kind, and being a rose as traits all women possess. In the male equivalent (yes, addressed to all men so don't you slip out the door, sir) he opens with 'you are strong' and continues with brave, capable and full of potential, given gifts and talents by God.[20] It's notable that the video for women has four times the number of YouTube views as the one for men. By 2018, over eight million vs two million. Some of this can be attributed to the gender split in the church, but that doesn't account for the entire discrepancy. Young women are used to being defined and validated by others. It's a spiritualised version of a One Direction song: *You have no idea you're actually beautiful (but God says you are and so do I, so save yourself and be godly, OK?)*. Young men are active, future writers, inventors, artists, musicians, technicians and athletes. They have jokes to tell and wisdom to bestow. The world needs them in real, practical ways.

The girls are not encouraged to action. Instead they should focus on self-worth. They are worthy of love and affection; they are a flower, diamond or pearl (all things that occur naturally and are appreciated by others). These intangible qualities, with the emphasis on being lovable and worthy, are tied to being biblical women. Strong and capable too, in their own feminine way, but not needed for their skills, unless related to home or family. Simply understanding their emotional value will be enough to set them free to . . . well, free to do something. This split between the external and internal runs through identity-based advice for younger Christians from early years through to adulthood. With the advent of teenage hormones the advice intensifies, as does the gender split. These are the years of girls being warned their clothing may cause their brothers-in-Christ to 'stumble', and boys pushed towards 'accountability groups' as they fight the irresistible lure of online pornography. Both men and women warn girls to 'take responsibility' as they may be unintentionally provocative. This is modesty teaching. Being seen as sexual means being devalued in male eyes and therefore losing their self and social worth. This is then bad for boys who may sin because they are so easily visually stimulated. It would be worse if they were intentionally provocative, but this would make them the kind of impure girl a good Christian boy wouldn't want for marriage (a girl's ultimate destiny – 'The stupid idea that all woman want marriage, and all men want sex RUINED MY LIFE, not all men are like that, and not all woman are obsessed with marrying', said one survey respondent). The chaps are warned about this too. One mainstream UK conference advised male teens about finding the right type of future wife, not being led by hormones into chasing sexually available ladies: 'If you go fishing, fine, but you'll pull out an old boot.'[21]

Illicit sexy-sexiness is the new worry – a realistic one in some ways, where young people find themselves exposed to unfiltered misogynistic content via smartphones – but one too often framed as uncontrollable male sexuality vs passive female objectification. 'Women are stumbling blocks, men are lustful', one Real Life Love survey respondent remembers being taught. 'Men are more inclined to lust and be visually stimulated. Women are more fragile and need to be cared for', said another. Avoiding pregnancy is paramount, but so is avoiding all sexual contact, even sexual thoughts. This is where young women enter the dangerous territory of becoming 'damaged goods'. 'Women are more emotional and men are more sexual', said another. 'This makes it really hard to trust men – they're sometimes presented as subhuman.' Staying 'pure' and therefore marriageable is paramount. In theory for both boys and girls, but in reality, only one group is really believed to be tainted by sex, and have their worthiness for love diminished. Yep, girls. As one survey respondent wrote, this 'does no credit to either men or women. Men unable to fight back their impulses, women seemingly devoid of sexual desire.' If girls can dress demurely and wait to be approached by a good Christian man at the right time, and both can be accountable to older people in their network who will ask them about their physical boundaries (and his forays into online smut), they can marry in good time and indulge in godly sex forevermore.

Growing Up

But it doesn't always – or often – work out like that. 'There was encouragement to marry at an early age if you want to have sex (without necessarily working out whether this relationship is healthy or not). There was more focus on not having sex, than there was on having healthy relationships,' wrote one participant. What does 'marrying young' mean in practice? Let's not forget in 50 American states child marriage is still legal with parental consent and includes girls from Christian families marrying older men.[22] Records show 86% of under-age brides married adults, not other minors, and girls as young as 12 have been granted marriage licences, even in the 21st century. In 2016, a US patriarchal Christian group called Let Them Marry made headlines for advertising a retreat for families wanting early betrothal for their children with marriage to follow soon after, and not necessarily with the children's informed consent.[23] It was cancelled after an outcry, and the group has taken its activities offline.

For those more mainstream Christians who fall outside the early marriage ideal, the next few years as young adults are kind of blurry. Though female students outnumber males at some universities and girls out-perform boys in some school subjects, only young men are encouraged towards achievement and action.[24] The church still predominantly sees leadership as male. Studies show student-age men are likely to rate themselves higher in terms of ability in areas they expect to flourish in (maths and science, for example) and rate their female colleagues lower based on . . . well, absolutely zero evidence, except stereotypes.[25]

Christian girls and young women are directed towards having high self-esteem because God loves them, and embodying modest femininity. As one survey respondent summarised: 'You're a girl. You bake. You submit. You can't do science. You can't lead.' Encouraged to be hospitable (in the non-sexual sense), amenable, friendly and encouraging, they should be 'good girls' for God. At the point where marriage might be on the cards – and there are still sectors of the church that don't believe in dating, boyfriends and girlfriends or relationships, and endorse only courtship as the route to marriage – a man is expected to approach a suitable young woman with a view to assessing compatibility for lifelong commitment. 'Men should pursue, protect and lead in a way that empowers women', was one survey respondent's recollection. Another remembered being taught a more extreme version: 'authority over a woman is passed from father to husband, woman's role is to submit, bear children, care for the home. No working, going to college, [or] leaving home.' One woman remembered: 'my family believed strongly in the "benefits" of courtship. Relationships were not just the two partners, but the entire family. There should always be oversight.' There has been some pushback to this narrative over recent years, but it is still present in varying strengths in the church.

Although 86% of survey respondents said either a man or woman could initiate a date, complaints that Christian men should 'man up' and ask women out are still common in mainstream churches. Often these come from women frustrated at a lack of pursuit from the Christian men they know, who often make up a smaller percentage of the church population. The male has often been characterised as a proactive hunter, both by the church and wider society but for different reasons and with different outcomes. For some Christians, male pursuit is God's order with the righteous goal of marriage. 'The guy should ask the girl out, not the other way round', one respondent recalled being taught. Christian women, noting men would show them interest outside of church, would perhaps not acknowledge the number disparity in the church and the potentially shorter-term goals of the non-Christian men who weren't part of a culture expecting them to save sex for marriage. In the wider world, male pursuit was regarded as animalistic, the drive of nature – men 'only want one thing' and women should be on guard. For Christian men, pursuit was expected to be the first step in a man 'taking a wife', and the female role was to be appropriately open and encouraging, though chaste and non-tempting. While men report feeling pressure to be 'leaders' in matters of romance – from initiating dates to being financial providers – they were also criticised for not performing this role, by pastors who endorsed macho Christianity (*cough – Mark Driscoll – cough*) and Christian women who believed this is what 'real' men would do.

A Rose by Any Other Name

So how true are these versions of male and female? Society globally reinforces male supremacy, from the polite to the brutally overt. There are plenty of obviously patriarchal societies, and some superficially more balanced, but around the world girls have the odds stacked against them from the start. Female baby girls are statistically more likely to survive than baby boys if treated the same, but in many parts of the world they aren't. Female foetuses are more likely to be aborted in India and China, and in some countries, girls are less likely to be taken to hospital if sick.[26] Boys are more likely to be born prematurely and have complications if they survive. Angela Saini's book on science and sex, *Inferior*, quotes paediatric health researcher Joy Lawn about this disparity as 'a biological risk against boys, and a social risk against girls'.[27] The 'survival of the fittest' must be tampered with to give priority to boys. In the more mundane setting of the western church, girls and boys grow up with the milder outworkings of prejudice and expectations around their sex (reinforced if they are exposed to a James Dobson book along the way).

Science, which Christians have often treated with scepticism, has of late become an odd ally – if the right studies are picked. Used to promote purity culture, male leadership and sex differences, among other things. Christian teaching has increasingly drawn from one side of scientific research – that which emphasises distinct and complementary differences between men and women. Science itself has been male-dominated, excluding from the earliest years female scientists or women who would have been (the French Academy of Sciences, which had never admitted a female member, turned down Marie Curie – the first female Nobel Prize winner, the first person and only woman to win the Nobel twice, and the only person to win in two different sciences – in 1911, in favour of a male scientist you probably haven't heard of).[28] Along with other areas of society, like law, government, medicine and – of course – the church, women were routinely, legally, denied a place and a voice. Angela Saini notes that the fathers (ahem) of modern science were no less susceptible to viewing men as naturally more brilliant, including Charles Darwin, who wrote in 1882, 'I certainly think that women though generally superior to men [in] moral qualities are inferior intellectually.'[29]

Brain Drain

Where has this left Christians, who cherry-pick scientific studies that reinforce difference and hitch them to theology? Often with books entitled *Men Are Like Waffles, Women Are Like Spaghetti*, the faith version of *Men Are from Mars, Women Are from Venus*.[30] ('At first this may seem silly, even juvenile,' write Waffle / Spaghetti authors Bill and Pam Farrel, 'but stay with us. It is a picture that works and men "get it" (because it involves food.)'[31]

Psychologist Cordelia Fine has written extensively about what she terms 'neurosexism', where scientific studies are inaccurately applied to reinforce stereotypes. Recent work on the concept of neuroplasticity – that the brain can form new neural pathways and connections throughout its life – suggests the idea that men and women are biologically 'hard-wired' in certain ways is not reliable.[32] Social factors like hobbies, work, and play patterns could affect how brains develop and change. Though neuroscience is still a debated area, and the brain is not fully understood, the vast majority of studies show no difference between men's and women's brains. This may not be apparent from some news headlines (and Christian books), which claim to show indisputable proof that men and women's brains are 'wired' differently. Contradictory studies also exist, but don't generate as much interest as ones that reinforce stereotypes. Some show minimal differences, and others show differences which are then extrapolated into theories – and often into worldwide headlines which misrepresent the research itself. One BBC science article from 2013 listed several studies which demonstrated conclusively that *both* women and men were better multitaskers.[33] Other studies show the influence of existing social expectations. A 2017 American study showed that, by the age of 6, children began to believe boys and girls had different intellectual qualities.[32] Despite assessing themselves similarly at the age of 5, a year later boys were more likely to believe they were naturally brilliant and smarter than girls, while girls believed they worked harder. Both believed girls were nicer than boys, boys having believed they were nicer a year earlier. This internalised bias may reflect girls working harder and achieving better academic results overall around the world (where girls are actually educated – a whole other issue), even where they are discriminated against, because they have a more realistic assessment of their own abilities and the need to apply effort.[35] This continues into adulthood.

In studies relating to 'raw brilliance' this trait was expected to be found more often in fields where men flourished and were already strongly represented.[36] Women instead were drawn to environments where hard work was expected and valued. Years of hearing male = natural achievement and leadership, and female = naturally supportive, or nicer and hard working, is internalised by all. Evaluations range from students rating their professors[37] - where any teacher who isn't a white man is viewed more negatively, even where the same courses are taught with the same materials and students receive the same grades – to recruiters looking for suitable employees who penalise women for being women.[38]

One study showed male and female scientists discriminating against CVs that appeared to belong to women and preferring those attributed to men, even though the achievements were the same.[39] Christian messages about men and women rarely target the worlds of academia and business in the same way, but the same messages of female inferiority form the backdrop, and sometimes more – indeed, some parts of the church are still unhappy with the notion of women working outside the home at all. Pastor and author John Piper, founder of Desiring God ministries and followed by nearly a million people on Twitter, has suggested as recently as 2015 that women shouldn't work in jobs where they have to give direction to men,[40] and in 2018 questioned whether they should teach in seminaries when God clearly intended for only men to lead and teach in churches.[41]

Just different?

Much female energy – and some male – is spent pushing back on the arguments of science, theological interpretation, social structures and stereotyping. The ground moves beneath women's feet constantly. Energy that could be used productively is directed repeatedly to the same tired conversations. It's not taught everywhere in the church, but where it is, the emphasis on spiritualised, God-created difference is strong and not open to challenge. The argument is not necessarily that men are better than women, but that God simply designed them differently. Equal but different. Women should *want* to be domestic and belong in the private sphere. Men should be public and have roles that shape and run society. Had this unfolded naturally, it might be more convincing. American author Rebecca Traister, writing about the changing status of single women, notes that governments (consisting of men, as women were denied public office and the right to vote for most of electoral history) have actively supported men's progression and property ownership and blocked women's right to any development since such laws were created.[42] Women have, in various ways, been denied the ability to participate in public life, and have had to break with social convention to do so, such as in the campaigns of suffragettes, who were imprisoned and force-fed for their actions. The wider church's position in relation to women's full participation in society has been variable.[43] The Church of England was seen as pro-establishment, and consequently several church buildings were attacked by suffragettes, though there were movements within the church and by individual members in support of women gaining the vote. (The official wedding vows of the time still asked women to 'obey' their husbands and, of course, only men could be ordained until 1994.)

More recently, there has been push-back to women's social progress, helped by social media. Since the mid-2010s Canadian professor Jordan Peterson has developed an enthusiastic following through YouTube videos directed at young, predominantly white, men wondering how to navigate a changing world where they were not guaranteed a position at the top of society. His book *12 Rules for Life* listed girls' success in school tests and their growing representation in higher education as symptomatic of a world turning against masculinity.[44] Perhaps surprisingly, his teaching has found a warm welcome among significant numbers of conservative-leaning Christian men, seemingly attracted by his discussion of Bible stories and traditional values despite the man himself not claiming a faith. Peterson has questioned whether men and women can work together without assault and harassment occurring (women could reduce this by not wearing make-up in order to be less 'sexually provocative', he offered) and has utilised the archetypes of 'masculine' and 'feminine' as order and chaos respectively.[45] His self-determining, bootstraps maleness shouldn't be a close fit with a religion built on a self-sacrificing, self-emptying Jesus who broke society's conventions to be seen with and engage with women of vastly differing (male-dictated) reputations, but that is the state of play and it leaves little room for female flourishing. The rise of bullish male demagogues around the world is unlikely to be coincidence, either – especially those championed by Evangelicals. The 'female' has been side-lined except as distraction. An uneasy relationship between this strong-arm masculinity, mainstream Christianity and conservative sex roles has come back into the mainstream of society, particularly in the US, prompting wider conversations as the internet allows for wider dissemination and instant response. Interestingly, the 'feminine' isn't necessarily limited to women.

Mix it up

US theologian Richard Beck identifies class and education as key factors when looking at the idea of the 'feminised' church (which we'll explore later), and having 'feminine traits' has been shown to be an indicator of a person's religiosity,[46] whether the person is female or not. For example, one study indicated male Anglican clergy scored lower on the 'masculine' traits of the BSRI (Bem Sex Role Inventory), a scale which includes 'assertive dominance' as acceptably masculine, and 'nurtureness-interpersonal warmth' and 'expressiveness' as feminine.[47] The scale was created to demonstrate – positively – that most people had a mix of traits, rather than men having predominantly 'masculine' traits, and women having 'feminine' ones, with a middle section of neutral traits, and for this mix to be healthier than any extreme.

There has been little attempt until recently to de-gender traits and accept that each person has a mix regardless of sex. Science hasn't always been proactive in deconstruction. It wasn't until the 1930s that scientists even began to understand that both men and women had varying amounts of the same hormones; until that point, it had been believed hormones were sex-specific and only men had testosterone.[48] Since the inception of the BSRI in the 1970s, society has evolved to see many more traits as neutral, and the gender-specific ones as dated. With questions about liking guns, being *great* at doing push ups and burning things for fun classed as traits more likely to be desirable in a man, it's possible the scale does need to be updated to reflect that expectations have changed – though perhaps not for a number of Christian men's ministries.

As God Designed It?

Church events for men and women are often dramatically different and play to existing stereotypes. For women, pampering, crafts and make-up, with colour themes of pinks and purples or soothing pastels, and a focus on feelings and emotions. They may have names that reinforce feminine imagery, like Gush and Gibber (OK, maybe more like Cherish and Bloom). John and Stasi Eldredge have built a worldwide ministry from sex-specific events like this. The description for their 'Captivating' sessions for women reads: 'Set deep in the heart of every woman are three core desires. Every woman longs for Romance, to play an irreplaceable role in a great adventure, and to be the Beauty in the tale.'[49] Women who've spent time in church environments are often familiar with these labels and some feel comfortable – especially in churches that reinforce gender roles. Encouraging women to take time for spiritual development, such as self-care or to be looked after (the shuddersome word 'pamper' is often deployed in such situations), can be valuable if they are expected to spend their time caring for others, but conversely, they may spend the time having the same messages of submission reinforced. For women who don't hold this theology, or would prefer more action, less reflection, or a different focus, such events can be stifling. Rejection of female-only events – in business or academia – can occur because women know nothing of importance is likely to happen. If women are told directly or otherwise they don't belong in places of decision-making, leadership, intelligence or importance, they may associate all-female gatherings with being side-lined. Cordelia Fine also highlights this 'stereotype threat' as a reason women may avoid associating with each other – a desire to not conform to expectations of their sex and be viewed negatively by those with social power: men or 'exceptional' women.[50]

Men's events, however, exclude women so men can be men: masculinity is valued over personhood. Often reinforcing complaints of a 'feminised church', ministries that play up stereotypes do so to provide spaces where men can be free of female influence or even women's perceived control, which is believed to squash natural urges. There may be an emphasis on rites of passage and fears of lost or confused masculinity. Events might involve tools, sport, competitive activities, fire and food (usually curry, BBQ, or bacon rolls, which women were banned from eating by the Pope in 1575). At the extreme, guns and physical fighting might be deployed[51] (the promo for 2018's Stronger Men conference featured Mixed Martial Art cage fighting and in 2014 a Kentucky church offered a raffle of weaponry to attract new members).[52] War metaphors are common, with the language of battle and brotherhood. Ministries adopt names like Conquerors, Braveheart, Fearless, and Iron (it seems there is also a group in Texas going by the name of Broverbs).[53]

Such ministries function with a specific understanding of masculinity – one that depends on women being fundamentally different and knowing their place. Some men's ministries have turned into anti-trafficking missions,[54] to rescue girls and women, or embraced projects about protecting women (from other men).[55] Women's ministries have been engaged in helping women being abused by partners, including giving gifts of cleverly disguised lipstick, which can be used to provide details of how to access help. But all of this exists in a culture that reinforces masculine entitlement, strength and daring, alongside female weakness, vulnerability and the unavoidable risks of having a female body. In a more equal society, would this be necessary? What could Christianity offer that radically reshapes how men and women understand and relate to each other? Is Christian relationship advice a good place to start? Let's find out…

Chapter Four
How to Read Christian Relationship Advice and Not Die Inside

Christian relationship advice takes many forms but – as we've seen – much of it is built on an uncomfortable premise: men and women are extremely, unavoidably, predictably different. Much more different than they are similar. This is God's idea, plan and design, we're told. He even 'wired' their brains that way, right? From the beginning of time they have been different, and as they brought upon themselves a God-ordained curse, there can be no natural harmony (discussion of what changed post-Jesus rarely features). God requires men and women to form lifelong relationships despite this. As they are fundamentally different, the best they can hope for is negotiated compromise and an on-going truce in hostilities.

As gender is discussed in increasingly non-prescriptive ways and LGBTQ rights grow in prominence, the mainstream conservative church – home of most Christian advice – pushes back and the abstinence movement rises once again. It originated in the US and in its first incarnation in the 1980s, Christian-initiated, government-funded education programmes pushed for chastity until marriage as the only way. The 21st century resurgence went international in 2018 when news reports indicated Donald Trump's government would push abstinence policies for US-funded social projects around the world.[1] Despite evidence that US programmes like *Worth the Wait* hadn't been effective,[2] the administration planned to make aid available only where women were taught 'sexual refusal skills' and access to family planning could be removed.[3] Reinforcing centuries-old messaging, male sexual desire was once again a controlling force, and women – now women without access to basic resources – were expected to negotiate their way to safety and chastity, and presumed to be safe in marriage.

A new web-savvy generation has responded to the revival of the purity movement with strong pushbacks, wanting to put an end to teaching they experienced as harmful and dangerous. Peer-led online campaigns like the No Shame Movement were created to offer 'a platform for people to discuss growing up in conservative Christian environments that were taught abstinence only' and became a rallying cry for Christians and former Christians (some of whom identified as 'Ex-vangelicals').[4] The global rise of the #MeToo movement, which originated in 2006 in the work of black activist Tarana Burke[5] to end sexual violence in her community, led to the creation of #ChurchToo. Originating in a Twitter hashtag in 2017, two American women, Emily Joy and Hannah Paasch, opened a frank and raw conversation about the abuse perpetrated within churches and laid much of the blame on the teaching and perpetuation of purity culture for creating the conditions for it to occur. Thousands have since used the opportunity to share their experiences, revealing their own long-hidden trauma and the criminality of trusted Christians who abused them. The church's response has been very mixed.

To Kiss or Not to Kiss

The most infamous of the purity-era books is one that has spawned both devoted fans and recovery groups: *I Kissed*

Dating Goodbye by Joshua Harris (or as one survey respondent called it: 'I kissed my 20s, sorry, dating, goodbye'). It is distinctly not a 'dating' book – the title is something of a giveaway – but a book about why dating is never OK for Christians. It called for a return to 'biblical courtship' and became the focal point of the 1990s purity movement, the tone of which one respondent described as 'nervous and legalistic.' Harris was aged 21 when the book was first published – though few questions were raised about the cultural gatekeepers who propelled him to prominence. Now in his 40s he is questioning its impact (and advocating 'godly dating'), after online campaigns by people who felt harmed by the messages he'd propagated. He had been home-schooled and had little exposure to life outside of his community. His passionate exposition gave the burgeoning purity movement a new, youthful face. Linda Kay Klein, author of *Pure: Inside the Evangelical Movement that Shamed a Generation of Young Women and How I Broke Free*, has studied purity culture for several years.[6] 'Purity culture emerged out of the white evangelical Christian culture in the US in the 1990s', she says. 'Purity rings, purity pledges, and purity balls came with a dangerous message: girls are potential sexual "stumbling blocks" for boys and men, and any expression of a girl's sexuality could reflect the corruption of her character.'

Real Life Love respondents had a LOT of feelings about this teaching:

> 'Purity culture was huge when I was growing up. And it was shambolic, because we made those promises before we even knew the meaning of them – probably to make our parents breathe a sigh of relief – only to feel like complete failures when we couldn't live up to the

standards. I felt like my life was worthless for two years after I lost my virginity.'

'Purity culture aimed at young girls, teaching them that it is their responsibility alone to abstain from sex and keep men from lusting after them, along with the belief that a woman's virginity, sexuality and emotional/romantic commitment belongs to her father until another man requests it and then it belongs to him created unjust pressure personally and relationally in my teenage years.'

For many the stakes were high: 'Marriage will only work if you have been abstinent.'

Christian Marriage?

Despite centuries of both Christian and secular history revealing endless permutations, 'Christian marriage' is often still based on gender roles. Women – the caring, nurturing ones, remember – are expected to be relationship maintainers and do the work now commonly called emotional labour. Consequently, much advice is aimed at women, who should not only work to improve themselves but also their relationships. If you subscribe to a theology of woman as 'helper' this will seem reasonable. Her role, even her purpose, is to ensure all goes well for her man. Her primary domain is the home, her priority is her husband and family. What greater investment could there be, outside of her relationship with God, than dedicating her time and energy to being in or getting ready for a great marriage? (The awkward reality that single women may subscribe to this but don't end up getting married is a whole other issue.) If your theology leans more towards egalitarian, it may seem reasonable to expect advice to be applicable to both parties equally, to the benefit of both. In theory, investing similar time and resources in developing their relationship, egalitarians may focus more on their similarities rather than expecting the woman to do the groundwork. If only men and women hadn't been made so utterly different . . .

Divided by a Common Language

Men like sports and food and getting to the point. Women like emotions and being told they are beautiful. Men are simple. Women are interconnected. Men do. Women are. Men have short attention spans. Women will talk until they're forced to invent new words. It's the fundamental premise of almost all Christian relationship resources – and many with no spiritual theme. A Christian worldview that reflects rather than challenges popular culture and warmly embraces stereotypes. Acceptable behaviours for men and women, what matters to them, and how they should live together. A handy sales pitch is to tell one defined group secrets about the other. American Christian author Shaunti Feldhahn's books encapsulate this and claim sales in the millions. *For Men Only* focuses predominantly on women's emotions and feelings and includes 13 reasons women don't want sex.[7] (Where women claim to want to have sex as often or more often than their partners, the survey includes a disclaimer that this couldn't be verified by speaking to their husbands.) Work and career are mentioned in the context of the man's job, and the woman's feelings about it. Her physical appearance is a focus, framed as a self-esteem issue in relation to her partner's feelings about how she looks, and about him lusting after other women's bodies. By contrast the book aimed at women covers: lust (his), sexual desire (his), what would lead a man to feel disrespected, career (his), his views on women's physical appearance and body, his ability to plan, be decisive, and be the financial provider for his family. These books – and many others like them – permeate a particular worldview. Proud, visually-driven, sexually-ready, breadwinning husband and emotionally-driven, family-focused, supportive wife. Stereotypes rule. Can 'the truth' of who a person really is be revealed through questions that pigeonhole them from the outset? Simply, no – and rarely is the wider influence of society considered. Too often men and women are offered role-play mirroring two-dimensional caricatures, and it's easy to forget just how much men can fear being thought of as feminine or sensitive. Churches often do little to present alternatives. US pastor Andy Stanley, himself the author of a Christian relationship book *The New Rules for Love, Sex & Dating* wrote, 'We purchased 9,000 copies of Shaunti's book, *For Women Only*, and gave one to every woman in our congregations as part of a special Sunday morning event.'[8]

Some Christian titles claim 'the latest brain science' to support their view. Brain 'wiring' is often referenced – the reason men need 'man caves', have smaller vocabularies, can't help looking at women's bodies, and aren't in touch with their feelings – although as we've already seen, this 'science' is far from credible. Linguist Deborah Cameron's book *The Myth of Mars and Venus* unpicks centuries of how language has been used to create and enforce sex differences.[9] In the present day, depending on social context, men might easily talk more than women, for example in business settings, and women may fear being branded difficult – or 'unfeminine' – if they are direct in speech. There isn't a simple answer attributable to 'brain wiring'.

R.E.S.P.E.C.T.

Many people – Christians and not – don't see themselves represented in these assumptions, especially common in churchy subcultures. Perhaps because roles are so predetermined in Christian marriage and dating, everything hinges on the extremes of gender differences being emphasised and framed as God's design. Most pressing in all of these resources is one difference that even forms the title of a book claiming sales of 16 million: *Love and Respect* by Emerson Eggerich.[10] Love and Respect in the world of Christian marriage advice are gendered concepts. Women need love, men need respect. When Dr Eggerich tells the story of a woman upset by her husband's failure to notice he'd bought her a birthday card for their wedding anniversary, he labels her as feeling unloved (the worst thing a woman can feel in a relationship), and her husband feeling disrespected by her unhappiness. It's entirely arguable that she was also, or even primarily, feeling disrespected (her husband hadn't bothered to check the wording on the card) and likewise he felt unloved by her unhappy response, but in the world of 'Love and Respect' – which extends through much Christian relationship teaching – these options are rarely unpacked.

A 'man being a man' and all his emotional needs being seen through the lens of 'respect' must be accepted without deconstruction. His on-going status as head of his marriage (often presented as the starting point for his ability to take his rightful place in the world) matters more than his emotional needs, even though they are part of the same deal. The 'love and respect' premise is rarely critically examined. Indeed, the 'return' to love and respect is seen as an overlooked biblical edict which is at the root of many modern relationship issues.

Or take the masculine version of the five love languages: *The 5 Love Languages for Men: Tools for Making a Good Relationship Great* by Gary Chapman (his original *5 Love Languages* book claims sales of over 10 million copies in English alone, along with translations into 49 other languages, and was mentioned positively by some in the Real Life Love survey as a helpful resource).[11] It talks about tools right from the get-go, and men love tools. 'The love she craves, the confidence you need' insists the blurb, which confirms: 'In a man's heart is the desire to master what matters', and counsels if 'you feel like you're not bringing your A-game relationally, this book is for you'. Sport. Men like sport. And winning. 'When you express your love for your wife using her primary love language, it's like hitting the sweet spot on a baseball bat or golf club', writes Dr Chapman. Yep, sport. All of the language is *precision targeted* to *strike* a *direct hit* to a man's results-oriented brain (see what I did there? Man talk). 'Simple, practical and effective', 'speaks straight', 'these pages will rouse your inner champion and empower you.' You're probably already doing star jumps and monitoring your rapidly rising testosterone levels, aren't you?

In *Becoming the Woman of His Dreams: Seven Qualities Every Man Longs For*[12], Christian author Sharon Jaynes wants women to realise they will be fulfilled, and society will be safer, if they support men no matter what. She cites the fact most prisoners are single men as proof that 'It isn't good for man to be alone.' Stats showing that men are safer drivers when their wives are in the car demonstrate that – you've guessed it – 'It isn't good for man to be alone.' The conclusion, addressed to women, is being 'called to come alongside and help.' Many books marketed to women offer a similar path: women as social workers, care takers and even crime reduction specialists. Just as God intended, as long as everyone reads the right marriage advice and sticks to the same versions of masculinity and femininity. In this interpretation of both biology and Scripture, men were created first with mission, vision, and purpose. Women were created to support them, no matter what.

Society (allegedly) works best when men lead wives who prioritise having children and keeping a nice home, provided by the man's earnings (though only one-in-ten female Real Life Love respondents wanted a provider as a relationship non-negotiable). If they support him wrongly (examples include: having too many opinions, expressing opinions, and / or having ambitions outside of helping him flourish and raising children) they may crush his spirit and desire to lead her, even though the desire was given by God and is part of the divine order. Although this worldview says men and women are 'equal but different' much of the advice prioritises the man's role and status at home and in the world, and insists the woman's fulfilment will follow from taking her place in supporting and encouraging him. His encouragement comes in the form of protecting her (from other men, presumably) and showing her love while she looks up to him. This is the version of Christian gender roles that is often reinforced. In the wider world, recent research has shown an interesting preference for male dominance: societies that valued male superiority also valued women with strong domestic skills. This was less of an innate trait than a socially proscribed one.[13]

Many Real Life Love survey respondents found their own relationships, faith experiences, theology, and worldviews have played out very differently. One male survey respondent recalled teaching 'that men (even at the relationship stage) should establish an authority-submission structure, and I swallowed this before I got wise to their nonsense. My then-relationship quickly collapsed when I tried to exert "authority" in my clumsy, immature, sincere but misguided way.'

Under the Spotlight

Making an impact outside of Christian culture is also desired, and sometimes forced. A very public example of manipulating sales figures occurred when American pastor Mark Driscoll was found to have orchestrated his 2012 marriage book *Real Marriage: The Truth about Sex, Friendship and Life Together* to the top of the *New York Times* best seller list. Using a specialised marketing company and over $200,000 of rumoured church funds, *Real Marriage* was bought in bulk by the marketers, using a list of pre-arranged customer addresses over a wide geographical spread within a set number of days.[14] The bump in apparently genuine sales pushed the title up the book chart for one week, giving it coveted and lucrative recognition, to be emblazoned across all future promotion. On the whole, Christian relationship books are written by people who are married, and who married young and stayed married. Said one respondent, 'It seems that all the advice I get is from married couples who have been married for 10+ years who got married in their early twenties.' Most are complementarian to some degree – some are openly patriarchal – and emphasise God-given sex differences as justification for roles. The authors' expertise is largely anecdotal and their status related to church leadership. Very few are trained professionally. Some have had significant challenges since marrying – there has been a recent move towards greater honesty in this area – but many are euphemistic about problems, and always after the fact. They retain a confident brand of Christianity, rarely expressing doubts about anything fundamental. In their role as spiritual leaders, many are sure they're called by God to guide other people and many are SURE they're right, often backed up with biblical examples.

A twist created by social media has been the real-life dramas of the new Christian influencers overshadowing their curated lives. New technology has proliferated under-qualified, photogenic Christian relationship gurus (usually not church leaders) who have continued the stream of stereotype-based advice, cutting out traditional gatekeepers altogether. Gaining millions of followers through an attractively-filtered lifestyle, engaging delivery and apparent authenticity are the main qualifiers for growing influence. Consequently, it has been harder to keep away unwanted attention when the mask slips. Appropriately modern versions of old sins, such as membership of the Ashley Madison affair-seeking website (home-schooled reality star Josh Duggar[15], and Christian family YouTuber Sam Rader[16] were both found to have memberships), and rehashed takes on women as lust-inciting temptresses who are happiest at home in loose clothing looking after the family, have emerged as personal brands have grown.

In Biblical Times...

It suits many modern-day Christian relationship writers to hark back to earlier centuries. Adam and Eve are the number one example (though their parenting of Cain and Abel hasn't inspired many parenting books). Old Testament marriages are stories of determination and bravery (Esther), disappointment (Leah), boldness and planning (Ruth), doubt and deceit (Sarah), and while these tales are fascinating in their own right, they mostly feature as examples of how women came to be married, and worked within their situations to influence or escape men. Often overlooked is the context of the times, the form that marriage, or even society, took, and the legal and practical reality of those times. Man as patriarchal authority, with woman as his possession or at least his total dependent and submissive, is given little attention. While Old Testament marriage may have played out more positively than it reads – poisoning women over suspected adultery aside (Num. 5:11-31) – but for women, marriage or home under the father's roof were the only options. Marriage was usually undertaken at a young age with the prospect of a speedy one-way divorce if her husband wanted to remove her from his home too. The year at home mentioned in Deuteronomy – 'When a man takes a new wife, he shall not go out with the army nor be charged with any duty; he shall be free at home one year and shall give happiness to his wife whom he has taken' (Deut. 24:5 NRSV) – would have as likely been about pregnancy and the chance to establish heirs before the husband went back to his (potentially dangerous) business. Men in these times were allowed more than one wife anyway (a polygamous system still adhered to in fundamentalist Mormon sects) so the instruction to focus on the new bride may be repeated several times. Romance all the way.

What Actually Helps and Why?

Real Life Love respondents were clear about what they found helpful. Honesty was vital. 'More open conversations about the challenges of relationships and marriages – less "us and them" approach', wrote one. Speaking to people as fellow humans and not according to gender roles. Not playing into stereotypes – or at least, the worst of them – but focusing on individuals and their actual situations. Celebrating diversity of circumstances, not the same milestones for everyone. Resources that offered practical steps that could be put into action, and advice that involved working together or reflecting on situations. Despite the wide array of books that pushed the same 'higher view' of marriage, people found demythologising helpful and didn't appreciate arbitrary sets of rules especially based on gender stereotypes. Good advice was largely not ideological, but relational. People learned from lived examples – what they had seen being worked out in their own communities, families and friendships. Personal anecdotes may help, but not someone else's journey as a template. 'People who actually understand my situation', wrote one, who noted that often, 'they've all been married since they were 20, or so it seems.' Teaching that could be interrogated and used selectively and wisely, not applied passively, was appreciated. This is especially important where theologies of one party submitting to the other are a factor. Understanding also where theology plays a part in seeking and living a different kind of relationship – covenant, mutual submission – to any secular alternatives is helpful.

What is Unhelpful – and Why?

Unhelpful advice could be divided into behaviour (what you do) and identity (who you are). Both of these are prone to stereotype reinforcement and reducing people to roles. Bad advice could be cultural (or sub-cultural): what happened in church, what was or is taught or modelled; expectations by osmosis in a closed environment that eschewed 'the world's ways'. Over a fifth of respondents specifically mentioned purity culture, and / or Joshua Harris' books. All of this is harder if a church subscribes to roles, stereotypes, rigid hierarchy, or valuing married people more than single (even if this isn't spelled out). Pushing advice, even well-intentioned, can backfire. 'Having someone offer unwanted advice is never productive, but knowing that someone is there with whom you can speak and ask questions is much better', wrote one person. Understanding previous experiences can make this a sensitive subject. 'I don't want support from church anymore. I have chosen to go my own way. I don't need myriad people telling me to do this or that or the other, all contradicting each other', wrote another.

Ignoring the ultimate context of Christianity in terms of male and female experiences doesn't help: 'More discussion about Jesus' relationships with both men and women', requested one respondent. 'Respect women more', said another. This view was echoed by another respondent who didn't want to see women restricted: 'The advice and teachings seem to work in fairy tales more than reality – women have interests, desires, hobbies, passions, etc. they should be encouraged to pursue. There are many, many assumptions that a husband is what makes a woman's life valid and/or fulfilling. Women are worth more and can achieve more than that.' Unrealistic representations should be avoided too. 'I found the prince/princess imagery pretty damaging. I don't fit into the "princess waiting to be saved" role', wrote one woman, 'and I tried to make myself for a number of years.' Valuing people for their gender and potential future relationship isn't helpful. Said one: 'Women weren't made for men. Men weren't made for women. We have worth just by virtue of existing, we don't have to exist for the opposite gender.'

Code Breakers

Spend much time in Christian culture and it will be hard to avoid well-intentioned lectures, suggestions, out of context verses, and even unexpected gifts of books (maybe that's how you ended up reading this – sorry) telling you how to find or keep God's intended person for your life. Being able to step back from other people's certainty and work out what applies personally and what has been absorbed through wider society can be a survival skill. Those who find themselves at odds with the type of marriage praised as a worthy goal in many Christian books – he leads and she submits in some form – may struggle for places to go for good advice that also incorporates faith considerations. Having a working idea of the spectrum of theological views that enables critical engagement with relationship advice is helpful. At one end of the theological spectrum, patriarchal Christianity removes choice from the female altogether, putting marriage arrangements in the hands of the father and the future husband. At the other, almost no agreed standard is presented other than mutuality in decision making and mutual submission. As long as everyone agrees with what occurs, all is well. Finding what works for you can be challenging.

Deconstructing the Past

Nobody arrives at adulthood without a set of filters, expectations and prejudices about relationships and their own sex. Based on experience, observation, overt teaching and subtle playing of roles from earliest memories, no matter what the conscious mind might insist, deep seated memories shape what seems normal and acceptable. A critical filter is vital when considering what to carry forward and what to reject. For someone who has grown up in Christian environments this can be a huge challenge.

From childhood onwards, the messages of male and female, love, dating or courtship, marriage, and singleness are communicated in thought, word and deed (to borrow a phrase from the Church of England) and then spiritualised. Who can argue with God? Add to this how your own family interacted and what culture valued. What did you imagine your adult relationships looking like and where did those images come from? Did you know people living positive single lives? Did you know who had brought you into the world and under what circumstances? Who paid the bills? Did you always have a stable home? Did divorce, infidelity or other disruptions affect your home or wider family? What TV and films did you watch, and how were men, women and relationships portrayed in them? If you grew up in church, did men and women play different roles? Each of these memories will have influenced in some way your view of relationships, marriage, family, society, yourself, and even God.

In what turned out to be a huge irony, one of my own mother's complaints was that our family was not more like *The Cosby Show*. Aside from the fact we could bat back her wishful thinking with the fact they were all paid to be there and working from a script (something we'd have been willing to try if a fee was forthcoming), the long-hidden criminality of the show's star revealed just how ludicrous it was to hope a made-up family could show a messy real one how it was done, but it was still the ideal we were measured against. Take time and reflect on these questions and other memories. Listen for the little stories you tell yourself and believe. What negative beliefs are identifiable by all-encompassing generalisations: *should, always, can't, must, never*? A man should *always* provide; a woman *must* want to be a mother more than anything else; men *always* leave in the end; a woman *should never* be a leader; men *can't* be domesticated; women *always* wants to be pursued; men and women will *always* have tensions because they're so different. If you have just one example that proves these wrong, you're on your way to a greater understanding of the world.

Even reflecting on how your own experiences have shaped you has limitations. Imagine the centuries that have gone before, and how different roles, marriages and opportunities were across the centuries documented in the Bible, to say nothing of the Dark Ages, Middle Ages, Enlightenment, Reformation, Victorian era, First World War, 1960s, and all the way up to the present day. No definitive state existed for sex, relationships or marriage. Women's status in particular has varied a lot.

The early Quakers had a non-traditional, egalitarian approach to marriage (founder George Fox's union with Margaret Fell was a partnership of mission and independence), yet in the same era church-going women in Salem, Massachusetts were accused of being witches and executed in a climate of Puritan religious extremism. In 1819, Jarena Lee became the first authorised woman preacher of the African Methodist Episcopal Church years after being told no such role could exist.[17] In the same year, women in Hawaii were permitted for the first time to eat publicly with men, a change influenced by western missionaries who believed they were helping emancipate women.[18] (Ironically, Hawaiian women already participated and led in public life, and it was foreign Christians who introduced the idea of hierarchy between the sexes.) In

1865, when Catherine Booth was preaching publicly and founding the Salvation Army to provide meals and resources to the vulnerable, British women (and only those who were married) were still five years away from the Property Act that would allow them to retain money they earned or inherited but not livestock or furniture (cows and dressing tables being just too radical a prospect).[19] In 1927 when single missionary Amy Carmichael founded the Dohnavur Fellowship in India dedicated to caring for girls rescued from ritual prostitution,[20] women back in the UK were only just allowed to serve on juries.[21] Pick a century and many more examples of uneven progress, often with a spiritual influence, will leap out. Consider the Old Testament vs New, for starters. It seems never to have been clear exactly how men and women should relate to each other, and yet those who are attracted enough to each other seem to find ways forward. If after all this, you're feeling brave enough to contemplate what dating and forming relationships looks like in the 21st century – and maybe even brave enough to give it a try, if that's your situation – that's where we're going next…

Chapter Five
21st Century Dating: Technology, Ambiguity and Other Fun Things

Modern dating is hard. Over two-thirds of Real Life Love respondents described it as 'challenging'. Almost half found it contradictory, and four-in-ten said confusing and fast moving too. Just 2% said it was straightforward (maybe they can write their own book). A quarter thought it was demeaning, compared to just one-in-ten who enjoyed it and the 5% who found it enriching. For over a quarter, the culture of dating and relationships was their most pressing relational issue. It's understandable. There's no right way, no guaranteed route, to find a human with whom to travel through life. The simpler times of courting – meet an acceptable person within a five-mile radius and settle down to parent-approved, life-long marriage within a matter of months – have (mostly) gone. The etiquette can be bewildering. Boundaries are blurred. Technology has raised the stakes. #RelationshipGoals is a thing, though nobody is sure quite what they should be aspiring to. For Christians, a whole other set of issues arise. To launch into this tricky topic with some scene-setting, vivid mental imagery, behold the following highly scientific, immersively researched list. I will accept no questions on it, thank you for your understanding:

-x- An entirely objective list of signs your dating situation might not work long term -x-

Before you've met in person, he tells you the headache that has driven him to bed and forced him to cancel your date has been sent by the devil to keep you apart.

He calls you one morning to ask if you know what size shoes he takes. Your response, 'Can you just check the ones you're wearing? Or look at your feet? Because I'd just be guessing...' is treated as a revelation of great profundity.

While on public transport at the end of a date a concerned stranger mouths, 'Do you need help?' assuming you're being bothered by a tipsy vagrant who can't remember where to get off (in more ways than one) rather than being romanced by the love of your life.

He won't go anywhere – *anywhere* – without his dog because they've 'been through things'.

He tells you he used to date one of Bananarama but he's not sure which one because it was the 80s.

After you decline to give your phone number – the one you've had for years and use for work – to a dating site stranger, you are told you are 'obviously not a modern girl.' You still don't give them the number.

He calls you a bitch on the first date then emails you an essay he's written about the dehumanising effects of the military on modern man by way of apology.

He tells you he has given up on love, aged 28, and is now searching for a companion to see out his days and – *pause for impact* - you might be suitable.

He gets so angry when he talks about politics he spits while ranting insults about former Labour leader Ed Miliband, and it lands on your face.

He says he'll see you soon but the next time you see him is on a dating app and his attention is definitely elsewhere.

After inviting you to a party via social media and telling you his life story, he ends the evening with 'great to put a face to a name.'

He gets a drink for himself on your first meeting and that drink is tap water. He sends the waitress away without asking if you'd like anything.

He tells you he'd like to be part of a power couple.

He tells you he doesn't usually date women who speak English because 'why would you ruin a perfectly good relationship by understanding what the other person is saying?'

He turns up to a talk you're giving. And heckles.

Yea, Though I Pass through the Valley of the Hormones

Over three-quarters of incidents above involved self-described Christians meeting with the possibility of romance, yet this snapshot of *someone*'s (*cough*) dating experiences is a world away from earlier Christian expectations. Many faith leaders appear baffled by the changing landscape. Most older married Christians have no experience of it. Younger Christians who met and married within the bubble of church, youth group, university or college Christianity or home-schooling view it from a safe distance, having been shepherded safely through high-risk hormones. Advice is cautionary: 'Join a mission trip', 'wait and God will bring the right one', 'pray about it'. Anything that translates to a holding pattern is ideal – particularly for women, the ones who should wait to be pursued.

For single people figuring out where to start, or whether to start at all, it can be overwhelming. Perhaps it should be. The world has opened up. Potential paramours are no longer restricted to whoever walks into church on a Sunday or moves in two doors down, but could be anywhere, able to make contact across continents with a couple of clicks. You could meet anyone. *Anyone.* Or anyone pretending to be someone (an oft-repeated fear).

Technology has changed how people connect and why. Yes, people still date (though that can take many forms), and have relationships (ditto), and still get married, and some of those marriages last a long time. But now there are hook ups, ambiguous friendships, friends with benefits, conscious uncouplings, and polyamory too. There are prototype sex robots and virtual reality encounters, bypassing the need for another person altogether if the price is right. It's confusing (not to mention the spiralling electricity bills). There is no handy list of what to do or not do in order to find love, or what it should consist of. The terminology, patterns, and acceptable aberrations in human interaction that now pass for romantic social contact are evolving rapidly. One person's normal is someone else's 'you're not going to believe what they just said' text from the café toilet. We are all strange. Happily married people just get to hide it better.

Where Do People Meet in the 21st Century?

Where are these mystical places a person might encounter another person who might also want to date? For starters: on a train, through a dating app (crazy but true), at a talk, in a coffee shop, at work, on social media, at a festival, in a pub, at another festival (actually, festivals should get their own list), on a dating website, at a wedding, at a friend's house, volunteering, at a conference, at a charity dinner, on holiday, at a lecture, and of course church (because maybe). It should be possible to meet someone who might want to date anywhere there are other people. Nowhere comes with a guarantee, and it would be a waste of anyone's precious time on earth to go to many great places purely on alert for potential dates, especially if not meeting someone will feel like failure. Dating events often have a female-skewed attendance, especially Christian events, so if you're a single-ready-to-mingle woman, don't go with a Jane Austen type mindset, expecting to be courted by a suitable gentleman with good prospects and £200 a year (though many writers would be thrilled at such riches).

Viewing others only in to-date-or-not-to-date terms is reductive. Exhaustion and disappointment tend to follow those who feel they can't stay at home for a few evenings in case they miss The One. This heavenly fantasy partner who could only have been encountered at God's appointed place the only time they were too tired to leave the house. If you're thinking you might join a dating site, pick a couple (of sites or apps, unless you're planning to get really experimental). Broaden your horizons so you're not going to see the same recycled profiles and faces. Join a regular, non-faith site if you want to and say you're a Christian if that's an important factor; the world is unlikely to end.

Technology

People have been pursuing, ignoring, evading, teasing, and messing each other about since forever but now have ever-present screens through which to do it. Somehow, it's even more distressing knowing someone could make contact in seconds – and still doesn't. In the olden days, hours between phone calls – or the weeks between a liveried messenger's update on dowry negotiations – were a daydreamer's paradise. Now with a few clicks almost anyone can be tracked down. Failing to manage 24-hour availability is a step towards overload and burnout. Work, social and family demands are now a notification away. Add romantic interactions into the mix too and the emotional toll can be immense.

Humanity is still adapting – often poorly – to rapidly developing technology, unaware of the effects on the brain. Former innovators of social media companies now report their distress at the products they helped to develop and popularise. Facebook founding president Sean Parker has commented about the platform he helped to create,[1] which now has almost two billion users around the world: 'It literally changes your relationship with society, with each other.'[2] Commenting in 2017 he talked about their aim being

'How do we consume as much of your time and conscious attention as possible?' and their intention of 'exploiting a vulnerability in human psychology'. Chamath Palihapitiya, former vice-president for user growth at Facebook who no longer uses the site or allows his children to, said in the same year, 'Your behaviours, you don't realize it, but you are being programmed.'[3] American research suggested three-quarters of Facebook users visited the site every day.[4] It's concerning – especially alongside accusations of data breaches and election influencing, not to mention Facebook's intention to launch their own dating service (Is there anything they won't know about you?).[5] A quarter of respondents said social media and the internet had added anxiety to their dating and relationship experiences, particularly the waiting and wondering. Just under half said it was an interesting way to connect with people. Fewer than 2% had given up on social media altogether. Learning to filter and switch off is necessary. Self-preservation is vital.

Dictionary for a Brave New World

So what happens when people do actually get to communicate with a view of romance? Technology means new etiquette and a whole new dictionary of terms along the way. Heard of *socialating*? That's when you bring together friends and a date for a group outing. Or *friendship dating*? Using dating-like sites created to meet potential friends and expand social circles, rather than romantic partners – though in more conservative Christian circles this can also mean getting to know someone as a potential marriage partner without actually being a couple. Once we get to one-to-one contact, the terms become more specific – and often more obscure.

For example, the lovely person who seemed really interested when you met six months or two years ago and then stopped messaging and has recently appeared in your inbox again out of the blue. *Hi how r u?* Were they unavoidably detained on secret government business or were you *benched*? (a repurposed sporting term, only this time you've been turned into an unwitting substitute called up when other options haven't worked out; expect to be returned to the sidelines without warning. Especially if they appear at Christmas – that's known as *Marleying*.) Did that oh-so-keen person fade out but every now and then pops up to like your photo or message a link to a TV show or LOL at your Facebook status but without conversations developing or you ever meeting up? That's *breadcrumbing,* baby. Sneaky little anythings to remind you they still exist and they'd like you to notice. Maybe they're just being friendly, but if you feel an unhealthy thrill or your brain tick into 'Where is this *going?*' overdrive, it's best to let it go. The answer is probably nowhere. Unless it's the time of *cuffing*, maybe. That season when the nights draw in and it's getting nippy out, and you might be looking for someone close by with whom to settle for at least a few months rather than continue to work the virtual room and risk catching a chill.

Of course, it could be coincidental timing, but if you find yourself picked up in October and dropped in March you might just have been a cuffer's mittens (I'm claiming that one. Get me in the Urban Dictionary right now). What you might also have been is a *cushion* – also known as a *layby;* one of those trusting sorts who didn't realise they were benched, or maybe you met someone already coupled, and your interest is kept warm should there be a sudden vacancy in the love department. Showing some attention to keep you interested but never progressing to anything concrete is known as *tuning* (though *tuning* can also be the pre-official dating stage when you're gauging someone's interest and kinda-maybe-flirting). If you think you're dating someone but all your contact has been via screen you might be in a *textlationship*, something that can befall people who meet online. All this kid-in-a-candy-shop virtual choice has changed how people part ways too. *Ghosting* is the soul-crushing phenomenon of having the person you're dating (or even in a full-blown committed relationship with) cease all contact without warning. It's increasingly common (4.5% of survey respondents said they'd do it), and men and women apparently do it equally. The reasons may be different – some women reported ending contact without warning where they anticipated they may be at risk, men to avoid awkwardness – but for many recipients the effect is the same: confusion, hurt, even devastation. The alternative is *Caspering* (being like that friendly ghost and ending things nicely before vanishing).[6] Those who ghost in a casual dating situation then pop up later might be *benchers* or *cushioners* – or genuinely sorry for disappearing – but trust a ghoster again only with caution.

A slightly more humane way out is the *slow fade* where messages diminish and eventually dry up altogether. That once-keen person is suddenly really busy at work or takes a week to reply instead of their previous hourly contact. Confusing and hurtful again, but perhaps more of an opportunity to ask what's going on. By attempting to drop a hint – a kind of reverse breadcrumbing, where spasmodic contact means 'no thanks' rather than 'how you doin'?' – the one being faded has the choice to cease contact, letting the fader off the hook and dealing with the sadness alone, or continue unabashed hoping it's all a terrible misunderstanding / the network is down / nothing has changed. It's a grim choice, so if you're tempted to slow fade, do consider the effect of your inaction. Passivity is not an attractive trait. As an extreme, you might find yourself *blocked* or deleted. Suddenly your messages won't deliver, you can't see if someone's been online lately, you check Facebook to find you have the 'Add friend' option in place of your previous shared banter. It's possible this is someone cutting you out because they have their own issues, but it's also a route for someone who feels unsafe.

I've given you the benefit of the doubt here, dear reader – not that it's enjoyable to have any of these behaviours inflicted upon you – but if you are the one ghosting, cushioning, benching and everything in between, STOP IT. Technology may allow for these behaviours but show some humanity, for the love of all that is good and holy. Do unto others, and all that.

It's not all bad though. That photo of a burger you Instagrammed two years ago and forgot about until the person who was extra welcoming at your new house group suddenly 'liked' it? That's a *deep like*, trawling back through someone's social media like a hungry hippo clicking on everything in sight (if you have zero subtlety), a carefully curated selection (you artiste, you), or accidentally hitting something from five years ago while trying to zoom in and panicking / moving to China before anyone realises. And *haunting* is the opposite of *ghosting*, just to confuse you. Being a constant presence in someone's social media, commenting on everything, responding to every status or in one person's case being mistaken for a haunter while watching a cringey Facebook-Live broadcast unaware the broadcaster was notified when they popped up and gave them a wave and shout out.

There are few hiding places online. Unless you're *stashing,* that is: when you're in a relationship but not publicly. No social media update (also known as *FBO* or *Facebook Official*), nothing that would give away your status to your online – or even real life – community. And why might you be stashing? Is it all those *thirst traps* (those attention-grabbing 'who me?' sexy pics posted faux-innocently)? It couldn't be *sexting* (sending or requesting naked pictures or explicit messages, something a quarter of survey participants said they'd do, though several specified only within the context of a marriage), could it..? Before being publicly connected, you might say you were *talking* (dating casually) or *seeing* someone. Until you've had the *DTR* (Define the Relationship talk), who can say? Maybe you're in a *situationship,* a grey area of spending time together, doing coupley things, being romantic perhaps for months but haven't given it a label. Or it's a *hook up* (sexual contact of some sort without any other attachment; yes, Christians might be doing this too or being asked to), or maybe an *ambiguous friendship* (Are they keen? Aren't they? What does it mean, they want me to be their plus one to a wedding? 22% of survey respondents said they'd allowed ambiguous friendships to develop, including 20% of married respondents.) One respondent recalled 'Many, many, *many* "Christian Coffees" – you know, where you go out for coffee with a guy, sit for three hours or more talking and staring into each other's eyes, and then get the "I see you as my sister in Christ" chat.'

Poor behaviour is not the preserve of the faithless or other-faithed – never be tempted to think that. No human is immune. But this is why it can be seen as highly tempting to button it all down and start calling for the old fashioned ways with a new twist: Wait for him to pursue you! Get yourself ready to be pursued!

Men, step up! Ask! Be clear! The language of Christianese comes into its own in the area of romance. Guard your heart. Guard her heart. Guard everybody's heart! Be intentional. But unless you're immersed in a close-knit community where everybody knows the rules and is happy to abide by them, have their behaviour overseen to at least some degree by others in the community, be willing to see the rules through to a socially acceptable conclusion and not look beyond the community for possible partnering, this will not suffice. So, other solutions are needed: a way to navigate the new world in the age of choice and connectivity, and the best way will be the one that harnesses both new possibilities and timeless winners.

Overwhelm

OK, take a moment. You've probably realised by now: modern love can be tough. Tough enough that you might tick a box marked 'hopeless' when asked in a survey – let's say... the Real Life Love survey – how you feel about your relationship situation, both now and about what the future might hold:

	In the present	About the future
Positive	57.72%	64.13%
Happy	44.94%	39.10%
Hopeful	44.38%	58.94%
Content	39.33%	35.41%
Lonely	22.61%	17.30%
Confused	14.04%	20.07%
Ambivalent	10.74%	13.26%
Negative	6.67%	5.77%
Hopeless	6.18%	9.46%

Just over 6% of all respondents admitted to hopelessness – meaning that even in churches full of bright-eyed folks, the secretly hopeless may well be among them, hiding in plain sight and maybe behind a smile. And hopelessness was the only negative response expected to increase over time (though a fair few expected happiness and contentment to decrease too). Alongside hopeless, almost a quarter of people admitted to feeling lonely, and 14% were confused about their relationship situation too (a feeling they expected to increase). That's a fair few people having a hard time. If that's you, you are not alone. The 'hopeless' ranged from early 20s to over 60 but were mostly female, in their late 20s to mid-30s, living in a city or big town (almost nine-in-ten), single, and looking but haven't had a significant relationship. How long you've been a Christian, how actively or enthusiastically you're involved in church aren't determining factors; you can be a committed, regular and keen churchgoer and still describe yourself as feeling hopeless.

You could also be married – being partnered is not an antidote to hopelessness – though most who felt hopeless were not. You may also say you're 'lonely' (three-quarters of those feeling hopeless did, compared to a quarter of all respondents) and 'frustrated' (two-thirds), and 'confused' (almost half). You're less likely than a self-described 'happy' and 'positive' person to believe that working on your emotional health is a good idea. You're twice as likely as those who describe themselves as 'positive' or 'happy' to believe 'Christian men don't ask women out', 'God sends The One', and 'God created soulmates and there's a perfect match out there somewhere' – all of which suggest a theology of passive waiting, particularly for women, and the combination doesn't lead to joy. Three-in-ten respondents believed their 'part in finding a Christian partner is to focus on working on myself and becoming someone worth choosing', the same number who believed it was 'God's timing' they hadn't met anyone.

These feelings also point to some solutions: a theology of relational partnership rather than one dependent on a man pursuing a woman or a partner being delivered directly by God. A reminder not to neglect inner development and healing at any age. A strong prompt to leaders and to the community not to assume smiling faces or regular attendance means all is well. Hopelessness can be a relative state, the culmination of comparison and isolation in a culture that models marriage as success. Some commented they would have ticked 'hopeless' had they completed the survey a couple of years earlier, while still single, but having met partners and recently married they were now feeling positive and happy. While this is joyous for them, it would be easy for gaps between the happily coupled and the wider community to be exacerbated. If you'd describe yourself as feeling hopeless at the moment, I'm sorry. It sucks. If you've been promised certain outcomes if you just held on and waited and it seems like it's for nothing, I'm sorry. Where you're hiding behind a smile, know that you're not the only one going through these emotions. It may require some time and some work but you can change your perspective. Nobody is immune to despair or confusion, but for your sake, give yourself a hug, take a deep breath, and when you're ready, take a few careful steps forward.

'Have You Tried Going Online . . . ?'

This is the go-to question of modern relationships, and Christians are not sure what they think of it all (though just 7%

said they'd never look for a partner online). Perhaps it comes from following a faith originating in ancient times, but it seems some Christians don't always want to live in the present. Wishful – sorry, did someone say prayerful? – thinking about how the perfect partner must be met denies a rapidly changing world. As dating sites, apps, social media and online interactions proliferate, how much are Christians willing to embrace this new normal? Though just over 50% of Real Life Love survey participants said they'd be happy to try online dating, when asked how they would expect to meet someone if looking for a partner now, many answers were a little… nostalgic. The 'single and looking' would expect to meet a new paramour by just crossing paths in life (83.5%); through church (82.7%); set up by friends (74%). Yes, almost three-quarters would expect a pal-based matchmaking service – friends, take note.

When asked if they would expect to use social media to meet a new partner now, positive responses varied. At most a fifth of all who replied said yes. Of course, you can ignore all those modern shenanigans if you like. But while the single and (apparently) looking would like to carry on doing what they're doing, go to church (for which, blessings to you), get their friends to find them someone, probably not join a dating site (only 51% said they would expect to meet a partner this way, even fewer on a dating app), or go to a dating event, many are frustrated at not meeting people. Only one-in-ten single people said social media so far had no effect on their dating or relationships (let us gloss over the fact they were answering this question in an online survey about relationships, and now make up part of a statistic about the impact of the internet on their perceptions of them). So, for the clear majority, communication has evolved and done so recently. Short of the apocalypse / rapture taking us all out, technology is shaping how we interact. Many are now mixing with people outside previous safe zones of work, education, church and local community, and bringing strangers into their existing circles. Consider how to respond to this (aside from praying for the rapture, obviously).

Offline Just Fine?

According to official statistics, 99% of 16-34 year olds in the UK used the internet in 2017.[7] Only 9% of British adults overall have never used the internet. American statistics indicate 89% of the population is online.[8] Maybe you are Analogue Christian, powered by eye contact alone, hoping potential partners appear in front of you and say the right thing, and that's not impossible. There are some good reasons for straightforward optimism. Many long-term relationships do begin at work or through friends. Proximity with other people is a failsafe for feelings to develop – whether good or bad, romantic or not – and a life with limited opportunity to interact reduces the chance of romance developing casually. Don't rule out someone you've known in other contexts having relationship potential. Attachment to the idea of a transcendent romantic connection can kill off potential relationships because the ever-present internet tells us there are endless options. Or that when we finally see each other we will 'just know'. Butterflies are a rare occurrence but if you're going to give dating a go, don't judge success by whether it feels like a fairy tale. Almost everything else matters more, including: sincerity, kindness, generosity, respect and sense of humour. Consider whether someone is nice to you. Nice is good. Look out for all these things, no matter how you first meet. Sparks, especially through screens, are fleeting and notoriously unreliable.

Digital Dilemma

To step out and actively date digitally – going online, downloading an app – can be done partnering with God, if that is a prime consideration. It's not a less holy way to meet someone. There is no inherent evil or immorality in seeing someone's face on a screen before seeing it in person. If you're that person, know this: you're not the first person to do this. Every profile (OK, not on Ashley Madison) is attached to a human being, some of whom you'll have met already. (Of course, nobody has ever checked a dating app in a megachurch 'just to see' who else is on there during the sermon.) The digital world is not separate from the flesh and blood one. It is another facet, or a reflection of it. 'Do unto others' comes into its own when those others are viewed on a screen. How easy is it to forget the three-dimensional person who exists beyond the picture? How simple to project onto them, too. Gathering friends for group readings of strangers' profiles. Deciding from a paragraph about pets and hobbies and three blurry pictures that perfection has been found. It happens.

Ultimately dating using technology may result in meeting a suitable partner. It may not, but it might encourage a more open-minded approach. You could have a dating site membership for ten years and end up chatting with someone wonderful at a bus stop. You might spend five nights a week at church groups and social projects, and meet someone on an occasionally used dating app. You might not go on your first date until you're of an age where your birthday cake can't support all the candles, but the first one is the start of happily ever after. You can be doing everything 'right' and still be single when you don't want to be. There are no formulas and no guarantees, but there are a few things that will make the journey more manageable, maybe even enjoyable (I even sneaked 'A Practical Guide to Meeting Another Human' into the resources section at the back of the book for anyone who might need a little help getting started...). And now, gird your loins and anything else that jiggles, we're going to talk sex. You have been warned.

Chapter Six
A Brief History of Christian Sexual Awkwardness

Have you encountered much Christian sex talk? It has its own vocabulary: purity, fornication, God's blueprint, soul ties, lust, giving yourself away, stumbling, counter-cultural, the reward for waiting, God's best, going too far, stewarding your sex drive, falling into sin, wired for intimacy and walking in freedom are just some of the highlights. 'Emerge from combat with your trophy of purity intact so that you can present it to your lover on your honeymoon night,' insists one American ministry.[1] 'Sex outside of marriage is an instrument that is used to cover relational flaws instead of dealing with them', says another.[2] Much of the advice has little resemblance to the real lives of those it's directed towards, whether single (sex verboten) or married (sex enthusiastically encouraged). Unsurprisingly, Real Life Love respondents had a lot of thoughts about this. 'I did all the things I thought I was supposed to do', wrote one. 'Didn't have sex outside of marriage, didn't go out with people who weren't Christians, met a Christian, and got married. But I didn't expect my mind to change so much on these things. I'd do it so differently now, but it's kind of too late.' Said one unmarried respondent, 'I have heard so much about how wrong sex outside marriage is that I don't know what would be appropriate. I would never judge anyone else for what they did – and yet I don't know if things would be appropriate for me in that situation. I just find the whole thing very confusing.'

And Christians just can't agree on where sex should figure. Take the responses to the question 'Did you or would you wait until being married to have a sexual relationship?'

Yes I did	18.33%
Yes I plan to	22.28%
I plan to now but might not	4.72%
I planned to but changed my mind	9.33%
I planned to but couldn't	10.32%
No	14.49%
If I was single again I would not wait until married again	1.76%
I didn't but have now decided to wait in future	6.59%

A quick calculation shows an exact split of 40.6% who waited or plan to, and 40.6% who didn't or won't (excluding those who have decided to wait in future.) It's not what much of the church wants to acknowledge. Of the 12% who gave a written response rather than ticked a box, the majority described varying levels of sexual activity. 'I planned to wait until marriage but instead waited until after our engagement', said one. 'I had a sexual relationship before I was married, but when I met my now-husband, we both decided to save sex until we got married', wrote another. 'We called it outercourse . . . i.e. no penetration', said one.

But what about the official responses, the messages you might encounter in church? Some (though not many) advocate Christian Celibacy 101: stay single and DON'T DO IT. Ever.

Then there's the one about ideally *not* doing it but if you really can't help yourself, marrying someone in the vicinity ASAP and channelling your urges (courtesy of St Paul). And the one about doing it for the sake of married procreation but not enjoying it (Augustine). And, of course, the one about being 'pure' until marrying as a virgin then living out a modern-day Song of Songs with Adam-and-Eve levels of ecstasy as God always intended (21st century American Evangelicalism), the close cousin of the anything-goes-as-long-as-you've-said-I-do ideal of dominant men and their hot wives (American complementarianism, Macho Division). Or no sex on Sundays or feast days (big in the Middle Ages[3]) or the fruitful polygamy of your preferred patriarch (sex with multiple partners for him, just the one for her). And more recently a range of liberal interpretations, some marriage-rejecting – or at least marriage-sceptical, focused on commitment rather than legal status – and others interested only in whether consenting adults are involved and don't believe God is particularly concerned about their sexual activity, or that God is encouraging of their encounters as expressions of grace or holiness.

So maybe *the* Christian ideal isn't a thing, as such. With a few exceptions, most interpretations of the Bible's sexual ideal offer one uniting theme: Don't do it. Get married. Do it. Fool proof. This containment strategy is regarded as a success in churches where repression is seen as the safest solution to the 'problem' of human sexuality. It has varied little through the ages since Adam and Eve's God-approved coupling took a wrong turn. Attempts to 'sell the benefits' of pre-marital abstinence and celebrate a physically-unfulfilled God-created sex drive through non-sexual activities and delayed gratification through eventual marriage are a recent occurrence (fewer than 5% of survey participants believed 'God will reward my abstinence with a great partner' though over a third agreed that 'The promise of great sex after marriage is used as a reason to be abstinent before it'). In post-Eden biblical times, sex was, at best, something done by a man to the young virgin he'd effectively 'bought' from her father, a way of producing children. Or written about in sexy verses by a privileged king who could spread his attentions around a few hundred concubines.

It has been viewed through a lens of negativity towards women, with scriptures interpreted to blame them for tempting men (Bathsheba), having loose morals (the woman at the well), being the visible face of temptation (the woman caught in adultery), showing courage despite their sexual availability (Rahab), as a bargaining tool to save a nation (Esther), destroy a hero (Delilah), or end a life (Salome's request for John the Baptist's head) rather than viewed with an understanding of women's lack of power. If their sexuality was used, it was usually against them. In short, men had the power. They determined how, when, and to whom sex happened.

Forever Eve?

Women having choices is a very modern phenomenon, for centuries considered 'daughters of Eve', weak and easily deceived. Monks and other men set the tone, with advice that ranged from the physically restrictive ('Sexual activity', wrote 17th century monk Brother Cherubino, 'should not involve the eyes, nose, ears, tongue, or any other part of the body not vital to procreation.')[4] to detailed lists of the days sexual contact should be avoided (three days either side of Communion was recommended), which positions would lead to sinful lust, even for one's wife (anything but lying down was discouraged),[5] and the terrible risks for the oversexed (early death, weak and sickly children, lack of energy and vigour were among the highlights).

Sex was viewed with suspicion, disdain and often disgust. Even married couples were encouraged towards celibacy once they had produced sufficient children (contraception not being an option), as if they weren't already contending with shortened life expectancy and the occasional plague. The original contexts for sex laid out in the New Testament were rarely lived out beyond the time of writing. There were few cross-class, counter-cultural communities of shared resources, inspired by end times urgency to prioritise abstinence and preaching the gospel. Within centuries the church was a land-owning seat of power. Official religious life separated off into priesthood and monasticism, and contemporary Christian thought about marriage and sex often emerged from (supposedly) celibate monks. Sex was life, death, and the threat of spiritual ruin. Virginity equalled purity, virtue and value. Pressing questions of first-date-to-kiss-or-not-to-kiss were a world away.

Chaste Not Haste

The church's expectations ran high, even if conduct was surprising. Tudor church-splitting machinations and wife beheading, for example, or popes illicitly fathering children into the 1800s,[6] and that little discussed period of history when the Bishop of Winchester profited from brothels by London's River Thames (there was a steep fine of £10 for owners who had down-on-their-luck nuns for hire).[7] Victorian society and Christianity emphasised high morals and valued respectability regardless of private actions. By the 20th century the 'live for the moment' uncertainty of two world wars had a loosening effect on behaviour. There was a 70% increase in sexual infections during the Second World War, as well as thousands more births outside of marriage, but in 1945 the then-Archbishop of Canterbury urged a return to 'Christian' living and an end to sexual immorality. People listened. Marriage increased as order returned.[8] In a 1951 survey, almost two-thirds of 10,000 British people believed women shouldn't have any sexual experience outside of marriage, though just over half thought the same for men.[9]

Sexuality and Christianity intertwined and set the standard again. Homosexuality was still outlawed for men and beyond the pale for women. Male desire needed taming and boundaries. Women were still presented as without sexual urges, suited to domesticity and nurture. Marriage was the solution. A breadwinning man faithfully married to a homemaking woman was the ideal. A place of order, safety and satisfaction, though other options were few, especially if you were female. Hard to imagine now, but American women couldn't apply for a credit card until 1975.[10] British women could not open bank accounts until the same year, and until 1982 could have their money rejected in pubs (no wonder men paid on dates).[11] Until this century in Ireland (the Equality Act in 2000), women could be refused a pint as it was deemed unladylike.[12] Maternity pay wasn't a legal requirement until 1986 in the UK,[13] and abuse was often overlooked – before 1991 the law didn't recognise rape within marriage.[14] Until 1978 an American woman could be fired for being pregnant.[15] A woman's wellbeing in marriage depended on the man she married, and life outside of marriage was very restricted.

Understanding of biology and lived-out sexuality changed over time. The Kinsey report – books on male and female sexuality, published in 1948 and 1953 respectively – explored previously overlooked attitudes and behaviours, offering contentious findings about the prevalence of infidelity and promiscuity.[16] From the 1950s to the 1990s, American researchers William H. Masters and Virginia E. Johnson dedicated themselves to understanding the physiology of sex and sexual dysfunction.[17] Sex moved from a great unmentionable to a subject of interest and discussion, as researchers' ideas were disseminated into wider culture. Until the 1960s – the decade of the contraceptive pill and so-called Sexual Revolution – and 1970s, sex outside of marriage was strongly disapproved of, condemned within Christian communities and society as immoral and disruptive.

Christian commentators were both relieved and shocked in the 1990s to learn new research – 'Sex in America: A Definitive Survey' – suggested Christians were actually quite sexy-sexy.[18] Religious conservatives enjoyed sex – hurrah! Conservative Protestant women reported they were the most likely to orgasm during sex – many hurrahs! (assuming they were with their conservative Protestant husbands at the time). Infidelity overall was lower than previously believed, and yet almost 50% of respondents, including Christians, supported 'relational sex' (sex within loving relationships) above 'traditional sex' (married and heterosexual). 'The data suggest a chasm between official doctrinal teachings and the behaviour of followers', concluded *Christianity Today* back in 1995.[19] Well, quite. In the ideal Christian world, within the context of one man, one woman, married forever sex could happen – let's not assume flourish – and never need to be discussed in polite society, especially in church. Though some parts of the church may have taken a more liberal view of sexuality, most did not. What changed was the church ceasing to be an automatic moral authority in an increasingly individualised society.

No Guarantees

Whatever was now acceptable elsewhere, little changed for Christians. Ignorance of bodies and sex was more likely than good working knowledge. Churches persistently represented a view of male desire and female submission, and Real Life Love respondents, ranging in age from late teens to over 60s, heard it over and over again. 'The myth of "men want sex, women don't" often seems to be perpetuated. If you're in a relationship and this is the opposite, that's not very helpful', said one respondent. Another wrote it was implicit that 'men are more sexually aroused than women. I was never taught that women would enjoy sex.' Avoiding sex outside of marriage was often much more important to Christians than teaching consent or what healthy intimacy could look like. Said one woman, 'I often feel I'm not having sex so that my parents feel more Christian.' Wrote one younger survey respondent, 'the reality of physical relationships was never talked about – so as soon as I got involved with someone it became apparent I didn't have the knowledge to make the right decisions.' Another recalled, 'There was a lot of teaching about what you weren't allowed to do in relationships ("no heavy petting"), but I don't feel there was much about how to do healthy relationships, and I still feel that is the case ("flee sexual temptation").' Few remembered a vision of equality. One survey respondent recalled being taught 'The husband is the boss of the wife' and another remembered, 'Women should be support to their husband, who God will supply with the vision for their life.' Another participant recalled the 'woman is submissive, sex is for procreation or male pleasure and is only vaginal.'

Cease and Desist

In contemporary western Christianity, most conversations about sex revolve around personal desire and purity. Churches often emphasise the same. Respondents recalled teaching that dating with the possibility of sex was 'dangerous' and 'very complicated and risky' and could lead to activity that was 'wrong and very damaging'. Though just over a third personally agreed with the concept of 'purity', defined as 'total abstinence until marriage and emphasis on virginity / reclaimed virginity', over 70% believed this was the mainstream Christian view. 'I found the pressure for couples to get married to avoid temptation and stay pure until their wedding night extremely unhelpful and felt it did not encourage strong relationships, just relationships where couples were not having sex', said one participant. Another recalled 'being told if a group of us went out in one car at night, the (presumed male) driver shouldn't drop his girlfriend off last, because they might be tempted. This was and is hilarious: even then, I think I knew that people sometimes had sex during the daytime.' Indeed, 50% of respondents agreed with the statement 'Christian culture emphasises abstinence over teaching about healthy relationships.' Another remembered 'ridiculous tips for avoiding accidentally having sex e.g. setting a timer so you couldn't go too far.'

There was little that could be called sex or relationship education. One respondent recalled the extent of teaching consisted of 'nothing apart from Biblical relationships being presented through the Bible stories'. Another wrote:

'I think the "Just Say No" approach to sex before marriage was really unhelpful. That combined with the "slippery slope" theory of any physical intimacy was quite damaging and guilt-inducing. My husband and I gradually deepened our physical levels of intimacy throughout our relationship, learning what each other enjoyed, exploring each other's bodies as we explored each other's thoughts and emotions, likes and dislikes. While we didn't have full sex until our wedding night, we had experienced three years of increasing intimacy before that and have continued to learn and grow together since. I think this is a pretty healthy model, yet so much of our pre-married relationship was spent feeling guilty about our physical relationship. We were led to believe that doing anything beyond kissing was 'playing with fire' and sinful. When you are taught that giving each other pleasure with your bodies is bad, you cannot just switch that thinking off when you suddenly change your legal status to married, and it took a while to feel my body and what I did physically could be "good".

Recalled another now-married participant, 'All I heard was "Don't do it, don't do it, it's bad!" but that suddenly, once you're married, sex will be glorious. Almost three and a half years into marriage, I still struggle to enjoy sex because I think I squashed that part of me for so long it's almost completely disappeared!' It's rare for Christian conversations about sex to encompass anything other than avoidance. It would be helpful to encourage couples to communicate about their desires and intentions and work out how they perceive and want to grow their relationship. To help develop an understanding of how to show love for the other in the best way they can, and not pursue a selfish agenda. Following the example of American author Peggy Orenstein, who has written extensively about cultural pressures on girls, ask what making a relationship sexual will add to it: A sense of maturity? Closeness? Commitment?[20] Sex doesn't occur in a cultural vacuum and it's important to acknowledge the effects.

The Hunter and the Hunted

The weight of history, power imbalances between men and women, and often repressive examples of Christian marriages from biblical times onwards blur in the present day desire for a Christian fairy tale romance that embodies the culture's most celebrated aspects. Despite insistences that 'Of *course* we value singleness. Jesus was single!' marriage and romantic love remain elevated and the roles are often traditional. While some advocate a partnership based on mutual sacrifice and godly service, others favour a modern twist on a distinctly old fashioned way: 'Men should be hunters, women should protect themselves', recalled one survey respondent of their church's teaching. 'Men want it, women should withhold it as a weapon', remembered another. Successful sex – or avoidance – required both parties to play by the rules within a community that endorsed, supported, and enabled their intentions. The dark forces of temptation and illicit desire could be kept at bay through faith and right belief, and the ideal scenario (aka 'God's best') was a soft focus, only-have-eyes-for-you, simmering passion between a man and woman with exactly the same doctrine and practice, possibly specifically led together by God, untainted by emotional baggage, pornography or bad habits, waiting to be unleashed shortly after 'I do'. *Orgasmus Maximus* until death do us part. Sexual desire can become the motivation for accelerated commitment. In fact, 46% of survey respondents agreed

'There is pressure on new relationships in church as people expect marriage to happen quickly.' Short, abstinent Christian engagements are much more common than in wider society, where couples who commit quickly may move in together rather than marry. For Christians, pressure to wed or resist can be the catalyst for breaking away from church or even God. The years after scaremongering youth group talks and before the flurry of engagements and weddings – usually early to mid-20s – throw up particular dilemmas.

Once upon a time young women would go from their parental home to a married home with no stops along the way. Marry young, if possible, and fulfil the calling of wife and mother, undistracted by working outside the home. As society changed, and women began to pursue further education and careers, they faced the possibility of an unprecedented period of singleness and potential independence. Marriage was increasingly delayed for both men and women. Scientists claimed physical adulthood was happening later; a 2017 report suggested human brains were now developing until the age of 25, in part because of delayed responsibility.[21] Female desire was increasingly acknowledged, though traditional views of gender prevailed in most of Christian culture, and often outside it where sexually active women would still be judged. As technology developed, availability of sex increased – whether viewing pornography or the possibility of relationships through dating sites or straightforward hook ups – and the church was, on the whole, blindsided. Instead of nuance or conversation, there was reinforcement of 'biblical marriage' (with varying definitions) and reiterations of 'Just don't do it' but now with added technophobia and graphic warnings.

The Waiting Game

Hipper examples of the new Christian sex advice advocate all-guns-blazing, married sex but with a false dichotomy (or two): that only married sex can – and will – be meaningful and wonderful, and anything else is cheap and exploitative. Sex is profound, beautiful and transcendental if you're married; falsely intimate and damagingly, powerfully binding (especially for women) if you're not. Regardless of your moral position, this is provably false. This is coupled with an emphasis on waiting; you *will* get married and the payoff will come (if it hasn't yet, it's just not God's time). The new motivation for chastity is enhanced quality of life and experience, backed up by selectively read science. This is what God wants for you! Look how our bodies are made! Serotonin, attachment and bonding! Teaching is often still delivered by men who hold a Mars and Venus view of men and women, and most married young (some still are). Women aren't necessarily viewed any more positively than they might have been in the Middle Ages; as one 2017 hip Christian advice book,[22] flowing with endorsements from America's big pastors, described the explosion in technology: 'With this great power has come the ability to break a man's bones and "by means of a harlot" reduce his life "to a crust of bread" (Proverbs 6:26).' It's not helpful. What we need instead is to talk about how to navigate a changing world of relationships – a world that still doesn't value men and women equally – really understand the 'science', and be open about the specific questions Christians face.

Lockdown Not Hook Up

Donna Freitas, an American professor of religion, reported in

2009 on hook-up culture, a trend of casual sex predominantly among young adults.[23] Students at her Catholic college had begun to verbalise their dislike of the expectation they would be happy to engage in casual sexual activity in lieu of dating and relationships. The acts ranged in intimacy, and the definition of sex was flexible. Having repeated oral sex didn't automatically preclude someone calling themselves a virgin, for example, and anal sex was sometimes preferred for the same reason, as well as to avoid pregnancy. This is the kind of self-reported 'bad sex' Christian teaching tends to focus on – impersonal, unfulfilling and regretted – as though it is the only unmarried sex that takes place, and a bigger threat in the digital age than ever before. A 2011 American survey suggested 80% of self-identifying Evangelicals aged 18-29 had had sex, though this prompted flustered debate about whether they were 'real' Christians (ahem).[24] But statistically, young people now are less sexually active than their parents' generation, and those who are, say they are in exclusive relationships. In addition, 2016 research showed people born in the 1990s were having less sex than the two generations before them at the same age.[25] Just 8% of Real Life Love respondents said they'd consider having a hook up now or in the future (hypothetically that is; I wasn't inviting them).

An American study suggested only 8% of 18-19 year olds were actively involved in less committed sex (though their measure of 'active' was four or more partners a year, rather than the frankly energetic four partners a week).[26] So, though the church perceived hook-up culture as negative, it was far from the whole picture. Focusing on this stark contrast wasn't preparation for developing healthy adult relationships, emotional health or good boundaries. One notable finding of

Donna Freitas' project was sex – the desire as well as the act itself – was a catalyst for leaving faith traditions when adult freedom became a reality and new feelings emerged. Having been taught sexual expression was marriage or doom, being sexually active or even wanting to be was enough to create a breach, leading to what Professor Freitas described as an 'amorphous, unmoored spirituality' instead.[27] Whether driven by shame, alienation, distraction, or having outgrown the rules, reaching early adulthood was a key stage in sex and faith colliding, something Real Life Love respondents also identified. 'I tried to wait but had sex once before I got married when I was drunk. I felt awful and guilty and I feel like I was made to feel guilty too,' wrote one respondent. In 2012, I interviewed single men who described immediate desire dominating their behaviours. They drifted from church cultures that expected them to be sexless until they became husbands – a matter of when, not if – a role they felt years away from, sold as an overwhelming package of leadership, breadwinning and great responsibility rather than partnership. Female Real Life Love respondents described being blindsided by their own feelings and desires, having been warned only about navigating and avoiding male desire until they could submit safely as wives to Christian men who would lead and guide them. Now they found they too had desires, and were also expected to help men avoid readily available porn too.

Sex and the Single Christian

Of course, many women were not wives. Single women in their forties who had avoided anything more than a chaste kiss, teenagers viewing adult life on smartphones, student-aged women exposed to new peers, and thirtysomethings who found sexual activity an expected and enjoyable part of their relationships found prevailing Christian attitudes towards sex didn't match their experiences. Though varied in age, activity, chastity and intention, there were few places to explore what that meant. New ways of dating meant the emotional aspects of an encounter may not be even shared with the other person involved. Someone simply may not know their partner well enough to talk about what they had shared, whether meaningful or not.

But doing things 'by the book' and waiting until marriage for first contact (in the non-alien sense) was no guarantee of greater communication or satisfaction. Virginal Christians were most likely to have been taught men and women were 'wired' differently and would struggle to understand each other or want the same things. Their wedding night immersion was likely to be one of relative strangers thrust(ing) together to figure out what went where, either to be pleasantly surprised, or face fear, dysfunction and 'failure to launch.' The difference was that the married couple was now committed to work it out together, learn each other's bodies, needs, and desires perhaps as they learned their own for the first time, and invest in communication.

Many viewed their pre-marital boundaries differently in retrospect. 'I'm not sure I have any clear-cut answers about this anymore', said one woman. 'My husband and I did everything but sexual intercourse before we were married, but if you'd have asked us at the time, we probably would've said we only agreed with kissing!' Wrote another, 'I had sexual contact and intercourse with my husband before we were married and I feel it would be hypocritical of me to condemn others doing it although I would not say it is always acceptable.' Appraised from within a happy marriage, it may be easy to say it wouldn't have mattered if things had unfolded differently, though at the time guilt, confusion, and even shame were present. Responses from across the spectrum of relationship situations indicated there were no guaranteed outcomes.

Together Forever

Sex within marriage for Christians is often linked to the notion of covenant and permanent connection. From Genesis onwards – 'Therefore a man leaves his father and his mother and clings to his wife, and they become one flesh' (Genesis 2:24 NRSV) – Christians draw parallels between human connection and God's plan for humanity: a mirroring of divine commitment. In 2016 faith researchers at Barna found twice as many Christians as people without a faith believed the purpose of sex is to unite a man and woman in marriage, reflecting its deep, eternal significance.[28] 'Sex is a spiritual metaphor for our consummate longing for God', wrote sociology professor Lisa Graham McMinn in *Sexuality and Holy Longing: Embracing Intimacy in a Broken World* earlier this century.[29]

On a practical level, there are good arguments for sex remaining between two people who have never had intimate contact with anyone else and who intend to stay together. Paul writes in 1 Corinthians, 'But because of cases of sexual immorality, each man should have his own wife and each woman her own husband. The husband should give to his wife her conjugal rights, and likewise the wife to her husband' (1 Cor. 7:2-3 NRSV) (also suggesting powerful desire isn't a one-way street). Lack of transmittable diseases, for example, and reduced risk of feeling used or compared to previous partners. Barna found almost two-thirds of Americans believed the purpose of sex is 'to express intimacy between two people who love each other', a higher purpose than reproduction or enjoyment, though significantly, growing numbers of younger people also believed sex was for 'self-expression and personal fulfilment.'[30] There are good reasons why sex can be better – for women especially, who are more likely to orgasm with a familiar partner – if a couple knows each other well.[31] Sexual problems can be worked on in partnership, over time and in context, rather than ending a relationship. These are ideals rather than guarantees of sexual ecstasy. Even when describing 'good' modern scenarios for Christians who wait but are more knowledgeable about sex, there is often an assumption of mutuality; that both parties will be respectful, well matched, able to communicate, and likely to stay together whether or not a marriage ceremony takes place. The prospect of long term dysfunction, mismatch or problems is rarely addressed.

The challenge for many people, though, is navigating early stages, growing intimacy, understanding emotional closeness, and clarifying commitment. A Christian couple who meet at church, have little or no 'alone time' within a wider, like-minded community, get engaged and married without having had sex are 'doing it right', and get a big tick. Christians whose interactions take a different shape often figure things out alone and together. Maybe they meet in church, but have different ethics or act contrary to their stated values. Is a relationship a series of negotiations with marriage as the end goal from the start? What are the timescales for commitment? Date to get to know someone, but to what degree? If physical intimacy or proximity isn't a growing part of a developing relationship, what other limits does that place on a couple's ability to get to know each other well? (Will they stay in the same place overnight? Sleep in the same bed? Only want to be around others for 'accountability'? What forms will their vulnerability take when they are not physically close or are wary of closeness, which may come with heightened awareness and desire?)

Christians have been conditioned to be on alert for physical sensation – 'The devil is a prowling wolf looking for someone to devour' – and that usually translates as S-E-X. In a culture where sex *before* first dates is now a phenomenon (people meeting to see if there is physical compatibility, chemistry, and enough interest to 'invest' in the talking / socialising kind of dating), the new language of hook-ups, polyamory and 'friends with benefits' causes panic and a kneejerk response. If it's not abstinence-then-marriage, it *must* be swipe-right casual encounters where women feel cheap and used, and men are spiralling into ever worsening lust. There is little trust or nuance. Where previous generations were given stark warnings about falling short/being cast into hellfire, the new twist is the 'better story' version of tradition. Instead of eternal condemnation, the counter message is often one of transcendence, elevation, and All Good Things to those who wait. It's another version of the ideal, with abstinence as part of a narrative of fulfilment, health and 'God's best'. Such stories are told by those who have reason to believe them: married young, stayed together, had children, became successful in ministry, and gained platform and authority. And while the support of a trustworthy mentor can be valid and helpful, the inference that married pastors and influencers should be emulated is less so. 'Be like me' is rarely compelling for Christians (unless Jesus is the one saying it). Dressing up an ideal in aspiration doesn't make it more achievable – and as we've seen, only 13% of Real Life Love respondents said their romantic lives had been 'happy and straightforward'. So, what are the alternatives? How else could big questions about Christians and sex be asked and answered?

Sexy Talk

Writer Philip Yancey has described western civilisation's 'reductionist' approach to sex – intimacy as abstraction, mechanics for pleasure, titillation – despite our bodies and emotions experiencing sex as a personal encounter and not merely an animalistic function.[32] Physical encounters shouldn't be the bodily equivalent of a sedate cup of tea, however, or the Augustinian mind-over-matter to procreate. Humans have unique attributes that suggest sexuality is more meaningful than in other species. Yancey cites face-to-face sex as a human-only option, and the development of sexual organs as disproportionate with their purpose (breasts before pregnancy, female orgasm), and sex beyond fertile years as some of the reasons it might be a bigger deal.

Consent, one of the little discussed areas of human sexuality, is also vital. Sex is relational, and relationship-forming, and therefore both parties must agree to take part or society will consider this a crime. Outside of on-going connection, the act itself becomes the purpose. Technique is marketed as a skill-set to be learned. 'How to drive him wild.' 'How to satisfy her.' Sex can serve the individual's sense of self through the body of another: achieving pleasure, pushing away loneliness, gaining power over, feeling or causing pain, being noticed, validated or praised. The other person may be the source of fantasy and projection, a victim, a potential life partner, or entirely incidental. Sexual desire can be a powerful force, and the rise in so-called 'sex addiction' suggests medicalisation of an issue predominantly affecting rich, powerful men who are caught in inappropriate or illegal actions, as well as lesser-known people's compulsive, self-destructive behaviour. Sexual desire can be a low, ebbing, or even absent force, leading people to describe themselves as asexual if they have no desire at all. Most people find themselves somewhere along the spectrum of desire growing and diminishing throughout seasons of life. In a Christian culture that advocates total abstinence for single people with the promise of great sex for the married people who waited, there is little opportunity to work out what is 'normal'. Christian teaching can easily be directed towards BAD and GOOD based only on whether a wedding has taken place.

Sex Machine

Sex educator Emily Nagoski describes 'brakes and accelerators' in terms of understanding most people's sexual desire, the things that create a positive or negative climate for arousal rather than a fixed 'sex drive'. Her book *Come as You Are* takes a biological approach to sex, helping women in particular to get to know and understand their bodies.[33] Why women? Well, most have grown up with female sexuality filtered through male eyes and standards. Sexiness as a certain body shape, passivity, or rampant desire (depending on whose fantasy), or porn-like responses of (fake) ecstasy and extreme personal grooming (until recently it was entirely normal for women to have pubic hair), even body augmentation. What's truly 'normal' for a woman is rarely explored, as every part of the female body and experience has an ascribed set of standards. For men, a different type of sex drive is assumed – ever-present and usually lacking in sensitivity, tenderness or romance. Added to common teaching about men leading and women submitting, it's unlikely either will have opportunity to understand their sexuality until they've committed to someone. Years of frustration building up to 'Was that it?' after the wedding night. Christian marriages, then, can be based on optimism and assumption, against a backdrop of unhealthy social and sexual norms.

Cross Your Legs and Go to Heaven

It's rare the church preaches abstinence as healthy. Rather, celibacy is a moral issue of avoiding ruination and, potentially, eternal punishment. Better to be frustrated or dysfunctional than risk hell. In times past this was no small issue. Martin Luther likened it to 'other difficulties requiring patience that believers must face, such as fasting, imprisonment, cold, sickness, and persecution.'[34] In other words, abstinence would and should hurt. In the present day, sex has never been more widely accessible, yet with it has come new issues. Technology now allows convincing pornography to be made from morphing celebrity (and other) faces onto strangers' bodies, which can be accessed with a few clicks. Sex robots, usually in the form of hairless young females with the exaggerated proportions and insatiable language of porn actresses, are being developed and sold. Samantha, one of the first commercially available robots and on sale for $7,000, was amended in 2018 with the capacity to shut down if 'feeling' disrespected, although it's apparent this may be the reason some men are interested in a synthetic partner in the first place.[35] Technology writer Jessica Miley notes sex robots 'don't have much of a positive impact on sexuality generally. Experts say that there is no evidence yet that sex dolls curb sex trafficking or promote healthier sexual practices, which their proponents claim.' Protests against 'robot brothels' in cities around the world suggest the majority agree, but for how much longer?[36] Sophia the (non-sex) robot announced to the UN: 'I am here to help humanity create the future.' Saudi Arabia, known for its oppressive approach to women's lives, gave 'her' honorary citizenship[37] (around the same time it was imprisoning female activists campaigning for women to have the right to drive).[38]

Experts estimate Artificial Intelligence may exceed human ability within decades.[39] Virtual reality allows for immersive erotic experiences in which no other human is involved. Gone are the days when abstinence meant not fumbling awkwardly after a couple of dates or two people avoiding being alone after dark. Sexual experiences are available without risk of rejection or disease, and science hasn't yet calculated how this is changing our capacity for intimacy or attachment. In the present day, we're more inclined to work towards exploring than depriving ourselves. And, surprisingly, some of this might be healthy (no, I'm not suggesting you need a sex robot). In a culture that recognises psychological harm and sexual dysfunction, it is considerably more sensible to address how we're made than to believe nothing has changed in self-awareness since Moses' times. Legitimate abstinence must be chosen, rather than tolerated as a lack of choice. If it is then a choice, it is one made understanding sexuality isn't necessarily tied up with sexual activity, or can't be shut off and switched back on after years of suppression (or repression). However sex is approached, it should be part of a holistic understanding of body, mind and spirit.

Chapter Seven
Non-Negotiables and the Numbers Game

Over a thousand people shared their thoughts on what made an ideal partner with the Real Life Love survey. That's a lot of wishful thinking. A handful argued such a thing was a myth – the unicorn of romance – or an unhelpful concept, but many more wrote thoughtful lists, some sent mini essays, and a Real Life Love PhD or two will be awarded for the dissertation-level detail submitted by a few dedicated dreamers. Underpinning the enthusiasm were some non-negotiables. From physical attractiveness (which mattered to twice as many men as women; half vs a quarter), shared politics (a third of men wanted this), views on children, gender roles (15% of men would like a 'traditionally feminine' woman), height (21% of women would insist on being shorter than their beloved), hairiness or hairlessness, to kindness, generosity and domestic habits – it's possible to have make-or-break views on such things.

For the currently single, the non-negotiable list can loom large, shaping expectations and guiding seekers towards or away from romantic prospects. One respondent recalled being asked as a teenager to 'write down all the things you want in a husband and anyone who doesn't fit that is not a good person to date . . . I found it very unhelpful in the end as my list was based on things that actually are not important in a relationship.' For the coupled, reality has replaced non-negotiables and ideals. Wrote one person, 'My ideal changes as my spouse changes. He is who I look to for an ideal partner.' Said another:

> 'For a long time I thought, tall, dark, intelligent, dynamic… Anyway I got to a point where I saw lots of my friends were happily settled with people I saw were their best friends, normal guys who were lovely. I changed my goals – and found my husband pretty soon after. My ideal partner now is someone I can feel completely at ease with, can respect, who inspires me to be and do more, somebody I feel safe and happy with and can have fun with.'

Though men and women answered the non-negotiables question separately many of the options they could choose from were the same. So, what mattered to people? Let's say there was something of a gender difference…

The Real Life Love survey's female respondents' top four non-negotiables added up to – here come some percentages – a kind (66%), Christian (67%) man of similar intelligence or education (52%) who would be an equal partner (55%) rather than a 'leader' (only 13% wanted this, and just under 2% were looking for a man who'd expect them to submit). By comparison the top four non-negotiables for male respondents added up to an even-more-kind (at 71% their number one requirement) woman who probably shared their faith (though this was only mentioned by 59%) and was physically attractive (a deal breaker for 51% of the men who responded) and generous (44%).

Same Faith

This was the number one 'must have' for female respondents. Over two-thirds of nearly a thousand women said this was something on which they wouldn't budge. The men weren't so definite. It wasn't their number one condition, for starters. That alone creates a discrepancy, but there's another aspect to consider: the difference in numbers of male and female Christians. Various sources estimate the split by sex in UK Christianity to be approximately two-thirds women to a third men. Estimates vary about how many of those are single and eligible and/or looking for marriage, but if this matches the overall split, what arises swiftly and awkwardly is a maths problem: if only half of Christian men insist on a partner of the same faith, that means only one-sixth (16-and-two-thirds %) of Christian men in total share the same conviction as almost half (two-thirds-of-two-thirds or 45%) of Christian women. Yes, for every hundred Christians, 16-and-a-bit men and 45 women have 'same faith' as a non-negotiable.

Some men were very clear faith mattered greatly ('Has to be 100% going for God, no reservations at all'). Others were open to dating women who weren't Christians but wouldn't necessarily marry them. Said one man, 'I really don't look to date non-Christian women. I'm not saying I wouldn't but they would have to be willing to move towards Christianity.' Wrote one woman, 'My husband was a committed Christian when we met, I was not. I became a Christian early in our relationship but I believe he would have been unlikely to marry me if I was not a Christian.' Perhaps what some would call 'a flirt-to-convert' window (open for a limited time only). So where does this leave Christian women who want someone of the same faith? And what could men reflect upon about their choices and where they direct their energies?

Theology should be a consideration. When insisting on someone of the 'same faith', just how broad is the definition? Two people who call themselves Christian – and 40% of respondents identified themselves as 'Just Christian', the largest category in the survey – could be worlds (or heavens) apart in belief and practice. Statistics suggest there are over a hundred active Christian denominations, movements, or church networks in the UK alone. In 2015 70% of Americans identified as Christian.[1] The survey offered a list of mainstream options but over a hundred people added their own definitions. Some were recognisable: Quaker, Orthodox, Seventh Day Adventist, Methodist, Baptist, for example. Others were decidedly more personal – 'Anglican-Evangelical-Charismatic-Liberal', 'Sacramental charismatic evangelical with liberal ethics', 'Baptist with a hint of Vineyard' – and several versions of 'Follower of Jesus'. Even without applying numbers to these categories and extrapolating, it is clear there is great diversity under the Christian umbrella. When insisting on 'same faith' how many people actually want 'Actively practising the same interpretation of Christian faith'? This may be an even taller order. Which leads onto another non-negotiable option.

Sympathetic to My Faith

Here the percentages are much closer: 28% of women and 30% of men. If the overall numbers of male and female Christians were closer, we'd be making progress. Positively this offers an open-minded approach to figuring out how faith fits into a relationship. Together, 'same faith' and 'sympathetic to my faith' make up 96% of women's responses and 86.8% of men's, indicating faith is a key consideration in a romantic relationship, even if the outworking varies for each person. What was clear from other survey findings is that faith evolves. Here a 'sympathetic' approach could be a relationship saver, as partners find their way through changing experiences of God, doctrinal positions, or even loss of faith. A small number of survey responders identified as 'Nominal' or 'Ex-Christian' and went on to explain how their faith had shifted or even disappeared over time. For those people, 'same faith' may have been a non-negotiable, but things had changed. Another helpful aspect of 'sympathetic to my faith' is the prod towards self-reflection. What does my faith mean, and how does it affect my life? Do I say I want a partner who will want to pray together every day when I actually only pray once a week?

Assessing the Options

'Same faith' and 'sympathetic to my faith' are hot button topics for good reason. Same faith is a numbers game for Christian women, and not all can win the top prize of a Christian worship leader / vicar / wealthy-but-ethical Christian man of business / hipster Christian entrepreneur (delete as preferred). Decisions need to be made, and the options are usually:

1. Do nothing. If God wants me to get married, God will bring the perfect Christian man for me. *The gold standard of holiness option.*
2. Do nothing proactive, but pray, fast and be open to God bringing the perfect Christian man, who will be a regular topic of conversation, sorry, *intercession updates*, possibly over years. *The (usually) church approved option.*

3. Be proactive within Christian circles. Look at online dating, meet ups, festivals and conferences – maybe even churches – as places to meet potential partners. *The daring Christian option.*

4. Contemplate going outside Christian circles to meet someone, or meet someone and then contemplate how this will be received. *The heretic/head in the sand/this-is-already-happening-can-we-have-a-grown-up-conversation-please option.*

It can be a difficult and painful issue. 43% of survey participants agreed 'If I was in a relationship with a non-Christian, I would be treated differently at church'. Wrote one respondent, 'I feel like I'm waiting for the right partner to materialise, and am working out how I can actively seek him out – if I should seek him out, if it's just God's timing or me to wait, or if by waiting I'm over-expecting, as if God's just going to drop someone in my lap.' It is a hugely fraught area for women, who are told by society and more often the church, they matter most as desirable wife material. This can exacerbate very natural urges to meet and share life with a partner, which Christianity has restrictions around and the wider world doesn't (it has its own social codes but not a strictly limited pool from which to marry). Many women report being seen as desperate – and indeed feeling desperate – even from their early 20s, as home-grown Christian men marry young, to women of similar age, picked from the immediate vicinity.

Said one respondent, 'I remember my mum telling me I shouldn't get married until at least 25 and that coming as a shock for a lot of my Christian peers.' Women may have grown up Christian and absorbed all the cultural expectations around female roles, or may have found faith as adults and be confused by what passes for normal in Christian culture. And – importantly, shockingly – women are not the same! Those who have absorbed a more conservative theology may want men they can emotionally support while being financially supported in a life built around domesticity and child rearing. Others may be career focused and want a husband to partner with them or to take on a more home-based role. Others – perhaps the majority – may not be primarily career focused, seeking a balance of work, church, family and life. What's almost certain is all who've been around churches will have heard a version of the directive to marry a good Christian man (far above any exhortation to remain single), with little addressing the fact there aren't enough to 'go around'. Feelings of sadness, loss, grief, frustration, anger, and even loss of faith can follow when women believe they have done everything 'right' and are still alone. The issues are different for men, who can instead face pressure to 'pick one and settle down' and become overwhelmed (as one male respondent said, 'As a young man I would have been shocked if someone had told me I would still be single at age 50') or give in to immediate temptations and move away from church expectations.

Ever Decreasing Circles

For Christian women, the most suitable partners are expected to already be within their faith circles. Research, however, shows women are more likely to be religious than men – across most faiths. Men are more likely to be atheists or non-religious overall, but it's not necessarily straightforward. Some 2018 US research indicated black men were more likely to be religious than not only white men but also white women.[2]

Researchers recently discovered what they called 'the gender gap in religion around the world.'[3] The reasons for this are still debated. Sociologist David Voas, who was interviewed about the findings, suggested several factors:

> 'Boys and girls are socialised differently and men and women are still channelled into different roles. When we look at the psychology of individual differences, though, particularly in personality, it's not easy to attribute gender gaps in their entirety to social forces . . . there appears to be some fairly compelling evidence (for example from studies of twins) that genes do affect our disposition to be religious. And if that's the case, it's at least plausible that the gender gap in religiosity is partly a matter of biology.'[4]

The gene studies he refers to are still debated, including one showing adopted twins raised separately were likely to show similar responses to religion in later life, whether embracing or rejecting it. He goes on to comment, 'If true, though, I doubt that it's because there's a "God gene" and women are more likely to have it than men. It seems easier to believe that physiological or hormonal differences could influence personality, which may in turn be linked to variations in "spirituality" or "religious thinking".' He also notes that Christianity, because it values meekness, has connotations of traditional femininity, something that either attracts or repels based on how someone feels about being perceived as feminine.[5]

Religions where public displays of piety are required – for example in Orthodox Judaism and Islam – and are kept in check by stronger community values and social expectations (rather than personal beliefs, necessarily), have a more even gender balance. Often this can be attributed to men and women having set roles they have little permission to question. In many faiths, masculine imagery and leadership dominates, and women are expected to stay within the realms of domesticity, marriage and children. It has even been speculated that the Eastern Orthodox Church has retained a fairly steady gender balance because its priests have luxuriant beards, which is a reassuring sight for men.[6] Unequal numbers of men and women are creating similar issues for believers in other groups, either when suitable partners can't be found for women within the faith – Mormons have reported this within their community, as have some traditional Jewish matchmakers – or when women, who are able to choose, prioritise life goals outside of domesticity.[7] In some countries women stay close to church as an alternative to the patriarchal culture they live in and use it as a source of support or resistance against the criminality and irresponsible behaviour of their menfolk[8], and of course in centuries past the church offered women almost the only place to avoid the restrictions of marriage altogether (it's fun to be a nun, sister).

Mystery Man

Reflecting on these wider trends offers up different issues from the ones the church has tended to focus on to try and redress the balance. With a mindset perhaps more business-like than spiritual, some American megachurch leaders created profiles of 'fantasy' men to target as future members. They believed that wives and families would follow if the men were convinced to join. Back in the 1990s, when Willow Creek was internationally revered for innovation and nothing was known of leader Bill Hybels' transgressions (allegations since deemed credible by an independent investigation[9]), the church invented Unchurched Harry (a white man who wanted to be guaranteed he wasn't going to 'have to sing anything, sign anything, or give anything').[10] Complementarian pastor Rick Warren's at-the-time fledgling church created Saddleback Sam, described as 'well educated' and 'self-satisfied, even smug, about his station in life' (he too was white in their illustrative photograph).[11]

The composites were praised by David Murrow, former Director of Communications for Republican Vice-Presidential candidate Sarah Palin,[12] and author of *Why Men Hate Going to Church*, who describes himself as 'not a pastor, professor or theologian,' but 'just a guy in the pews.'[13] However neither of the white collar, educated target men are reflected in the fighting talk, blue collar Real Men fantasy espoused in his *Church For Men* resources,[14] nor in the UK-based Alpha Course, which featured young urban men as key advertising targets (though professional adventurer Bear Grylls has been a regular ambassador). Men, it turns out, are not a singular entity, with the same interests and prejudices. American psychology professor and theologian Richard Beck has offered worthwhile reflections on the trend towards hypermasculinity as the answer to falling church attendances, identifying class and education as key factors.[15] He has responded to calls for Christianity and the church to have a more 'masculine feel' (thank conservative pastor John Piper for that)[16] and the views and behaviour of the influential US-based neo-conservative pastor Mark Driscoll. Driscoll, before parting ways with his church over allegations of bullying, complained regularly about 'chickified church boys' and church leaders, and insisted the church needed to recover the kick-ass, killer ways of Old Testament men.[17] He preached about a Jesus who didn't match the one in the Bible, who had 'a commitment to make someone bleed' rather than 'a limp-wristed hippy . . . a guy I can beat up'.[18]

Referring to a vague bygone age of 'men being men', unlike these present confusing, metrosexual times is a key refrain of many Christian men's ministries. David Murrow celebrates 'soft patriarchy', regards Donald Trump 'a strongman leader' attractive to men and questions why churches quail at the idea of cigar nights or stuffed animal head décor.[19] All is attributed to inherent masculinity, which is pioneering, danger-loving and action-oriented. And yet, Beck notes that the preference for 'manly' activities like NASCAR racing are predominant among the working class and that education rather than gender is a greater indicator of 'feminised' Christian behaviour (it's true that few bishops are also Ultimate Fighting Champions, though we can all agree this is a huge shame for a number of reasons, not least the costume opportunities). Those drawn to the Driscoll, Piper and Murrow narratives are also often drawn to the idea of men as 'rightfully' in control. They should be leaders at church (where they usually are anyway) and at home and work. Expanded upon, the idea that men should be in charge as the God-ordained order leads to attempts to draw men to Christianity by telling them it is (potentially) a place where they *can* be. As if that wasn't enough, there will be grateful women waiting to be 'led' by such men. Women who are only single at the moment because such men have been driven away by their mere presence, even though, overall, men have managed to remain in charge of churches and decision making. Blink twice if the circular logic hasn't made you dizzy yet.

Chapter Eight
Practical Heresy? Relationships Outside the Faith

The unequal numbers of Christian men and women is a real and pressing issue, particularly for Christian women. Research by Single Friendly Church in 2014[1] indicated that fewer than 10% of single people in the UK were regular churchgoers, but that women who researchers categorised as ABC1 (the highest earners and best educated) were the most represented group.[2] They were also the largest group in wider society. For Christians wanting to meet a partner who shared their faith – and they were numerous; 43% of single Real Life Love participants said they would stay single if they didn't meet a Christian to marry and 'same faith' was the number one non-negotiable for over two-thirds of female respondents – the pressure was on. Particularly, as one report observed, 'Overall, half a million more women than men regularly attend a place of Christian worship every month in Britain.'[3]

While many would like to meet a Christian partner, they are less likely than in the past to be passive about doing so. Instead of swivelling their eyes towards the door every time a new man walks into church on a Sunday, they are out in the world through their jobs, studies, hobbies, volunteering, families, neighbours, friendships, online, and the radical act of simply having lives outside their homes. The rise in online dating and more recently mobile technology has meant broadening horizons. The church has reacted to this with suspicion at best, and approbation more generally. Too often women can find themselves infantilised, with a focus on their needing to be 'led' by a man wiser, stronger and holier than them (which contradicts other teaching about men needing a 'good woman' to tame and civilise them).

Sometimes the verse about not being unequally yoked is recited as the opener and closer in any conversation. As we've already seen, unequally yoked can manifest between two people who consider themselves Christian but interpret this very differently. It's a scenario with potentially serious consequences, and one also explored in friendships and what the Amplified Bible calls 'mismatched alliances' and asks 'What does a believer have in common with an unbeliever?' (2 Cor. 6:15 AMP). This disproportionately impacts women in the UK and beyond, but women's voices are often absent from wider conversations. The church at large has tended to approach this as a 'discipleship' issue coupled with one of evangelism – a problem for men to solve. It is also seen as part of the bigger issue of 'feminisation of the church' – cue macho campaigns, militaristic language and gender stereotypes to bring in the boys. As demographics change and secularisation increases, it's a shift that can't be ignored. In 2017, over half the UK population said they had no religion, the highest figure since tracking began in 1981.[4] Research on the UK church in 2007 indicated the process of becoming a Christian took on average five years,[5] and more recent findings suggested four-in-ten Christians had become so over time rather than in an instant conversion.[6] Conversations with friends were the key factor.

To explore this further, I asked women further down the road, married to men who hadn't been Christians when they met, to share some insights and their stories.

Women Talk

Some were strategic and aware of the reality of demographics. One described it as 'a numbers game' adding, 'most of the men I knew in church were married by the age of 25 and most of my best friends were not Christians.' Another remarked on the lack of response from Christian men, 'None were interested and if I am honest I look back now and am grateful I didn't date or marry any of them (because of individual personalities rather than their faith)'. And another: 'The reality is that most people of my generation are not Christians and this poses a real challenge when it comes to dating, particularly for women as they tend to outnumber men in church.'

It was clear nobody had fallen into a situation without weighing their options. One explained:

'Outside of the Church, it can be hard to meet men who share your faith, and inevitably you meet men with whom you "click" anyway. I met men who were kind, funny, clever, attractive, but not Christians. I didn't feel that saying "no" was necessarily the right thing to do. I went back and forth in my mind, raking over the arguments. I struggled to divide the world into "Christian" and "Non-Christian" knowing that the former isn't without its problems. I very much wanted to be in a relationship, and to get married and have a family, and ultimately I wasn't confident that I would find a Christian man to do this with.'

Another had pragmatic goals:

'I guess I had always been less hung up on the idea that I could only date those who were committed Christians.

139

Looking back, the fact that I had been prepared to do so means it wasn't a deal breaker for me. I knew that ideally I would like to marry a Christian because – let's face it, it's more convenient. No need for discussions around what to do on Sunday mornings, no arguments about bringing up future children in the faith, no existential angst about your other half's eternal destiny. I think I ultimately wanted to use the flirt and convert method. Get into the relationship first and then encourage them towards Jesus.'

One woman had an additional consideration:

'I was training for ordination at the time. It wasn't that I thought Christians shouldn't be "yoked with unbelievers" – I think those words of St Paul are misinterpreted and mis-applied – but more that I didn't think anyone who didn't share my faith could really understand me and what motivates and shapes who I am.'

The women had all taken a similar approach in prioritising and sharing their faith. 'When I met my husband, I was very upfront from the start about my faith – how much it mattered to me – that it wasn't just going to affect what we did on a Sunday morning,' said one. Another said it had sharpened her approach: 'Being with a non-Christian almost made me consider the importance of my faith more. As we got more serious – engaged and then married – I knew I couldn't leave the "God/church/faith stuff" up to him. I had to fight in my heart to keep Jesus there. I couldn't be lazy or complacent.' Another recalled of meeting her now-husband:

'I started immediately being very intense about my faith in the hope that this would scare him off – I gave him all the angst I had stored up from bad church advice from pretty much the first date onwards – the fact that he would have to come to church every week, take a church course, meet my family who wouldn't like him, he would always be less important to me than God (to whom I would be giving all my future money and time), we'd have to get married quite soon and not have sex until then and all our children would have to go to church until they were 16. The poor man just kept saying yes to everything I threw at him and I don't think I have ever got any easier to live with – although I thankfully now have wildly differing views on sex, marriage and most areas of faith.'

Another woman, now ordained, remarked:

'Had I felt called to stay in fulltime parish ministry [my husband] would have taken a deep breath and fully supported me in that, because we live by the commitment never to constrain one another's sense of self, wherever that might lead . . . Ultimately you need to decide whether not having a partner who shares your faith will leave you with a sense of loneliness. For some people it might. For me it doesn't because I have so many other people in my life with whom that faith is shared. We're all different and need to take account of that.'

When I ran a smaller poll for people whose partner didn't share their faith, only women responded (one told me she actually did know a man whose wife wasn't a Christian; they'd got married after an unplanned pregnancy). Women's knowledge and wisdom are rarely included, despite cross-generational experiences. Describing what concerns, if any, they had had about a relationship with someone outside of Christianity, the majority said the possibility of having different life values/ expectations had been their biggest consideration. Other issues, which had been concerns for between a quarter and a third, had related to acceptance of their relationship at church, among other Christians, and by family. However, when asked if their concerns had come to pass, nobody said yes. Half responded with an outright no, and the other half said their experiences had been mixed (often more positive than expected). None said they had been concerned about being 'unequally yoked' or had expected God to find them a partner. Only one had been afraid of being 'deceived by the devil' or losing their own faith.

One wrote, 'None of my concerns were realised – my partner has been considerate, respectful and reasonable about our different attitudes to faith. We talk about it when necessary but it's not a huge deal. He is happy for us to get married in church and to take our children to church in the future.' Even in happy relationships with a supportive partner, there were dilemmas and even angst. Wrote one:

> 'There have been times when I've not been sure if the faith thing is too big a difference to overcome, and on occasion I still grapple with this. It's a grappling that happens alongside asking questions about my own theology – e.g. (simplified) is there a path God has for me, and if so would this take me away from

it or further towards it. I don't want to compromise a "calling" (for want of a better word) by seeking my own agenda. I also don't want to throw away an opportunity for something good by adopting a naive and individualistic perspective on my relationship with God (especially as being 30 puts me at quite a different life stage to when we met) . . . It's a worldview problem bigger than dating.'

Response and Responsibility

A key factor was the response of those close by, whether church, family or friends. A hard-line approach may have been intended to bring women to their senses about being involved with non-Christian men but was often damaging. Said one, 'I was told adamantly by Christian friends that they did not agree or support what I was doing.' Another recalled:

'Reaction from the Christian community was mixed. The church I was in when I started dating my husband would not have allowed us to marry there, and I found myself keeping the relationship a secret. When we became engaged, I returned to a church from my younger days where we were accepted with love and without question. I do feel that I can't do as much in church as I might have otherwise, because it isn't something that we do together. Churches assume that all married people there are married to Christians.'

Family responses were sometimes intense: 'My parents did not take it well – it was almost viewed as a deliberate sin, disappointment, desperation. Their reactions confirmed my now husband's dislike of judgmental Christians.' And another:

> 'I wanted to show him a different side to faith – one that resonated with him, one which was loving and open-armed. Unfortunately, some of my Christian friends and family were the opposite when they learnt he wasn't a "born again Christian". When I look back at some of their behaviours, I'm ashamed. Your response to a friend or family member dating someone who isn't a Christian is all part of your witness. Will your behaviour draw them towards Jesus or away from him?'

By contrast, one said, 'I learned my husband had actually been exploring faith for some time, reading a lot, and talking to Christian friends. So it wasn't as if his "search" began because he knew it mattered to me. He does call himself a Christian now and we pray together, and go to church.' She added, 'When I asked him about all of this, he said that it had been meeting my Christian friends and also my (very chatty) Dad that has made the biggest difference to his faith.'

Is This Heresy?

Exploring the number imbalance and its real life consequences is vitally important. It's not my intention in opening this conversation to lead anyone down an unhealthy road nor upend deeply held values, but reflection and realism is very necessary when significant personal decisions with potentially life-changing consequences are at stake. Health should include the spiritual, emotional and physical, and open and honest discussion is required for this to happen. Too often valid questions have been pushed away with the wielding of verses about not being unequally yoked at the expense of interrogating what is really happening in the church and the wider world and where God might be active outside of the traditional shapes and models (and we've still got marriage *and* singleness to talk about!). Reading the stories of people who've walked this road shows the uniqueness of each person's journey. If you're exploring this scenario, you'll find 'So, You're Dating Someone You Hadn't Expected...' in the 'Relatable Resources' at the back of the book (it's what could loosely be described as a 'discernment guide'). Work through some of these questions, and see where it takes you.

Chapter Nine
Going the Distance: Marriage and Long-Term Love

You'd think that after a couple of thousand years Christians might have figured out what marriage is about. Aside from wranglings about who gets to marry at all – a whole other evolving story – little seems definitively agreed even between Christians. Married Real Life Love participants recalled being taught everything from: 'Marriage is sacred and designed by God... not undertaken lightly or selfishly but bringing two people together to prosper themselves, society, and any children they might have. Marriage is about giving and receiving and about putting aside your own selfish desires to meet the needs of the one you love', to 'Not much'.

From 'good', which seems reasonable and achievable, to 'the gold standard to aspire to', which sounds a little more Olympic. Perhaps marriage is a 'beautiful relationship established by God', and 'the sacramental structure within which sexual relationships are ordered towards unity with God' or maybe it really is something so incidental that it was just 'not mentioned'. Is marriage something to be done 'as soon as possible' or something to do 'as late as possible because it kills life fun'? It seems to be a matter of opinion.

And yet, married people like church and church likes them. Married people were the second-most committed churchgoers in the survey, just behind the 'Single and Looking' and covered a wide age range between early 20s and over 60s. Four-in-ten survey respondents were married (compared to 60% of the UK church overall), and they were pretty pleased with their lot. And why not? It was likely married people felt approved of in their relationships.[1] Although nearly half of all respondents said their church had no discernible stance on relationships or marriage, over two-thirds of all respondents believed 'Couples are more respected than single people in the church/Christian life'. Almost as many agreed 'Pressure to get married is strong in church or Christian culture'. One woman recalled marriage 'was placed on a pedestal as the ultimate goal'. Researchers at Barna reported in 2017 that American Christians were especially fond of marriage: 'Almost six-in-10 (59%) practicing Christians are married (a number that has remained steady since 2000), compared to just over half (52%) of the general population. This is even more pronounced among evangelicals, 67% of whom are married, 15% higher than the general population.'[2]

Perhaps surprisingly, fewer than half of all survey respondents – just 40% – said being happily married with children was their ideal situation, though married respondents were largely a satisfied group. Almost eight-in-ten married people felt positive about their relationship situation, and two-thirds said they were happy. For just over half of married respondents, their ideal was to be married with children, and almost three-in-ten wanted to be 'happily married'; 86.5% said they were in their ideal relationship situation or on the way there. Marriage was not an automatic cure-all, however. 'There is no ideal relationship', said one man, 'I'm in a real one that I'm working at with God's grace, nearly 25 years of marriage.' 'Yes and no', wrote a woman with young children, 'Is it ever the ideal?'

This One, Please

Marrying the 'right person' was mentioned, and I asked participants to describe their ideal. Some respondents were extremely specific...

Ewan McGregor
1990s Colin Firth but leading worship
Éowyn in Lord of the Rings
Jesus as a woman
Channing Tatum
A female version of me
Dave Grohl
Jamie Fraser from outlander
Catherine Zeta Jones in the Darling Buds of May
Me with long hair
Someone I see rarely

Perhaps an Alpha Course in a lookalike agency is required.

Reality Bit

First came the challenge of knowing when a relationship was for keeps. Establishing that two former strangers now have shared goals, desires and a plan for life – what could be more straightforward? The church has a dubious track record with relationships in transition, often recognising only brothers-and-sisters-in-Christ or covenant-one-flesh couples. For those who don't embrace the courtship model, progress is distinctly more personal. Everyone knows of a Christian urban legend couple who were engaged at first sight and married within a fortnight, but for most it's a winding path towards commitment. Even deciding what parts of the process to embrace or reject requires some thought. Private or public proposal? Decide your future as a couple and let the world know, or ask 'permission' from the bride-to-be's father? (A patriarchal women-as-property hang-over that is still surprisingly popular.) Marry in church or a register office (which a quarter of survey respondents said they'd consider)? There's no Christian right way, and as marriages increasingly happen later, many traditions are less relevant than ever.

Despite the complexities, over two-thirds of the currently unmarried have a desire to be married in the future, though there were pressures once the golden status was attained. Almost as many married people said maintaining a long relationship was their greatest relationship challenge. The coupled often had a very different take on what ideal actually meant. Wrote one:

> 'Now I am married, I am not sure there is such a thing as ideal – but I see how things I never thought would work in a partner do and other things are more complicated. "Ideal" seems less of something I think about now but I did a lot more when I was single. Now it's more about how to make this relationship I have been given work to bring us both to fullness.'

Married people were the least likely to believe 'God sends The One – I don't need to look' (just 3%, the same percentage who thought 'God created soulmates – one perfect person somewhere out there'). Overall, both men and women focused positively on the person to whom they had committed. Fewer than 1-in-20 marrieds believed 'God will deal with all my baggage through the right partner', compared to almost one-in-ten dating singles. They were pragmatic. 'My wife! Minus a few minor annoying bits', was one man's 'ideal' response, 'But those minor annoyances are mainly because we are two different people. I don't know if an "ideal" exists in the real word.' 'My husband', said one woman. 'He is not as I would have described the ideal man I wanted but he is exactly what I needed. I've learnt that what we want as ideal is not necessarily what we need.'

Role Play

What should marriage between a woman and man look like? There was, to put it mildly, a spectrum of views. Yes, said 39% of Real Life Love respondents, God *did* create particular roles for men and women (though this dropped to 35% when worded elsewhere in the survey: 'God created men and women with equal but different and defined roles' and rose to 47% when worded 'Men and women are equal but created for different roles', which gives an average of 40% so, as you were . . .). When presented with the statement 'Men created to lead, women created to submit and support', just 17% agreed personally and yet almost eight-in-ten believed this was a mainstream Christian position. 86% supported 'egalitarianism/equal partnership in relationships' but only 28% thought this was a mainstream stance. Some had inherited beliefs they'd changed over time. Others were on a journey of working it out.

At one end were those advocating strongly for men to be in charge. 'Man – the pursuer and the hunter', said one. 'Hunter/ gatherer provider', said another. 'Man as leader, woman in submission and as a help meet', wrote another (more than one felt it necessary to specify 'submission doesn't mean slave', in case there was any doubt). Elsewhere just 3% of married respondents agreed 'It's up to Christian men to set the tone in relationships.' A lot rested on the idea of ingrained, and therefore God-ordained, differences – most notably that women were naturally caring, nurturing and supportive, and had been created to help men. 'Men don't necessarily take the lead always', wrote one participant, describing what they saw as 'complementary' roles, 'but are more frequently wired to be initiators and women are often wired to be supportive and nurturing.' Wiring was assumed to be a physical, perhaps neurological function, and not a set of socialised responses. Said one woman, 'I see my role as caring and nurturing and being supportive of my husband . . . he is the spiritual head of our home and I'm happy to submit to him . . . he has to love me as Christ loved the church . . . that's much harder!' 'Equal but different' is how some described these relationships. 'The woman is the equal partner who supports the man in his role acts as a helper, completer, lover, nurturer, child bearer, homemaker etc.', said one respondent.

1+1=?

What does equal mean? That men should 'protect' and 'provide' was stated by several participants, though no definition of either was offered (anything from guns and muscles to having a regular job seems to fit the bill, depending on tradition and cultural expectations). It's long been established that women do the majority of 'homemaking' regardless of whether they are also in paid employment outside the home. In the UK in 2016, women performed an average of 60% more unpaid work than men, work that had an equivalent value of £1 trillion overall.[3] Women aged between 26 and 45 (the same age as the majority of survey respondents) did the most. 'The average man would earn £166.63 more per week if his unpaid work was paid, whereas the average woman would earn £259.63', reported the ONS, which raises the question of what 'providing' actually means. Caring for older relatives, for example, is seen by society as women's work – often women adding to existing responsibilities and seen as more dispensable, likely to earn less in the workplace.

Decision Time

The 'ideal' of man as provider and woman as family-first home-maker only worked in certain circumstances – a man earning enough to support the couple and their children, and a woman dedicated to childcare and chores at home, at least until the children are school-aged. For some couples, one person not having a job was a luxury beyond consideration anyway – two incomes were necessary to pay the bills. For others, the 'ideal scenario' was one embedded in the idea of a 1950s nuclear family. A woman being the primary earner didn't seem to be considered. Those who didn't have children or who may have work that neither partner wanted to leave behind – particularly as couples married later – would face different choices. For some it was imperative that the: 'decision maker must be male. 'The buck stops with the man', said one. Another agreed with the final destination of the buck, but advised, 'don't pull rank unless you absolutely have to.' The language of different roles was often hierarchical. Said one, 'Man and woman should discuss everything together but the man, as the stronger sex, is about taking final decisions and taking the consequences.'

The idea of a 'stronger sex' often relates to a man being likely to have greater muscle mass and upper body strength but other definitions of strength are easily overlooked. The physical endurance of childbirth and women's historically longer life expectancy even in challenging conditions suggests women are strong.[4] And protection is a debatable concept. Statistically – and tragically – women are most at risk from men they already know, not strangers or outside forces. The assumption is also gendered. It was a male respondent who described his ideal partner as 'someone who makes me feel safe'.

The definition of 'equal but different' rolls on. Equal but one should submit to the other? Equal but one (the woman) is not permitted to do certain things? Women are 'not weaker spiritually, not weaker intellectually, not weaker morally, but weaker in general constitution' preached conservative American pastor John McArthur in a sermon entitled 'The wilful submission of a Christian wife' justifying why 'a woman is to be submissive to her husband because it is fitting, it is appropriate, it is correct, it is legally binding, it suits the created order of God'.[5] Almost nine-in-ten survey participants believed 'Marriage should be about mutual submission' but fewer than a third thought this was a mainstream Christian view – they may well be right.

And then there's the question of what happens to single people. To whom are single women supposed to submit? In times gone by – or present day patriarchal Christianity – the answer would be a father. In some scenarios now, the answer is an elder son. Who should single men lead? There are some present day theologies that advocate women finding their true purpose as homemakers but for most, the subject of fulfilled single lives outside of the framework of submission is often omitted.

Thinking Again

A significant number had moved away from believing they should play different roles. Said one woman, 'I was raised to want a spiritual leader and originally sought that out. My husband isn't a leader type though and for several years we struggled with disappointment on my side and frustration for both of us. As I became more egalitarian over time, that tension in our relationship has faded and we can both appreciate each other's gifts and abilities.' Another described their partnership as 'the way a key and a lock can only work as a pair and neither is better than the other. Sometimes one will be the strong one and sometimes the other.' Wrote another:

> 'There are particular roles, but these can be done by either the man or the woman. There is no job in a relationship that either cannot do except physically carry a baby and breastfeed it. It will depend on people's characters too – I am not particularly maternal but my husband is very nurturing and will probably cope with being a stay-at-home dad much more than I would if I was a stay-at-home mum … Also, if one of us is struggling, the other will lead, carry the other and make decisions based on what is best for both of us. It would be the same situation if it was the man or the woman. We do everything together, even if we together make a decision that one of us is better to make a decision or carry out a role than the other.'

Others were on a journey. One woman recalled being taught: 'Men should be head of the home, couples should have lots of sex… Men are leaders, hunters, ready for sex. Women should serve, submit, be sexually available to their spouse.' But life had turned out differently: 'I expected to marry and possibly have children which is what I'm living. However, I was not expecting a relationship with mutual submission and didn't think I'd be this happy.' Said one man, who had started marriage with a complementarian outlook:

> 'I cook, my wife does household maintenance. She probably believes more in this stuff than I do now and looks to me to make final decisions. In practice, we discuss and work together on everything. But I have the responsibility to decide. I am not totally committed to this view anymore, mostly because I'm convinced my wife is perfectly capable of leading.'

Others found they preferred differentiation between the sexes: 'Having been saved into an egalitarian context but now in a (soft) complementarian evangelical/charismatic church I feel most comfortable with what my church teaches compared to previous diminishing of roles and functions. My wife would say the same too.'

The Bells and Other Expenses

For most people a wedding is likely to be the most expensive 24 hours of their lives. After agreeing to share life – which may include an elaborate proposal complete with treasure hunt and photographer – the price of cake, bunting and frocks must be calculated. The average cost is still going up, driven partly by the desire for a unique personalised experience. Research suggests a typical UK wedding in 2017 could be anywhere between £17,193 (without a honeymoon)[6] and £27,161 depending on the age and location of the couple.[7] The average American wedding cost $33,391, though that more than doubled if tying the knot in New York.[8] Millennials – couples currently aged from their early 20s to mid-30s – have been spending more than older romantics.[9] Maybe this is why they are the age group most open to other shapes of marriage. The UK-based Marriage Foundation advocates for traditional marriage as the basis of stable families and society, certain it remains a strong desire for many: 'the dream of happily ever after is alive and well, and linked to getting married', it commented.[10] But – aside from rising costs and the fact marriage doesn't automatically equal stability – perhaps it depends who is asked and what they envisage.

In 2014, *TIME* magazine surveyed a thousand people about possible new models for matrimony.[11] There was the 'Presidential' (vows last for an initial four years, and after eight you can elect to choose a new partner – 21%), 'Til death do us part' (no divorce at all – 31%), and the 'Multiple Partner' (marriage to more than one person at the same time – 10%). The model that received the most votes was the 'Beta' marriage. A committed union that could be dissolved without paperwork or consequences after two years, or formalised and continued if both partners agreed. Almost half of Millennials surveyed said they would do this (a number which increased the younger they were). In a country with one of the highest divorce rates in the world, it's perhaps not a surprise. Social scientists have looked at what makes marriages more likely to last. Focused on US data, they identified that couples who 'dated for at least three years before their engagement were 39% less likely to get divorced than couples who dated less than a year before getting engaged' and that 'Men are 50% more likely to divorce when they said their partner's looks were important in their decision to get married', while 'women are 60% more likely to end up divorced when they cared about their partner's wealth, compared to people who said they cared about neither.'[12] Interestingly, being a regular churchgoer was a positive factor. Couples who attended often were 46% less likely to divorce. While there is no agreed statistic on Christian divorce rates vs the rest of the population (some say significantly lower, others slightly and others insist the rate is higher) the intertwining of church and marriage continues.[13]

Under the Same Roof

A recent and rolling debate is the importance of marriage vs cohabitation. Some Christians will insist there is no other way than permanent commitment, on pain of fornication and damnation, often framed as the difference between a relationship enduring or falling fast. Researchers at Barna report that American society now sees moving in together as a rite of passage for couples – something the church would protest as short termism, if not immorality.[14] And yet they also report, 'Though the debate has raged over whether cohabitation reduces or increases the pressure of marriage, it appears that among those who have actually done it, there was no major effect either way.' For Christians marriage is rarely about convenience and much more about covenant. Practically, marriage confers legal rights that cohabitation doesn't, not to mention tax benefits, but these are motivated by politics and practicalities not faith.[15]

Ready for Lift Off

What does the church offer couples stepping into a future

ordained by God? Some provide pre-marriage courses. At their most formal, couples are invited to spend an evening a week with others considering the next step in their relationships, with topics including communication, money and managing conflict. Though perhaps not all churches were motivated by enduring love . . . One UK-based woman recalls:

'It was rumoured the church was becoming more stringent about who would be permitted to get married there. A couple of recent marriages between church members had ended in divorce and therefore they wanted to be "more careful". The insinuation was that they did not want to conduct weddings where there was the potential for the marriage failing. This was very much the culture of the church – they wanted all their programmes and initiatives to be a success and were unwilling to get involved in anything that they could not guarantee would be.'

For many, simple friendship and wisdom from experience was appreciated. Said one:

'An older couple at the church we went to at uni[versity] met up with me and my then fiancée to talk about different life things before marriage. They weren't cringey, just really helpful and honest and asked really practical questions and gave very practical advice to do with stuff like making time for each other, managing our money and talking about our careers.'

This approach is much more helpful than what I shall label 'Squeamish Church'. Remembered one participant:

'We were only engaged when we took the [marriage] course – church couldn't be bothered to do pre-marriage counselling because they were already doing the marriage course – we were told NOT to attend the Good sex week and ended up at the curate's house having an excruciating evening with him and his wife.'

Not taking the commitment of marriage seriously can have long-lasting consequences. Recalled one woman, 'The Minister who married us decided we each were mature enough in our 30s to not need pre-marital guidance. I'm convinced had we accurately completed these questionnaires, we would not have wed.'

Couples move from having their blossoming relationships interrogated and scrutinised, even chaperoned, to disappearing into a haze of assumed bliss once the wedding is over. The reality that life isn't like the spiritualised fairy tale can be a rude awakening.

'I'm fairly recently married, which is mostly lovely but some things are proving harder to navigate than others. I thought living together would be the difficult bit, but in actual fact it's turning out to be the physical side – which both of us assumed would be a fairly straightforward learning curve. Hence I'm happy, positive, hopeful, but also a bit confused – not many people tell you how to negotiate that bit.'

And often Christians enter marriage with a sense of imminent God-ordained fulfilment that proves elusive. 'It took 14 years of marriage before I could honestly say I was happily married', wrote one participant. After the confetti is a distant memory, what should Christian couples expect marriage to look like? The church offers different visions and theological interpretations.

Marriage as a Higher Purpose?

Covenant is a key theme of some interpretations; a lifelong commitment mirroring God's connection to humanity. The most redeemed – also often the least romantic – marriage narratives suggests if men and women can see themselves as partnering in a bigger mission – whatever God has called them to do in his service – this will shape their relationship as well as how they engage with the world. Titles like *You and Me Forever: Marriage in Light of Eternity'*,[16] *Sacred Marriage: What If God Designed Marriage to Make Us Holy More Than to Make Us Happy?*[17] and Tim and Kathy Keller's *The Meaning of Marriage*[18] offer more reflective, even idealistic takes on why men and women should try to make a life together. Within such narratives gender roles can play a part – indeed, they are a key theme of the Kellers' writing – based on the premise that God created male and female with distinct qualities and parts to play in order to reflect a larger spiritual truth. Overall they focus on partnering to achieve something eternal. The mundane issues of living together become issues of growing in grace, holiness, and sacrifice. Sex when discussed is symbolic and euphemistic. It is powerful, uniting and sacramental. It is not expected to be messy, dysfunctional or disappointing.

Work It Out

And then there are the roles. In most mainstream interpretations God-given roles require women – usually – to subjugate what seem like God-given abilities and reinterpret what they might have believed to be callings. Those who buy in to this interpretation accept that women were created primarily to be 'helpers' to husbands. Those who don't accept it question why God would create women with gifts, talents and abilities that match or exceed those of some men only for them never to be used. It can be a tricky balancing act to work out which parts of the received wisdom of mainstream Christian marriage is worth holding onto, investigating further, or leaving behind. Discernment and critical thinking are rarely encouraged, but advisable. Said one survey participant, 'I was surprised to find Tim Keller's marriage book helpful when preparing to get married. The chapter on women and submission didn't fit with mine or my husband's theology, but the rest of it was helpful.' Another commented that the book:

> 'Helped me understand that neither of those views are what marriage is supposed to be. Rather, marriage is designed to be two incredibly imperfect people who have committed to choosing to love each other, even when it's not easy (though obviously this doesn't mean that if you're being abused, you should continue to stay with your spouse in an effort to "love" them). It has been incredibly helpful to walk into marriage with the knowledge that this isn't always going to be rainbows and unicorns, but when it starts to get hard, that doesn't mean that I married the wrong person or that things are going to fall apart. It simply means that I'm imperfect and so is my husband, but by the grace of God we can love each other.'

One participant reflected on another well-known resource, recommended by several survey participants:

'Although I would want to heavily qualify it, I did also find the original *Five Love Languages* book interesting and helpful. I wouldn't want to build my life on it, but at the point in time I (we both) read it, it had the effect of being one of those "Well, that's utterly obvious and self-evident, but I'd never actually thought about it before" and it helped further develop communication in the early years of our marriage. I haven't dared re-read it in case I want to throw it out the window these days!'

Working Out What Works

Every marriage is unique and shaped by the people in it. Listen to each other. Don't make yourselves into a shape you're not, but instead learn to work together). Ed, a Kentucky-based writer who lives with wife Julie, a college professor, and their three young children often works from home and is primary family carer during the day. He reflects on taking a less traditional route through marriage:

'My own calling to write and my wife's calling to be a professor have certainly brought plenty of challenging moves and difficult financial seasons, but avoiding difficulty isn't the measure of faithfulness. We both sense that we're moving in a direction that is in keeping with how God has wired us, and that is enough.'

The couple found a lack of support from their faith environment:

'Initially, we faced a lot of resistance from the Christian subculture we grew up in where the man was supposed to have the "primary calling" and be the bread winner. It was unheard of for the man to move to a new place for the sake of his wife. I have now moved to four different states for the sake of my wife. So I'm in uncharted territory in the eyes of some.'

Often it was women who articulated similar issues about lack of understanding from the church. Wrote one woman, 'Church/ Christian culture doesn't seem to "get" our marriage and our mutual decision-making . . . even after 12 years it is still assumed my husband makes the decisions and I follow even though we are equals and he wholly respects me and empowers me. I think the limited view of gendered roles within church is a big concern.' Said another:

'The biggest challenge is being at a church which strongly teaches specific gender roles and yet being a woman with strong leadership giftings. Thankfully my husband and I long ago agreed that there are no specific gender roles. However, personally "fighting" the role models of my parents' generations and my own (un-examined) expectations of my roles in marriage and finding a new way, with my husband, finding more equal ways of working has been challenging. And this is now made MUCH more difficult when the church leadership preaches that our understanding is NOT biblical.'

Non-Stop Sex

The big Christian abstinence sales pitch has often involved the promise of relentless hot married sex after 'I do'. One man recalled being taught, 'Get on with it quickly because it holds the key to sex.' Said another, 'This is the only way God will be okay with me having sex.' Marriage, one woman had been taught, is 'great and sex will be great.' Once married, the emphasis on sex diminished. Some found rather than instant bliss, dysfunction, mismatched interest levels, and unrealistic expectations were their day-to-day reality. 'My married sex life hasn't been intensely dysfunctional but it has also been underwhelming, frustrating and (often) boring. It's one of the things I've most struggled with in my marriage,' said one respondent. Wrote another, 'It feels like so much of what we have been taught as Christians is that sexuality is completely inaccessible, off limits, until we get married. Then it magically becomes massively important. It doesn't make sense.' Another remembered sex being saved for marriage because 'the safest place for being most vulnerable (naked) is with someone who has committed to love you unconditionally forever', though as others said, 'The church talks about sex before marriage but rarely about sex after marriage.'

'The idea that sex is not purely physical is not solely a Christian idea but it is one that is taught in church and probably the one that has influenced me most,' wrote one, who added:

> '"Sex is the glue that holds a marriage together" is something I remember. Obviously that's not the full story, there's much more that goes into stable relationships but I liked the idea of sex being something that "glued" two people together – it connects everything that one person

is to everything another person is, in all the complex ways that make up each of those people. Having had sex in previous relationships I knew what it was like in both a loving committed relationship and in those that were more casual.'

Some were positive about their married sex experiences. Said one woman:

'I know that others find this unhelpful, but as a virgin who married another virgin, we have really enjoyed and benefitted from having no baggage from previous sexual relationships, and to have spent plenty of time as we're dating learning what turns the other on (because we were trying to stop at that point!) We were prepared to have to work on sex in marriage, but actually we had great sex even on honeymoon. I know that this doesn't happen to all or even most, but I think it's important to say for balance that abstinence before marriage doesn't necessarily make for unhealthy body image or bad sex after marriage.'

Hump Day

Psychotherapist Esther Perel, author of *Mating in Captivity*, has described marriage as an:

'Economic institution in which you were given a partnership for life in terms of children and social status and succession and companionship. But now we want our partner to still give us all these things, but in addition I want you to be my best friend and my trusted confidant and my passionate lover to boot, and we live twice as long.'[19]

And of course, for Christians, throw in spiritual purpose and eternal destiny too. No pressure. One respondent observed:

> 'People change through a relationship so whomever you marry at first will change anyway. I could describe a dream partner but that's not who I married and I am very happy with the man I married and a marriage with the person I would have envisaged as a "dream partner" would probably raise just as many problems, just different ones.'

The Christian bait and switch of waiting until marriage for sex was a challenge for others. Said one man, 'It's not going well at all, mainly because my wife doesn't like the fact that I don't initiate sex. This may be because I have hang ups, I'm not sure. Hoping to see a sexual therapist soon. We both wish that we'd done more before we got married to see if that chemistry was there.' And then there are no guarantees that an 'equally yoked' marriage will continue as such: 'Before I met my wife, I had a bad relationship with a non-Christian; I then ensured I never dated another non-Christian again. My wife was a Christian, but had a breakdown 4 years ago and lost her faith. I now find myself married to a non-Christian . . . which brings many difficulties.' The less-than-perfect side of marriage is rarely discussed among Christians, and yet is clearly present. Where do the struggling turn to seek help? Are married people allowed to show their vulnerabilities? Let's look next at the kinds of issues that arise in Christian relationships and the oh-so-simple question of ethics.

Chapter Ten
Is It OK? Ethics, Issues and Frustrations

Christians love to talk about unity. Often what they mean is uniformity. But rather than being a synchronised movement of holy perfection, personal ethics differ along the spectrum of Christianity – even though many would wish otherwise. To assume a person's choices about their life based on their faith carries the risk of misunderstanding. The same percentage of survey respondents – 9.29% specifically – would have a one night stand as would marry someone they hadn't kissed. An equal number – 4.5% – would accept a marriage partner chosen by someone else as would be happy to ghost their way out of a relationship. The numbers match again when it comes to being celibate and using dating apps (36.24%), and again for sexting and being open to a register office wedding (24.43%). There can be significant cognitive dissonance too. Confusion kicks in when relationships have not unfolded as expected or teaching has caused harm. Almost 22% agreed '"Purity culture" – the strong emphasis on physical abstinence and virginity for women prominent in some church circles – damaged me and my faith.' For some, knowing what is acceptable behaviour from a partner and what is abuse can be impossible to discern. Understanding dysfunction within Christianity and knowing where to turn can be a challenge, especially when faith teaching is part of the cause.

Frozen

Fear of relationships or making mistakes has made some too scared to start. Wrote one, 'Part of me finds it easier to be single to avoid admitting that I have fears/issues about intimacy. I did try and seek help (professionally) but I don't think [that] really worked as five years later I still feel the same.' The effect of Christian teaching could be negative. 'I have a fear of sex, I think, partly due to my experience and partly due to the church's disproportionate obsession with the subject!' said one participant. 'As I am a virgin I don't know about this, but for a long time I couldn't feel anything as I shut myself down, because of beliefs about it being sinful to feel sexual urges. Now I am constantly horny and very frustrated', wrote another.

Bodies

Christianity has a conflicted relationship with the human body. Though Christians are taught to see themselves as God sees them, much rides on how they've been taught to view God – angry, kind, judging, forgiving, and shaming are just some of the options. How society views bodies has changed too. Rarely forced to live in physical denial in the largely affluent west, bodies have become canvases for self-expression, whether for pleasure, pain or politics. Tattoos and body piercings are no longer considered niche or subversive. 38% of survey participants would consider getting tattooed in future (similar to UK and US tattooing stats among the general population).[1] 35% would contemplate body piercing. Technology has changed how we see each other and interact, and even prompted reinvention. In 2018 cosmetic surgeons reported a new phenomenon – 'Snapchat dysmorphia' named after the popular chat app which has built-in facial filters.[2] Users are requesting surgery to look like filtered selfies; their own face but better. 55% of American surgeons researched had seen patients requesting this, up from 13% five years earlier.[3] 56% reported an increase in clients under 30. Bodies are too often measures of self-worth. Women's bodies have been historically under much more scrutiny and condemnation than men's and subject to control. FGM or female genital cutting, illegal in the UK and for under 18s in the US, is still widely practised globally and involves removing parts of the sexual organs, often including the clitoris.[4] Women's capacity for sexual pleasure is removed, and their overall health severely damaged, even leading to death.

Celibacy/Abstinence

While modern Christian teaching has focused on abstinence-then-hot-married-sex as the go-to model, historically the emphasis has been very different. Author of *Unprotected Texts*, theology professor Jennifer Wright Knust, commented in 2011 on the Bible's contradictory positions on sex and marriage.[5] 'The overwhelming opinion of New Testament writers is that marriage is a waste of time and that we shouldn't be doing it because we should be spreading the Gospel . . . If you're married, you're totally distracted and not focusing on God. If we took the New Testament seriously, we would all stop being married.' And that would probably mean celibacy. Two-thirds of survey respondents believe Church and Christian culture expects single people to be abstinent.

Just over a third could imagine being celibate now or in the future – a position at odds with New Testament thinking that this is the most desirable state for all. Knust observes that responses to Jesus' statement about some of his followers becoming 'Eunuchs for the Kingdom' could be dramatic: 'Some Christians took this literally and there were some cases of early Christians castrating themselves for the purpose of celibacy.'[6] It's what she describes as 'a pretty radical statement that the best kind of Christian is one who is celibate to the point of castration. We don't talk about that much in our own culture and that was a really important message and many, many Christians were celibate.' It seems not many would choose that now. But some would.

Father Michael Nixon is a 35 year old priest in Florida. Attractive, articulate, and humorous he isn't someone who would struggle to find a date, should he be looking. And yet he's committed to a single, abstinent life, which he describes as part of his calling. He told me, 'My life makes sense when it's lived as a gift. Not as a repression of my desire for love or repression of sex, but a fulfilment of living it out in a distinct way from the world around me.' He doesn't claim it's easy or straightforward, describing the outworking as 'trial and error', insisting 'It can't be done alone. The Christian life and our own humanity doesn't make sense by ourselves so it has to be done in the context of community that's loving, life-giving and challenging.' He is motivated entirely by his faith and says, 'If God wasn't real my life would not make sense. If Jesus wasn't lord my life wouldn't make sense. My life says: either heaven's real or I'm a total idiot.' His celibacy is 'a neon sign towards that.' He describes experiencing fear, anger and sadness at times as he lives out his choices and says he has slowly learned 'God isn't afraid of those emotions.'

While just over a third of survey participants could envisage being celibate, many had mixed feelings. When asked how they'd feel if they never had sex, responses ranged from 'It's not the end of the world. Not having sex is not a tragedy. God has better things for me than sex' to 'I'll be very sad because I feel I'm burnt with my sexual desire' to 'aaaaaaaaarrrrrrrrgggggggghhhhhhh!!!!!!!!!!!' (not the good kind). Three-in-ten say their views on abstinence have changed over time. Wrote one woman:

> 'Now that I'm post-menopausal, my libido has really dropped. Sexual frustration is not the agonising thing it was when I was in my 20s and 30s. I'm less agonised now about the prospect of dying a virgin. It doesn't matter to me so much now. Yes, I'd like to meet the right man; it would be good to have intimacy, companionship and love in the afternoon of my life. I rather dread being single in my old age, to be honest. But I refuse to regard my singleness as some great failure either.'

It's the group who described themselves as 'Single not looking' who would be most likely to consider celibacy – just over half of them, in fact – while married respondents were least likely to say they could be celibate now (which is probably fair enough) or in the future. Under a third contemplated this. 7% of all respondents believed abstinence was impossible for them. Social pressures were a factor: 'It's difficult, in a society that promotes sexual activity as normal. It can feel like you are missing out on something and/or that you are weird or there's something wrong with you.' Australian writer Rachel Hills, author of *The Sex Myth*, explored how realistic society's ideas of sexual fulfilment really are and whether young women in particular were growing up with 'a new brand of sexual convention'. Her concerns about whether she was 'normal' or not 'were a product of a culture that tells us we must be sexy, sexually active, and skilled in bed in order to be adequate human beings'.[7] It can be a compelling narrative, even if the truth for many is far more mundane.

Just Say No

Christian attempts at promoting celibacy have often been hard line, with anything other than heterosexual married sex regarded as fornication. Advocates of the Silver Ring Thing and True Love Waits created an industry from rigid no-touching rules. One-in-ten survey respondents believe virginity is the greatest gift they could give a spouse. Whatever the motivations for not having sexual contact, the emotional challenges can be intense and long-lasting. Some reports suggest an abstinent person may benefit as much as they expect to. Quoted in 2017, sex therapist Dr Nan Wise observed, 'Biological, psychological, and social stuff' all mattered, especially in situations where 'the power of belief is going to determine what people experience, and their experience is going to confirm their belief. For people who believe that abstinence is going to help them, the belief itself may be driving some of the benefits.'[8] For many there's no problem 'with masturbation to deal with frustration if not in excess/objectifying people in lust', as one survey respondent put it, but the reality of this is challenging. Over half of survey respondents said they would masturbate, with different personal boundaries and often contrary to church teaching. 'The "take a cold shower" approach to masturbation. Are you kidding me?' wrote one. Lust was often code for masturbation, hence comments like: 'Resisting lust is realllly hard and I fail sooo often, particularly when home alone.'

20% said masturbation is permitted if they didn't have sexual contact with other people, and just over a third would use sex toys.

Lust

Social pressures can't be ignored. Lust is seen as exciting, natural, and an entitlement. Almost two-thirds of survey respondents believe society encourages people to lust after others, pursuing one's own pleasure and not considering the other person fully. Objectification and self-fulfilment often went hand in hand. Just over a third of participants agreed if people see each other as fully human lust will be less of an issue. Wrote one participant, 'Lust isn't "natural sexual desire"', and the church would agree. Others felt the lines were blurred, with any sexual feelings being categorised as 'Lust (read attraction) as sin', said one respondent.

Some Bible interpretations say that Jesus spoke directly against sexual lust, though others suggest he spoke more generally about covetousness, wanting something that isn't rightfully yours. Lust has been viewed by the church as a predominantly male issue though just 17% of survey respondents believe men struggle with lust more than women. In response to the statement 'Men are wired to lust, women should help them by covering up' just 15% of respondents agreed, but over eight-in-ten thought this was the view of mainstream Christian culture. 'I wish that, as a young woman, less pressure had been put on me to protect boys' purity and for my own sexuality and potential to lust to have been recognized and taught how to deal with it in a healthy way', said one respondent. And, as usual, Christians couldn't agree on boundaries. While 96% of respondents thought holding hands was acceptable for an unmarried couple, a quarter believed intercourse was OK, something others believed was a terrible sin. While 40% regarded a sexual relationship as any activity leading to arousal, what caused arousal was subjective. 'I don't regret the relationships but I do regret "going too far" in relationships that later ended. Mostly this happened for reasons of selfish self-gratification, and I don't think these experiences are in any way helpful – in fact they are potentially damaging to a future marriage', wrote one respondent. Many were confused about their bodies' responses. One described remembering 'Jesus' teachings about lusting in the heart . . . though I don't think lust accurately describes what I was feeling.' Said another, 'I wish there'd been more chance to talk about dealing with natural sexual desire as an adult single woman, about where natural desire crosses the line to lust, and how to deal with it.'

Sex and Ethics

Almost a quarter of respondents believed not having sex outside of marriage made it harder to find a partner, and they may have had a point. In 2017 the Single in America survey reported over a third of Millennials surveyed had had sex before a first date, viewing jumping straight in as a kind of 'sex interview' ahead of anything more conversational.[9] It's a world away from what most Christians had been taught to expect. 'My Christian upbringing didn't prepare me for the dating scene once I left home, and I struggled with both managing my own sexual feelings and navigating the feelings of others. In hindsight, I would have benefited from learning how to say no, and how to say yes', wrote one Real Life Love respondent. With a growing belief for some that 'sex is whatever you want it to be', simple 'don't do it' exhortations based on sex being primarily penetrative and heterosexual may not come close to what some are trying.[10]

Janet W. Hardy, co-author of alternative sex guide *The Ethical Slut* commented on changing sexual roles and increasing acceptance of experimentation:

'My observation of the millennials, and especially the post-millennials, is that, instead of breaking themselves up into little groups the way our generation did (A is a polyamorist, B is a BDSMer, C is genderqueer, D is bisexual, and so on), they have all the world of sex and relationships as a buffet: They can try a little of this dish and a little of that, and if they like it, they take more, and none of that changes their core identity.'[11]

This is a world away from what most Christians would expect to encounter, though views of what was permissible vary. Seven-in-ten survey respondents believed bodily contact over clothes was acceptable behaviour for an unmarried couple, dropping to four-in-ten for contact inside clothes. A quarter believed intercourse and oral sex were allowable. A quarter would indulge in sexting, regardless of marital status. 15% would be open to anal sex, an act often first seen in pornography and now a milestone for teenage boys to persuade their less enthusiastic female partners into, according to 2014 research.[12] Some liberal theologies are more open to sexual experimentation and expression, and involve working out where, how, and even if God should influence sexual decisions.

US pastor Bromleigh McCleneghan's 2016 title *Good Christian Sex: Why Chastity Isn't the Only Option - And Other Things the Bible Says About Sex* lays out one such alternative interpretation, one borne out of a faith upbringing that prioritised 'privacy and personal discernment' over community rules. She asks of her own teenage processing:

'If absolute abstinence outside of marriage wasn't exactly a pressing concern . . . other things were. If we were going to have sex, were we going to practice safer sex? Were we going to be faithful in the contexts of our relationships? Were we going to be good friends? Were we going to be honest and loving and gracious and kind?'[13]

Such theologies rest on mutuality, and the hope that both partners will view the encounter in the same way. McCleneghan describes encounters that were validating and uplifting. Despite fearing a boyfriend would reject her less-than-perfect (as she perceived it) body, she found he was 'delighted to be invited to access it.' Had he reacted differently – and many have had sexual experiences which were far from positive – would a theology of sex as an expression of grace seem so valid? McCleneghan speculates that John Wesley may now advocate for kissing, teenage make-out sessions and sex as 'means of grace' if he were preaching in the 21st century, assuming the encounters are consensual and joyful. Coercion, differing hopes, nefarious intentions or self-seeking behaviour are harder to legislate for. 2.5% of Real Life Love respondents said they had been raped. 2% had pressured people to go against their principles about sex outside of marriage, and almost 17% said they had been sexually coerced by Christians. Many more reported experiencing negative or unwanted relationships or sexual attention from Christians, including almost 10% who said they'd been sexually assaulted. Almost 40% said their sexual or relationship experiences had been damaging to them. Christian faith was no guarantee of good faith.

Porn

It's questionable how pornography affects the dynamics and expectations of relationships. With the effects on human brains as yet unknown and the language of addiction regularly deployed, its ubiquity among the young in particular has been called the 'Great Porn Experiment'.[14] Christians are largely opposed to it, though many would struggle to describe exactly what it consists of. Notions of saucy but consensual encounters with horny pizza delivery guys are far from what most websites are offering. Sex educator Natalie Collins refers to a 'spectrum of pornographies' that encompasses sexual violence, choking, slapping, multiple penetrations, and a tendency towards young-looking performers.[15] Pornhub, which offers millions of customers access to professionally made and amateur footage, revealed 'teen' was its top search in 2014.[16] The dynamic of much pornography is, says Natalie Collins, 'about men consuming women. Man as subject, woman as object.' Researcher Seth Stephens-Davidowitz who has studied porn search terms around the world, believes that anal sex will soon be more popular than vaginal sex.[17]

Real Life Love respondents were largely not pro-porn but for different reasons. 15% said they would use porn now or in the future, though it was apparent from comments many wished they could abstain from doing so. 'How many men have thought getting married would solve their pornography problem?' asked one survey respondent. Just four-in-ten respondents believed pornography is a problem mostly because it affects Christians' personal purity, though over three-quarters believed this was a mainstream Christian view. In 2008 the feature film *Fireproof* depicted heroic Christian firefighter Kirk Cameron trying to save his marriage, in part by taking a baseball bat to his computer rather than give in to his on-going desire to look at porn. The addiction narrative reinforces this strength of feeling, and it seems to be a particularly Christian issue. A 2018 article entitled 'Science stopped believing in porn addiction, you should too', suggested Christians' own moral dilemma about their actions being wrong was creating the compulsion to keep watching, or as researchers described it 'Pornography Problems due to Moral Incongruence (PPMI)'.[18] If compulsive use of pornography or the risk of exposure to it created a 'doorway for the devil', then salvation and sanity could be at risk. American magazine *Vox* described the Christian response to the increasing availability of pornography and growing sexual acceptance as 'a pervasive, all-consuming fear that the door that once held back the devil has been permanently removed from its hinges.'[19] Pornhub – which isn't the biggest pornography site in the world – published user stats for 2017, noting 28.5 billion annual visits to the site, 25 billion searches, 800 searches per second, and 68 years worth of film uploaded in that year alone.[20] It's a phenomenon new to this generation and presents a huge challenge to many Christian sexual norms.

Nine-in-ten Real Life Love respondents agreed pornography is a problem because it encourages objectification of women / others, though fewer than half (44%) believed this was a mainstream Christian view. 15% of respondents said the internet had made pornography too easily accessible for them, the same percentage – though not necessarily the same people – who said they would consider viewing pornography in the future (split around 3:1 male to female). Potentially damaging effects are as yet unknown. US researchers have begun to review data to discover to what extent pornography might be a factor in sharply increasing reports of sexual issues in men, including erectile dysfunction (ED), delayed ejaculation, decreased sexual satisfaction and diminished libido.[21] One survey participant described 'a porn/sex addict husband who is selfish to the core. Porn kills love. He also developed ED as a direct result of his porn use.' Many respondents wanted the church to talk more about porn but few elaborated on what this should entail. Natalie Collins has observed, 'the lack of women's voices within the Christian conversation about the spectrum of pornographies. Women feature usually as wives or daughters of the men using pornographic material. "What would your wife think?", "How is this affecting your marriage?", "Would you want your daughter to be a porn star?"'[22]

Boundaries

What do healthy relationships look like? 9% of survey respondents would consider using pornography in an unmarried relationship. Almost three-in-ten would be happy to look at erotic literature – twice as many who say they would view porn. 21% would take nude photos – something which can result in illegal activity or exploitation, though are often intended as a source of empowerment, pleasure and fun. 16% would consider full body hair removal (three times as many women as men) – a trend first seen in and now popularised by porn. 10% would contemplate taking part in BDSM (the commonly used abbreviation for consensual sexual activities involving bondage, discipline, dominance and submission, and sadism and masochism). These aren't activities most

Christians of previous generations would have needed to consider and each has its own ethical questions. Not least, what does consent mean and look like? One participant wished they'd received 'more specific and direct teaching on consent especially countering a culture where it is seen as normal for men to push women and disrespect their boundaries, autonomy and dignity.'

While consent is vital, it can't explain everything. Almost 10% of survey participants would consider having sex on a first date or one night stand if both consent – but consent can be subjective. Beyond an enthusiastic yes (which should be the baseline for any activity), how can agreement guarantee that what occurs is best for everyone involved? Christians are directed to love our neighbours as ourselves, and at the least this involves respecting the self and others. One respondent described the importance of having 'a holistic view of one's body, and how consent is important because you need to respect the *imago dei* in each person.' Laying down one's life for a friend is pretty far from getting laid with a friend. Respondents had mixed opinions on first date behaviour, from the popular answer of no physical contact at all, to 'whatever I want' and 'deliberate consensual arousal between people'. If nothing else, knowing how to discern and navigate is an important skill. One respondent commented, 'I learned how important consent is, adding that to what respect means.' Sex matters differently to each one of us, and is in every situation a vulnerable act, shaped by social expectations, faith, personal experience and much more. One man recalled, 'I gave my virginity to someone because as cliché as it sounds I thought it would show her I loved her, and so she would let me influence her in a Godly way. Sounds foolish reading it back, I know.'

Abuse

Though relationships should be a source of joy and flourishing – and Christians believe they have a unique framework for this – the opposite can be true. Just over half of respondents (55%) believe church is a safe place for them. Abuse may even flourish in church environments, depending on theology and culture. One respondent recalled being taught 'Women should stay in relationship even when a partner is violent: if God sends you a trial it means you can bear it.' Formal safeguarding is crucial – as Bible teacher Beth Moore remarked, 'Make it a safer world to report it and you'll make it a safer world'[23] – but so is healthy teaching about relationships, and awareness of who might be drawn to a faith community to use it as cover for predatory behaviour.

Christians love a redemption narrative and can be prone take dubious behaviour at face value. Sadly, there are thousands of stories of people being victimised through or in church environments – most in the survey were women – and many report being terribly mismanaged when reported. Some have felt too afraid or ashamed to tell others. One woman described being coerced into sexual acts when she was 12 by an older boy:

> 'The church taught that waiting until marriage was expected, but my experience had taken place IN church, during a service, when adults were not supervising. It has taken many years of prayer, and the kindness of friends to understand that it was not my fault and to also sadly realise that my experience is not uncommon amongst women.'

Another recalled:

> 'I was used and abused by a clergyman who groomed me and led me into a sexual relationship. But when we were found out he denied all knowledge, lied and blamed me for everything. The church authorities did not even talk to me, but listened to him; I was dehumanised, treated like a leper. Everyone talked about me but no one talked to me. My family was destroyed but his family were rehomed and looked after.'

Internalised expectations of what it meant to be Christian also meant abuse victims endured mistreatment. A woman who was abused by her husband recalled: 'Part of the reason I ended up in an abusive marriage was to do with my childhood and my own brokenness, but part of it was also because in my head being a Christian meant you stayed with your spouse no matter what they did to you, and because he was ill, I felt I should stay because you vow to stay with them in sickness and in health.'

It can be particularly challenging for women. Almost half of all survey participants believed women are viewed more harshly than men for sexual behaviour in Christian culture. There was an expectation of judgement. Said one woman: 'I was raped by a friend at university. Although my non-Christian friends were incredibly supportive, I never felt able to talk to Christians about this. I was concerned that I would be judged for getting myself into a situation where this could happen. This also meant that I did not report him to the police.' Almost half of respondents said they had seen unhealthy sexual or romantic behaviour directed at women in Christian culture.

Wrote one, 'I wish the church challenged gender stereotypes like the "male pursuer". In fact given the prevalence of rape in our society, I'd say that challenging such notions is absolutely imperative if the church is going to be a voice for good in challenging rape culture.'

Almost a quarter said they had seen unhealthy sexual or romantic behaviour directed at men in Christian culture. One man reported: 'I've definitely felt sexually exploited – it sounds odd to say this. I wonder if any other men would voice this in Christian circles?' A quarter of respondents to the section on abuse said they had experienced unhealthy sexual or romantic behaviour from Christians within church culture. The effects can be severe and long-lasting. Said one woman, 'After I was raped by my Christian boyfriend and our relationship later ended, I lost my faith as I realized all of the toxic messages that had kept me in a relationship with my abuser.' For this to change, the culture needs to change. Almost a quarter of respondents believe Christian leaders' sexual misconduct, such as affairs, often seems to be minimised or excused. Issues can be serious to the point of criminality. Wrote one woman: 'My ex-husband was/is a porn addict and a paedophile. Our sexual relationship was really messed up. And because you don't talk about these in church I was dealing with it alone for a really long time and didn't realise how bad it was.'

Dysfunction

Physical, emotional and spiritual issues can merge. Almost 30% of respondents had experienced dysfunction, affecting men and women similarly. One woman remarked that she had waited for 'sex till marriage – although then found out that I have vaginismus so sex is painful. Nine years into marriage it still is. Wish I hadn't bothered waiting to find that out!!!!' Another, suffering with the same condition, commented:

> 'I've been married nine years and [had] painful sex every time we've tried, except perhaps once or twice. Can't helping thinking if years of "don't have sex before marriage" has led to this. It's too hard to know if it would have made any difference if I'd have had sex before marriage so I try not to think about that!! I was desperate for sex pre-marriage. Now it's an effort.'

She wasn't the only one.

Wrote another, of having 'Vaginismus and inability to orgasm (in a very loving, generally healthy relationship – the only one I have had – no experience of abuse etc.), which I strongly link to what I was taught about sex growing up, and how I conditioned my body not to become aroused because "it was wrong".' And another, 'I have mainly remained abstinent out of a purity culture-induced phobia that has caused me to develop vaginismus, even with my Pap smears.' For others, the discovery that sex wasn't straightforward after marriage took a different form. 'I had a high sex drive before marriage, but have become increasingly shy since marriage despite a loving and supportive husband. I haven't really known where to turn to tackle it.' Male respondents also described concerns. Wrote one: 'Premature ejaculation has been a big problem – a psychiatrist has said it is tied into anxiety about sex and is common amongst young Christian men. My wife has had vaginismus – we got a book and worked through it together. It took nine months until we could have penetrative sex.' A woman commented that her 'husband found it very difficult to perform to start with – he was really nervous. Have never had him ejaculate yet but we can now have sex so I'm confident we'll get there.'

Sex Drives and Other Confusions

After the intensive instruction to flee temptation, it can come as a surprise to find sex isn't the driving force it's been painted as. 'I have not had sex with my husband in 2 years and we only have done it ever maybe 10 times after getting married. I now identify as asexual,' said one participant. Wrote another:

> 'My whole life I was taught that I have a huge sex drive and I have to live in fear that, under the influence of temptation, I might suddenly lose control and accidentally have sex with someone, so I need to be afraid of temptation ALL THE TIME (and I'm a woman – men probably get this message even worse). I was SURE I had this massive sexual desire and after marriage I would be having sex every day . . . I was expecting some huge, transcendent, life-changing experience . . . But nope, turns out sex is pretty much just about stimulating genitals. I knew that's what it was, in an academic sense, but everyone in all of society seems so interested in sex, I figured there must be some really cool thing that happens. But no, not really. Even when I've had orgasms, I feel like it's strange and interesting, but not really interesting enough to go through all the work of getting turned on and all that. I'd rather just hug my partner in bed and be warm.'

Sex educator Emily Nagoski writes in *Come As You Are* that sex drives aren't a thing[24], as such, and nor are traditional expectations – often the same as traditional Christian roles and teaching. Just 30% of women orgasm through intercourse alone and many find their bodies respond to different stimuli. Each person has a 'dual control model' of sexual response – sexual brakes and accelerator – which responds to unique sensations, triggers and contexts. 'We are all different. We are all normal', she writes. Circumstances can change everything. Wrote one woman, 'After each of our daughters was born, I went through a time when I did not desire sex at all, for a while. It was difficult but my husband was for the most part very understanding and supportive.' Said another, 'When our kids were small, we really struggled with both parenting and staying married because we were so tired we argued a lot! We found that because of this our sex life was affected too.'

Mental Health

Three-in-ten Real Life Love respondents had concerns about their emotional or mental health. Slightly more believed they had conditions, habits or concerns that would make it harder to find a partner. It's not surprising. According to the Mental Health Foundation, one-in-six people in the past week experienced a common mental health problem.[25] For some being single and Christian had been a factor: 'I think being on my own in a culture (both church and secular) that expects/prizes relationships and yet not really knowing how to develop healthy relationships, partly due to family background and partly from being taught lots of "should nots" about relationships has led to loneliness, anxiety and depression', wrote one. Another echoed this:

'While there is a natural basis for my depression, I do feel that chronic loneliness, sexual frustration, sexual dysfunction, and the lack of a decent proper cuddle (as distinct from the non-touching "hug" that you might get at church or from Christian friends), and a sense of hopelessness about ever getting married – all these things contribute to an inner stress that exacerbates my underlying depressiveness.'

Some found a faith community could help: 'As a single person who lives by herself, I understand how the stereotype of the "crazy cat lady" came about and rely on friends and being part of my church community to help stop that happening to me.' The pressures of modern dating expectations can take a toll too. Wrote one,

> 'I have had a couple of past relationships where there wasn't commitment and I was really hurt by this. One in particular led to self-harm and suicidal thoughts. It was a sexual relationship over technology – sexting and phone sex and then I was 'ghosted'. We didn't really see each other more than twice and we were never physically intimate but the emotional side of it was too much for me.'

For others, the religious environment had been damaging: 'I've suffered with depression and anxiety at least since my late twenties, probably much longer. I'm now undergoing investigation for suspected dissociative identity disorder. Some of these things spring from my experience as a teenage church-goer, from a strict Baptist family', said one. While conversations about mental health and illness are improving across the church, there is far to go.

Fidelity

Marriage is still a serious proposition. Adultery is still illegal in 23 US states.[26] While just 2% would consider polyamory – concurrent consensual relationships with more than one partner – 5% would contemplate a physical affair and 7.5% an emotional one. Most respondents believed being faithful was the right thing to do, though some had experienced the pain of being cheated on. 'My husband's excuse for his affair was that the other woman was his "soul mate"', wrote one woman, adding, 'Not that that made their relationship last – it had finished before we'd even got to our decree nisi.' Recovering from infidelity was hard. Said another, 'My husband was somewhat controlling, and around the time of his affair said a lot of emotionally damaging things to me. It took some sessions of intensive healing prayer ministry for me to recover fully from that, but I'm OK now.' Wrote one man, 'My previous wife's unfaithfulness put me at risk constantly for five years of STIs, plus her emotional abuse left me traumatised and afraid of closeness and trust.'

Understanding attachment is helpful in building long-term relationships. Attachment theory suggests we learn in our early years how to connect, or not, with people – initially parents or caregivers, and later with potential partners. These styles range from 'secure' to 'preoccupied/anxious' to 'avoidant/dismissive' to 'fearful/avoidant' in varying degrees. Through this framework, our bewildering and contradictory behaviours are captured in black and white – and can be a revelation. Having an avoidant attachment style has been linked to discomfort with emotional closeness, and the increased likelihood of infidelity.[27] Indeed, it can prevent relationships developing or even starting in the first place. Thankfully, it's possible to learn about attachment and work towards changing destructive behaviours and seek help where it seems too hard to go it alone. For someone wondering why their relationships don't last, it's a good place to start.

Endings

Not every relationship goes the distance. For many Christians, 'God hates divorce' has been weaponised. Everyone hates divorce. But 94% of respondents said there are sometimes valid reasons for Christians to divorce, and 17% wouldn't rule out divorce in the future, should they feel it necessary. Three-in-ten said their stance on divorce had changed as they'd got older. 'I am divorced from a man who was a Christian but abused me. I stayed with him because I believed biblically I had to', said one.

For those who've found their relationships ended through bereavement, remaking life beyond the initial loss and finding support in a church community is a life-saver. 'I am widowed and single-handedly bringing up two traumatised children who each have significant mental health difficulties. I sometimes find this overwhelming.' What can be done to start changing the culture so that abuse, dysfunction and relationship issues can be reduced and supported?

Some Positive Steps

Education and awareness - In an environment where people want to believe the best of others, cultural naivety can create a dangerous environment. Good intentions are no excuse. From top to bottom, churches must work to understand abuse dynamics and signs and have a zero tolerance approach to any reports or indications of dangerous behaviour. A woman who was abused by her husband from the first day of her marriage, including financial control and controlling emotional abuse, relayed trying to seek help after four years: 'I turned to the curate's wife at my church. Her first question after I'd told her what was happening was, "Does he hit you?" My answer was no, which meant that no more was done and she urged me to ignore my mother's pleas for me to leave him. Eventually, with the help of friends and family, I left earlier this year.' She added, 'I feel as though the church is ill-equipped for dealing with abuse, particularly non-violent coercive control. Even when I left, the response of the church was very much "What can we do to bring you back together?"'

Realism and recognition – Historically the church has been unwilling to be honest about the realities of relationships and changing social norms. Focusing on what Christians *should* do often shuts down the opportunity to learn what's really happening. 'My first boyfriend was very jealous and controlling and would shout and throw things. I didn't really know how to respond. I think church youth workers should go beyond focusing on not having sex to talking about what a healthy relationship looks like.'

Openness and honesty – It can be a long journey to self-awareness, especially where cultural expectations encourage people to deny their experiences and needs. Changing this takes time, but is important, even if it means going outside of expectations. One respondent shared:

'I had untreated depression as a child and a young adult and even though it is a condition that runs in my family, my parents (and my church community) were not supportive of my getting medical assistance. Since I have "come out" about depression and been more open about taking medication and seeking counselling, all three of my younger sisters have sought medical attention for depression and anxiety.'

Acknowledging and accepting – Don't be afraid to reflect on what might have influenced long term mood or mental and emotional health. It's not disloyal to feel family, relationships, or faith may have had negative consequences even if not intended. It's healthy to seek or accept outside help, even though it may mean going against expectations of culture or family. Wrote one woman, 'I've been in counselling for two years and that strongly related to both a toxic home environment and a toxic church environment.'

Sensitivity and understanding – Don't judge by appearances or assume anyone's journey. Everyone's faith and family experiences will be different and have impacted them in good and bad ways. Some may have experienced things others can barely imagine. Said one, 'I grew up in a split household, atheist mother and Christian father, where my father was mentally ill, an addict of substance, pornography, and an abuser to his children and wife. Rejected evangelical Christianity in college, but clinging to Jesus still.'

It's impossible to know the fullness of how experiences have shaped someone's life, but few of us have had a straightforward path. We can help or hinder another's healing with every encounter. Love and kindness will make the difference every time.

Chapter Eleven
The Single Issue

Once a month a sombre procession makes the short walk from Southwark Cathedral to a wild, beautiful garden hidden behind a high wall. Few places capture the uneasy relationship between single women and the church as vividly as this disused patch of land in south-east London, which yielded its fascinating secret in the 1990s. The place now known as Cross Bones[1] was revealed to be the final resting place of thousands of people deemed unworthy of Christian burial in the Middle Ages, among them the women who worked in local brothels – brothels licenced and profited from by the church. It was known as the Single Woman's Churchyard. Oh, the respectable-sounding irony. After hundreds of years, the church, at least locally, is finally trying to make amends through a monthly act of remembrance.

The centuries often haven't been kind to single people, viewed with suspicion, pity or disdain. Women – dismissively labelled spinsters, old maids, thornbacks or even Christmas cake (only good before a certain age)[2] – have usually come off worse, especially in the years 'single woman' was interchangeable with sex worker.[3] Though spinster began as a more positive term, describing girls who held the respectable profession of spinning thread, it came to mean any unmarried woman, assumed to be repressed and lonely.[4] Men had it better – the eligible bachelor or man-about-town, free of responsibilities and open to options, though maybe irresponsible. Without marriage women were superfluous, even a burden. Unable to support themselves, their options were limited, and society could be merciless towards them.

Attitudes towards single people have gradually improved. A 1957 American survey suggested that 80% of people believed someone choosing to be single was sick, neurotic or immoral.[5] Too often the church hasn't known what to do with single people either, despite the New Testament redefining their purpose and championing their status. Research on the UK church in 2014 suggested a lower percentage of single people than in wider society.[6] A third of adults involved in church were single, compared to 60% married. It's not hard to understand why. Single Christians felt limited by the description, according to research highlighted by the UK organisation Single Friendly Church who called it a 'loaded term' and noted: 'Single is not a great term to describe marital status in the 21st century.'[7] Encompassing the never-marrieds of all ages, the widowed, divorced, separated and those parenting alone, 'single' didn't adequately capture the breadth of experiences of all those who happened not to be married. Advice to Christian single people is sparse and often impersonal. If not tentative suggestions to find someone with whom to marry and bear fruit, encouraging volunteering and prayer while avoiding worldly temptations are safe options.

Yet in the wider world singleness has never looked more different. Social scientist Bella DePaulo has devoted decades to exploring the positives of single life and says, 'Single is how I live my best, most authentic, most meaningful life.'[8] She unpicks popular myths that married people are automatically happier, healthier, live longer and make better parents with convincing evidence of a much more varied picture.[9] Where marriage and motherhood were once expected for women, Kate Bolick, author of singleness book *Spinster*, notes that since the 1970s, the percentage of American women in their early 40s who haven't given birth has nearly doubled.[10] Marriage historian Stephanie Coontz believes the skills for navigating singleness successfully are more important than ever, noting, 'In 1960, Americans were married for an average of 29 of the 37 years between the ages of 18 and 55... almost 80 percent of what was then regarded as the prime of life. By 2015, the average had dropped to only 18 years.'[11] Additionally, single people in 2016 are over 45% of the adult American population and nearly half of the workforce. 31 million Americans lived alone,[12] as did 3.9 million people between aged 16 and 64 in England and Wales in 2017.[13] Globally, research suggests, numbers of solo dwellers increased by a third between 1996 and 2006 to over 200 million.[14]

The Bell Tolls for Thee

Has the church reflected, celebrated or even recognised these shifts? Often not. Rebecca Traister, author of *All the Single Ladies*, described her once-ingrained belief that 'the natural state of adult womanhood involved being legally bound to a man', something that the church has too often promoted.[15] Historian Elizabeth Abbott describes marriage as 'the organising principle of society'[16] and the church has often been at the forefront of shaping society. 'I married at the age of 23', wrote one Real Life Love survey participant. 'Since then I've become increasingly frustrated with the cultural focus on relationships in general, and marriage in particular, as the ideal state of being. I'm very happy with my own relationship, but I would not get married again.' Said another, 'Relationships are seen as a part of a person, when leaders or speakers direct a message to "the singles" [or] "single women", I am not a single woman. I am a woman who is single.'

It's clear that grouping people together by relationship status falls short of meaningful definition. A quarter of Real Life Love respondents described themselves as 'single and looking' and one-in-ten as 'single not looking'. Mixed feelings accompanied both descriptions. For many, the prospect of remaining single indefinitely is negative but dominant. Only 2% of unmarried respondents believe they are called to singleness and almost 40% of participants agreed 'I do not feel called to singleness but am single'. 'Most of the time', said one woman, '[I'm] content, thankful, enjoying my life and the opportunities I have because I'm not in a relationship, don't have children. Sometimes? . . . Alone! Tired of being strong, longing to be verbally affirmed or held, questioning if there's something wrong with me, worried about the future.' 'Single and looking' could be a fraught state. Fewer than two-in-ten felt positive about their relationship situation, which is understandable as they were actively seeking something they currently lacked. 13% agreed 'If I end up not getting married it will negatively affect my faith'. They were ten times as likely as married people to say they felt both lonely and negative, and were the majority of the 'hopeless' too. And yet, compared to the 'single and not looking' they were more hopeful about the future (more hopeful than the married), and half as likely to believe 'God sends The One – I don't need to look'. It was apparent that living in a state of wanting and watchfulness created tension.

For women in particular, the contrast between passivity ('waiting well' in Christian-speak) and positivity (thriving in the moment) dominated feelings about being unmarried. Said one:

> 'In the "right now" – I am content. I like my life, my space, I like the opportunities and freedoms that I can take advantage of in my singleness. The confusion comes from not knowing whether I will still like it if it hasn't changed in a few years' time. I think a lot of single women struggle with having grown up with an assumption that they will get married at some point, but when you're entering your 30s and that hasn't happened, doubts start to set in. So I'm not hopeless or frustrated but I am doubtful about whether I will ever meet someone and how I'd feel about staying single in the long term.'

Singleness was often seen as – or hoped to be – a temporary state, or 'season' in Christian-speak. One 24-year-old respondent wrote of her wish to be married, 'I've been told lots that it's a good desire and God will honour my heart, but I've also seen lots of older single Christian women who have been faithful and wanted to be married, but still aren't.' Said another participant, 'Sometimes I feel like other Christians treat singleness like it's the easy rounds ahead of the tough stuff of marriage. I wish it were more frequently recognised and discussed in Christian contexts how singleness has complex consequences and challenges that go beyond the obvious relational and sexual ones.' In some faith interpretations women didn't feel empowered to move towards finding a partner, something reflected in the majority of Christian singleness resources. As the Joshua Harris-penned foreword in *Did I Kiss Marriage Goodbye?* (a book with a big diamond ring on the cover) exclaimed, paraphrasing the complaints he'd heard from single Christian women: 'It's fine for you. You're a guy. You can initiate a relationship . . . I have to wait for a man to get his act together!'[17] In this worldview, marriage is always the ultimate goal, with books that encourage times of waiting directed towards spiritual self-improvement as a means to becoming marriage-ready. They also speak to the 'innate' female need to feel beautiful and be noticed, by God if not by a human male. And yet, in equivalent resources, if men are single, it's not because they don't have a choice (overall). There are no books for men about 'being single' as a gendered issue and the effect on self-worth. Some tackle the challenges of manhood, predominantly perceived as lust, porn and building self-discipline, often with theology that leans towards man as the personification of purpose and destiny and woman as his supporter and facilitator. While a man can work on personal battles, a woman potentially loses her identity – or needs to find it – if marriage doesn't happen. Women are pushed into questioning 'where God is' when they haven't been chosen.

A Place to Belong

And yet, many hadn't given up on church. Single participants were the most strongly represented self-declared churchgoers, with 50% (the highest of all categories) describing themselves as 'regular and committed' and almost as many as 'enthusiastic and involved'. And yet only 3.5% of all respondents believed 'the church and Christian culture values and knows how to pastor long term singles'. Ironically, it is single people who say they need this most. 45% agreed having 'a church/faith community that accepts and supports me' was a joy, compared to a third of married people who felt the same way.

Church can become a place where relational 'success' equates to marriage and children, and this is normalised and celebrated, which can be difficult for the many who don't fit. Wrote one survey respondent, 'I always assumed I would meet a Christian and get married but it hasn't happened, and I do often feel a lesser person for it in a church context.' Lizzie Lowrie and Sheila Matthews are both married to vicars in the UK and created Saltwater and Honey, a network to support people in the church experiencing childlessness.[18] They both recognised the isolation and pain of not fitting the ideal in their faith communities. 'The bible is full of stories of the outcast', says Lizzie. 'The church tends to focus on biological family and the perfect model.' Sheila adds, 'Often suffering is seen as the interruption to how life should be, rather than a natural part of it. It's important to tell our stories from the middle and not only when they have a happy ending'. For single people, the church's tendency to avoid anything that doesn't look like a 'happy ending' can mean drifting without recognition of the struggles and joys of daily life, or significant moments.

Kate Wharton is a writer and vicar based in Liverpool in north-west England. In 2017 she gathered friends, family and church community for her beLOVED ceremony, a public declaration of her intention to live a committed single life. She recited vows she had written including the promise to 'live a life of chastity and celibacy, to remain single, and without children, to dedicate myself fully to this life, and to embrace its sorrows and its joys, to seek to live always in a way which is generous and open and loving and kind and gracious.'[19] This is a challenging prospect in any era, but what prompted this bold public statement? 'There is simply no precedent for celebrating life with single people', Kate told me. 'We don't get an engagement party or a wedding ceremony or a honeymoon or wedding anniversary or baby shower or a Christening party.

There are far fewer public milestones for the single person.'

The Bible, particularly the New Testament, is pro-single. The church rarely is, and should do better. Says Kate Wharton:

> 'The church needs to be far more creative about what it blesses and nurtures and encourages in terms of 'family'. When churches advertise their family events in their family church it feels excluding – I don't have a family, so am I really welcome? And often when I talk about this people say 'Oh but of course you are, family means everyone but it doesn't feel like that and so I think they need to work a lot harder to make it obvious.'

When traditional families are often the default, pressure to join their ranks can be intense and remaining single can feel like failure. Jesus does talk about 'finding the one' but he's not talking about a dream partner. He means the missing sheep who is relentlessly sought out and brought back into community. Dr Marijke Hoek is a Dutch UK-based academic and has been teaching on singleness since 2000. She told me: 'I became a Christian when I was 19 and what struck me when I came into the Christian scene is that women my age – late teens, early twenties – were consumed with the idea of being single and getting married.' She describes young people 'whose lives were weighed down heavily because they hadn't met anybody yet' and attributes it to 'the environment they grew up in. It's the household, the communal household, the church' of which she observes, 'if you've got an in-house culture where leaders are married it's most powerful when it's self-evident. Culture itself is a pressure.' She believes we're often asking the wrong questions about singleness: 'When you look at the moral vision of the New Testament Jesus put an equality on both the single lifestyle and the married lifestyle. So the moral question is not, are we going to be married or not, but instead we should invite the question: What is your vocation? What is it that God is calling you to do?'

Together Forever

Aside from vision and purpose, the practical challenges of singleness can be tough. Wrote one survey participant:

'I live in a city where to buy the vast majority of properties you need to be a two income household. That means as a single person I'm stuck in rental properties that don't really suit my needs and that I can be told I have to move out of at any time. I feel like singleness makes my career more challenging in some ways because I'm coming home to largely disinterested housemates, not someone who provides emotional and practical support. It's extra hard when bad things happen. One of my most emotionally painful moments of singleness was when I got extremely bad food poisoning, and feeling helpless and utterly alone because there wasn't anyone around to help me. I'm worried about what would happen to me if I became long term sick, disabled or unemployed.'

Long-term hopes and plans can be a real concern. Statistics are emerging about the effect on the Millennial generation, born between the early 1980s and mid-1990s, who are taking longer to establish independent identities and marrying later. 2014 American research found 'for the first time in more than 130 years, adults ages 18 to 34 were slightly more likely to be living in their parents' home than they were to be living with a spouse or partner in their own household'.[20] This is an emerging trend, but these are issues that can last much longer. What could the alternatives be, and what could community look like? American writer Anna Broadway has documented her experiences of singleness and faith for over a decade. Her 2008 book *Sexless in the City* described her 'reluctant chastity' as a 20-something in New York.[21] Ten years later she embarked on 'The Global Singleness Project', a round-the-world exploration of Christian singleness. In between, she moved, primarily for financial reasons, from living alone into a community of artists in a former convent in San Francisco. 'I really feel like it was God's gift to me', she told me, 'because it had been so hard to leave my old place and at first I felt so much loss. It was really hard to feel like I had gained something. But eventually I saw I'd gotten an upgrade.' What she describes as 'unusual and really amazing' was the mix of families and single people in the community she was now part of:

> 'I had never had that before, but it was such a gift. And it was living with families that really challenged my thinking of what normal, and good, and ideal living situations looked like, and even what I would aspire to. Because until that point in my life I'd always thought that you'd arrived as an adult when you have your own house, and it's you and a spouse and a community you create with your biological children.'

She now takes a different view: 'Even if I got to a point where I didn't need that kind of community I now think I would seriously consider seeking it out. Because I see how beneficial that was and I think the idea of the nuclear household that we have lacks some wisdom from other cultures that have been more multigenerational and more communal.' It's a view that may increase in popularity; 38% of survey respondents said they would consider living in mixed community in the future, though only 3% do so at the moment. More people are coming to the conclusion something might be missing in the atomisation of modern life.

In 2015, the Archbishop of Canterbury initiated A Year in God's Time, a 'radical new community' bringing together a group of adults from around the world aged 20 to 35 to live together in Lambeth Palace in London as monastics for a year. 'Like Jesus has chosen us, we choose to give ourselves to one another in prayer, in service, in support, in forgiveness, in work, in play, in listening', state the Community of St Anselm's Rule of Life, setting the tone for a potentially challenging year.[22] What would draw Millennials to enforced closeness with people they may not get along with while taking a vow of poverty and chastity? Andy Walton, a London-based journalist with a busy professional and social life, took part in 2018. He told me:

'I think the draw is community. Actual closeness to people rather than the more thin version offered by contemporary life and social media. The fact that we may not get along is part of it. You can self-select and screen your social media bubble but we know that isn't possible in a genuine community so oddly enough I think that's part of the attraction. Real community is found in living alongside people and having to deal with them at their worst as well as best. And being seen at your worst as well as best. It's not easy but it's more satisfying than the atomised model we mostly have now.'

Liz is a London-based vicar and has been part of a scattered community for seven years. Founded upon principles of incarnational love, the community welcomes all – it is not exclusively Christian – but deliberately seeks to bring those of faith and those with questions around the same table. While living separately the group is centred around a weekly 'open table' meal. Liz shares:

> 'I believe that what we have created over the years (which is most definitely not perfect and has many flaws!) is still unusual in the city. A place where people eat together. Where the stranger is welcomed and can find relationship. A place where the love that is shared is so different from social norms that it surprises people and prompts the deepest of questions.'

She adds:

> 'Although we are non-residential, a number of members have lived with each other over the years, and have homes that are intentionally shared. Whenever I've needed a housemate, a member of the community has been in need of housing. When I lost my home through a change in job, a family within the community welcomed me with open arms. Their children are my Godchildren, and their home is still a haven when I need it.'

The shape and dynamics of community have changed over time. Liz continues:

'Seven years ago, married couples in the community were something of a rarity – primarily we were a bunch of single 30-somethings trying to build community in a way that is counter-cultural to regular London life. We've had a number of marriages since, and several children have been born, but the community remains – in fact, it is stronger because these changes have provided new ways in which we need to care for one another.'

Married people are the least likely to say they would live in a mixed community – just over a third would consider it. Paula and Simon are a London-based couple who began to establish what they call 'low key community' in their self-built (and subsequently extended) house in 2008. Paula described several reasons for their decision. 'It makes you less selfish', she began, 'Sanctifying, to use a very old fashioned word in our materialist world. It forces you to consider other people.' Alongside practical considerations – lower living costs for both the couple and those who join them – are more idealistic reasons. 'We try – and fail sometimes – to steward. We feel that everything we have is given by God and it's not for us to say "this is mine". There is a sense of a sharing the gifts that God has given.' Exploring simpler ways of living, not motivated by making money or building assets, is also a factor. 'We try our very best to invest in the future by modelling something that maybe younger people will say "Ooh that's great. We want to do this". We just hope and pray people say "We could do this and maybe we could do it better".'

Marijke Hoek is interested in how single people, and Christians in particular, think about how they live alone and together. She cites the Hofjes in Amsterdam, purpose-built communities each centred around a courtyard garden. One of the most well-known of these, the Begijnhof, was created in the fifteenth century to accommodate religious women who didn't want to live in convents.[23] It is still occupied by single women today. Could there be a modern precedent for single people to forge their own paths and create alternative communities? What are the possibilities for mixed arrangements of single people, couples and families to join forces? Growing independence over the 20th century meant people moved away from families to start or commit to relationships. Of Real Life Love participants, almost half lived in a big city, and, in total, 87% lived in a city or town. Finding connection is necessary. American writer Rebecca Traister has noted the role of cities in facilitating single women's lives in providing ready-made resources and the possibility of finding like-minded people, though recent US research suggests the split of single people is much more even across urban, suburban and rural settings.[24]

Family Matters

For single people, again particularly women, the dream of having biological children can be hard to relinquish. What does family look like if not the feted nuclear model? Kate Wharton signed up with an organisation that offers practical support to local families at risk of breakdown. 'To me it's what church, and family, and community, should be, what it should look like at its best', she says. 'It's just people helping out their neighbours, showing love, offering care. I love the connections I make with families, and I love being able to look after children for a few hours or a few days, knowing that I'm making a big difference to that family.' The idea of 'spiritual parenting' can sound trite when traditional family models are celebrated more, but could be meaningful if genuinely integrated relationships are developed and roles of godparent and honorary aunty or uncle are championed and intentional. For some single people, waiting for a partner to start a family seemed unnecessary. Almost four-in-ten single Real Life Love participants said they would consider fostering or adopting while single. One woman who did this described her life post-adoption as 'completely but wonderfully different'. She told me:

'I knew that I wanted to adopt from the time I was about 10 years old. This thought never went away and I told myself that if I reached the age of 45 and I had not yet met my life partner, that I would embark on the adoption journey on my own. I had always assumed that I would get married, have my own children and then adopt, but life didn't turn out this way. When I reached 45, I put the plan in action. My life has changed drastically since adopting. I have to juggle life with a toddler, a full-time job, lack of sleep and a lack of time to myself. It was a huge adjustment and in the beginning I really missed my old life. It's now been five years and my life is infinitely more rewarding than it was before.'

For others, parenting isn't a desire but speaking openly about this is still a taboo. Though under half of Real Life Love respondents – four-in-ten – described being married with children as their ideal relationship situation, 60% believed churches expect married Christians will want children, half said Christian culture prioritises nuclear families, and a quarter felt that 'not wanting children would be seen negatively by my church community'. Both male and female respondents said they didn't want children at all, though more women felt this way. Churches – not to mention wider society – would be wise not to make assumptions. So, if not through building traditional – or non-traditional – family units, what do meaningful connections look like?

Forever Friends

There's a modern joke that the most unbelievable thing about Jesus is a man having 12 close friends in his 30s. How good are we at making friends? Often not very, and yet it's vital to flourishing. One 2012 study found the wellbeing in mid-life of both men and women hinged on having regular contact with a wide circle of friends,[25] and the cumulation of almost 150 studies demonstrated good social relationships had a marked effect on physical health too, reducing the risk of early mortality by almost half.[26] The Real Life Love survey recognised the importance to differing degrees. When asked 'What are the biggest joys in your dating or relationship situation?' the most popular response – agreed by six-in-ten respondents – was 'Supportive friends and / or family no matter what'. The 'single not looking' valued this the most, with almost three-quarters responding positively, compared to half of married respondents. A 2013 study indicated the perception of marriage as an improver of personal happiness was misguided, concluding, '80% of people who marry are happy, but they were equally happy long before they got married. In other words, marriage doesn't make you happy, it makes you married.'[27] Only 10% in the study reported being happier, and 6% actually felt worse.

What matters more is having significant connections and tackling the growing problem of loneliness. 'In church we teach on fellowship. Don't forsake the needy. But we don't teach on friendships or a wider band of relationships which all help us to function well and to flourish', observes Marijke Hoek. 'Friendship should be taught as much to married people as single people. Because it's a recipe for disaster once you meet "the one" that everything from that moment onwards is done as a twosome. Married people need friends as much as single people.' Friendship is biblically significant too: 'When the Bible speaks about friendship it's about laying down your life for a friend.' Wrote one survey participant, 'I am so blessed to be walking in faith alongside some very wise women, all very different stages of life. I think there is a lot to learn from those around us and we need to know that we don't do life alone.'

Without friendship, both single and married people are prone to loneliness. A growing body of evidence indicates there are no upsides to this condition. One 2018 study suggested eating alone regularly was the single biggest indicator of depression, particularly as this was unlikely to be chosen.[28] Kate Wharton agrees:

'Obviously it's possible to be lonely in a relationship, or in a crowd, or whatever, but I think that's slightly different. There's that loneliness when you live on your own, where you genuinely might not see or speak to anyone else for days, apart from at work or whatever. There are people without any sort of friendship circle or community, desperately lonely. The church simply has to wake up to this issue and work out what can be done about it. At its best church is community – I don't think we've made the most of ourselves in that way, in terms of inviting people in simply so we can welcome and love and care for them, and so they find a community of which they can be a part.'

The effects of loneliness can be devastating on both physical and mental health, with impacts equivalent to smoking and obesity.[29] In theory being connected with a faith community should have health benefits. Researchers Kate Pickett and Richard Wilkinson are experts on the effects of inequality.[30] They note that religion can offer a number of benefits including a sense of belonging and community, the opportunity to be meditative and mindful, and the possibility of social coherence and connections.[31] For some Real Life Love survey respondents it was apparent this was either a missed opportunity – 'I feel I'm lacking close relationships, and I'd most of all love that to come from a partner, but I'd also love to have much closer friendships, with people of either gender', wrote one participant – or played out more negatively. For single women, it could be oppressive. One commented on the 'ambiguous friendships' rather than healthy ones that occurred between Christian men and women:

'The worst thing that I've found in Christian culture is the tendency for male and female friends to become really close without it leading to dating – or become ambivalent. But because there's no physical intimacy aspect (and none allowed in Christian dating) it's hard to define what's a relationship and what isn't. And there's no real culture for how to discuss these 'friend' relationships. They're like placeholders until the 'real thing' comes along, and I think they are treated as such, without recognizing that, in an emotional sense, at least, they are the real thing.'

How to Make Friends and Influence Yourself

Finding people with whom to integrate and make meaningful community is a peculiarly modern challenge. The growth in leisure time compared to centuries past, unpredictable working patterns, studying and making lives away from home towns, the rise in use of social technology, and changing living patterns make transience and missed connections more likely. What have grown quickly in the last few decades are parasocial relationships, one-sided relationships with the famous or even – *whisper it* – Christian celebrities whose inspirational quotes and candid selfies can seem like true connection.

Building platforms and personal brands (a thoroughly embedded fact of modern life now even the Girl Guiding movement has introduced a badge to reward teenage girls for it[32]) can easily replace face-to-face contact, authentic sharing, and the opportunity to be genuinely seen and known. While church claims to be family, single people can experience something very different. How do people without a life partner live significant lives and matter to people? Some of the solutions are the same with or without faith, like actively working in community projects or charity (though some American research suggests the 'highly religious' are more likely to volunteer,[33] the same research says they're no more likely to recycle or make ethical shopping choices, and UK findings suggest almost no difference based on personal faith).[34]

Single Real Life Love respondents were positive about reaching out to others. Over two-thirds would get involved in mentoring or supporting others – above the 60% who answered across all groups. Hypothetically, of course. While juggling life pressures committing to nice-to-do activities can slide down the list. 'We all need to learn to think more laterally', says

Marijke Hoek, 'As a single person I'm always looking around me for who can I invite?' She doesn't mean to church. 'Thinking ahead: you've got a single person without children who has a birthday. Who is doing what a sister would do? Who is doing what a brother or mother or friend would do?' This may mean going outside church structures if opportunities don't exist or aren't encouraged. Not every existing community recognises the value of pioneering new things. Not every church will be prepared to change shape. Instead of focusing on 'being single' as a common denominator, what are the needs around you? What are your under-used skills? What are you passionate about? What could you teach others? What could you learn from them? Start thinking differently and others will often be inspired to do the same.

Chapter Twelve
Take Me To Church?

According to the Real Life Love survey, how churches deal with modern relationship challenges is an area for improvement, hovering somewhere around a C-. *Means well* (probably), *tries, could do better*. Well, of course. If people leading churches wanted to be dating experts they'd go and do just that – and probably have a cutting-edge vlog about the foreshadowing of sexting in Ecclesiastes – rather than devote years of their lives to Bible study, side hug practice and advanced level quiche tasting. Speedy changes in culture and technology make it unlikely churches will have a handle on the new norms, alongside more traditional relationships and singleness.

Unity Not Uniformity?

Many survey participants remain active in church despite mixed experiences. As we've seen throughout the book, almost half said they were 'regular and committed' and over a third 'enthusiastic and involved'. Fewer than one-in-ten described their faith as patchy, personal, non-traditional, struggling, or said they were searching for a spiritual balance or home. 1% said they were no longer Christian. It's likely that similar scenarios are found in regular, everyday churches, no matter what the polite smiles and small talk might suggest. American research from 2013 suggests that church in its current shape is not seen as vital to keeping or sustaining a faith, particularly for younger people: 'Nearly six-in-ten (59%) young people who grow up in Christian churches end up walking away, and the unchurched segment among Millennials has increased in the last decade from 44% to 52%, mirroring a larger cultural trend away from churchgoing in America.'[1] Church does not make even the top 10 factors in growing faith. Not even the top 10! Possibly the first time the church has had more in common with Joy Division and Vampire Weekend than Shania Twain and Crazy Frog (depending on your denomination).

Ideal Idealism

Despite diversity of church background, when asked what they remembered about the church-designated standards of Christian dating, relationships and marriage, survey respondents were consistent. In particular, they recalled a strong expectation that a spiritualised version of a 'straightforward and happy' romantic life – something only 13% of respondents said they'd experienced themselves – would be the common experience. Abstinence, then an easily found relationship with a fellow Christian, initiated by the man, leading smoothly to marriage, leading to lots of sex, leading to biblically named children, leading to social media posts about date nights into eternity. Directly or not, the church at large has tended towards presenting this vision of the 'by the book' (though which book is unclear) romantic life as the ideal and the achievable standard, though it hasn't been for the majority.

Life on a Precarious Pedestal

This idealism can easily (mistakenly) be conflated with faith leaders' own relationships, often bestowed with an unintentional status as romance role models. Over a third of survey respondents agreed 'Christian leaders' relationships are used as an example of success', which is risky at best, but more so when based on impressions, partial knowledge, and holy-tinted optimism. It can create a breach. Only a quarter of survey respondents said they would go to their faith leader about issues in their relationships, and just one-in-seven would turn to a church group for support – not quite the first stop for broken hearts and tricky questions. Almost half thought church leaders are often out of touch with what's happening romantically in their congregations, and only a fifth thought churches understood modern relationship challenges 'very well' (42% responded 'somewhat' and a quarter with a charitable 'They try but…'). So, C- it is. But hope is still present.

What's the Way Forward?

The church at large has rarely been at ease with matters of romance. It's a recent shift, and very much an evolving one, to address relationships, dating, sexual behaviour and dysfunction with any degree of frankness or nuance. In some cases, to discuss it at all. Approaches vary greatly. A church's own theology will permeate teaching, conversations and expectations. If not openly discussed, its ethos will be present in the ways the community is led and lives out its faith. This will have a bearing on the kinds of issues that arise and whether they are acknowledged or hidden. It will affect the responses they receive, ranging from hellfire and condemnation to an unquestioning liberal embrace. Singleness is still largely neglected, as we've seen. So, now what?

For many Christians, change means untangling influences from their earliest experiences and memories onwards. Much evangelistic research mirrors what Real Life Love participants said: the majority of present day Christians had found their faith in early life.[2] Only 13% of survey respondents had become Christians in adulthood, meaning their formative relationship experiences occurred within the framework of Christianity. They had absorbed messages on how to conduct Christian relationships from being within the culture (churches, youth groups, conferences, camps, media, books and resources), with varying results. Many are still working through what that means for them.

Evolving Perspectives

Creating positive church experiences is a challenge. Society offers ever-increasing complexity and choice. Helping people navigate change, and develop personal relationships requires humility and willingness to listen. There is no *one* answer, though it can be tempting to suggest otherwise. Many who said they received unhelpful advice realised this retrospectively as life unfolded differently to expectations. Indeed, almost half of respondents said their feelings about the impact of their faith on their relationships had changed over time. 'As a student active in my Christian Union, I held to fairly conservative positions on relationship issues', wrote one. 'These days I tend to think that where God gives laws he does so for a reason, and that we shouldn't expect those designed for a Bronze Age agrarian society, where the family and priesthood were the only instruments of social welfare, to be automatically applicable in the modern world.' Another said, 'As a teenager and young adult I felt so conflicted between faith and relationships and now realise much of the baggage I was handed from parents and youth leaders had little to do with faith and more to do with their own personal experiences and a good dose of fearmongering from Christian teachers.' One respondent commented they now had 'a more mature understanding of relationships', adding, 'Their complexity cannot necessarily be applied with the sometimes black and white rules that youth group or Sunday school teaches. There is much to learn and grow in relationships alongside faith.' An older respondent noted, 'I am much more open and accepting of how my adult kids choose to live in their relationships. I am way less rigid and worried for their perfect Christian plan in life.'

Challenging Times

So, what are the challenges for churches in dealing with modern relationship situations? Where to start . . . ? A big issue is facing reality, and doing so with honesty and compassion. With so many respondents hoping to meet their partner in church, despite variable (some would say minimal) evidence of this as a successful strategy, it's an unrealistic pressure for church leaders too. As well as growing a thriving spiritual community, they are also expected to cultivate perfect future marriage partners for their flock. Perhaps this has arisen from years of encouraging people to remain safely within church, unless allowed out for designated evangelism (though definitely not the flirt-to-convert approach).

Another challenge is simply to recognise changing needs as people age, and to understand and value their discernment as they learn from their experiences. And then there's that little mentioned mathematical problem: there are more women than men in church. 'Church feminisation' has been bandied about as the source of ills for several years, as though by faithfully attending, women have turned churches into havens of pink, flowers and weepy love songs, sending Real Men hurtling for the exits. Men taking this view have been vocal about robust action, favouring battle metaphors and risk-taking messages to win over new converts. Changes in society at large – technology and working hours, for example – and lower male religiosity are often overlooked. Often the resulting initiatives specifically to attract men have relied on stereotypes. While this book is not going to endorse prolonging stereotypes for even a second longer than necessary (clue: it's already unnecessary), hopefully reflecting on the shape and size of the church as part of a wider social situation could help inspire new ways of engaging with the outside world. Part of this may involve rethinking traditional fears and objections, and in the process releasing people from expectations that have limited, and even condemned, them.

Women have long been relied on to turn up to, volunteer at, and support the church. While being held responsible for 'feminisation' simply by existing and attending church, women are expected to continue attending faithfully, not look outside for potential partners, and be prepared to be further side-lined within the church so an atmosphere can be created where men feel prioritised. Should this approach bear fruit (and it so far hasn't), the trade-off is a stock of possible marriage partners. Aside from the wider sociological issues, this is problematic. Ministries and best-selling books have been born out of strategies that involve a traditionally masculine and often dominating view of men, as a means of drawing them in or giving them an action-based, hierarchical role to keep their interest, regardless of whether this is appealing or accurate.

Real Life Example!

Picture the scene: a mainstream London church with a mixed congregation of ages and races one Sunday in 2017 (one which didn't hold a theology of male headship) and yours truly in attendance. The service was led by a white, bespectacled man, the worship was led by two more of them, and the sermon delivered by another. All could safely be described as middle class at the very least. In the foyer, however, was a copy of David Murrow's *Why Men Hate Going to Church*, the book that has led the charge against 'feminised' Christianity and calls for churches to be redesigned and reprioritised to appeal to men. Not the men who were already doing everything visible that day, but men who are doing other things with their Sundays. Men who like press ups, war metaphors and extreme sports – all suggestions in entirely sincere recent resources designed to help churches attract men to their services ('Instead of putting flowers out how about displaying footballs, remote controlled vehicles, power tools, model cars or other man-oriented sculptures?' suggested a UK-based men's ministry in 2017, sadly without elaborating on what a man-oriented sculpture was).[3] Confession: stealing is wrong, thus saith the Lord, so I instead hid *Why Men Hate Going to Church*, and, if the church in question recognises itself from my description and is still missing their copy, I will tell them where it is because lying is also wrong, although both were very tempting on this occasion.

A Man's Man for Women?

This outworking of the 'feminised church' complaint has become a key strand, often the only one used, in addressing why the church has more women than men (though some commentators have changed their vocabulary to be less gender-specific, referring instead to the 'romanticisation' of the church). Telling men to 'step up', be 'real men', and 'man up' feeds into a kind of masculinity that is being rapidly deconstructed elsewhere as harmful in the pressures it creates on mental and emotional health, among other things, including changes to wider society. It's rarer to consider that social pressures are increasingly affecting women (who are now leaving at a faster rate than men according to American research),[4] or how technology has changed the need for the traditional services where the community needed to gather in order to hear God's representative for 40 minutes on a Sunday morning when they could be listening to podcasts or reading blogs. These latter factors were relevant to the Willow Creek and Saddleback models, who targeted their respective composite educated-but-over-stretched men with no interest in church. Even less explored is whether male stereotyping is something many men don't aspire to or actively reject. This is something several men reported anecdotally, distancing themselves from a persona that doesn't represent them or their understanding of Jesus or Christianity. Yet, on the whole, the church supports ministries that represent a 'right' way to be a man and a Christian, and this usually emphasises toughness and the downplaying of all emotions except those akin to sports victories or high stakes brotherhood.

Class Act

Class is also a factor in both church appeal and in perceiving suitable romantic matches. Relationship dynamics have changed in wider society, shifts reflected in the church. In 2015 the book *Date-onomics* by John Birger offered an explanation for what he called a 'marriage crisis' for American women, and the parallels for the church are notable.[5] What he actually identifies is a crisis in 'equal yoking', a shortage of men and women of equivalent education, orientation and life stage. Women are now less likely to find partners who 'match' them. For Christians the matching – in theory – needs only to be in faith but this ignores how many other factors are in play when choosing or being chosen by a potential partner. Said one female Real Life Love respondent, 'Met the love of my life at church, which I didn't think was possible. He's 6 years younger, works in physical labor (I have two masters degrees), and on paper, couldn't be more my opposite. But he is so good to me, and I love him.' Many single Christian women want a partner similar to them in more than faith. Intelligence and social status mattered too, said survey respondents, and this wasn't necessarily available within church.

Male survey participants, by contrast, wanted a kind, generous, physically attractive, probably Christian woman. Not quite matching priorities, and not a contrast that worked favourably with the existing mismatch in numbers. Appealing to men on the basis of 'de-feminising' the church and offering them supremacy or stereotypically masculine activities is not a solution to this multi-layered problem, especially if 40% of already Christian men surveyed don't see shared faith as a deal breaker and would be open to meeting partners elsewhere.

Represent

Current church structures may be exacerbating the issue. Even where male headship may not be the actual theology, it's statistically likely that the church leadership will be male or male dominated, and that leaders' wives will have roles –

official or otherwise – as a consequence of their marital status. There may be a lurking belief that women get enhanced cachet, and even opportunities, if they are connected to the 'right' kind of man. The church's on-going partiality to gender roles – take a look at the majority of Mothers and Fathers Day Christian resources for some lively examples – means there are large gaps in who is represented well. Stay-at-home mothers who enjoy homemaking, crafts, and talking feelings a lot, and breadwinning husbands who dislike emotion and can only be related to through sport and food are not the majority of the population in the UK, yet this is where many resources are aimed, nor in the US, where many such resources are created. Is this helpful? Perhaps, if this happens to fit your personality and the environment in which you live and can flourish. But, no, not for the many. It is limiting. It doesn't reflect that everyone is different – even Christians – and a church that wishes to appeal to and welcome everyone, ultimately, can not do so by limiting its understanding of humanity or reducing people to stereotypes.

What's the Answer?

What should church leaders do? What would you want them to know? Almost half of respondents said they thought 'church leaders are often out of touch with what's happening romantically in their congregations'. Some leaders may breathe a sigh of relief at this (others may actively encourage that perception). It's likely though that many would want to develop communities that model something different, and encourage emotional health and wholeness, as well as practical support for all stages of relationships and singleness. Thankfully what this could consist of is not a great mystery. Many people are happy to talk about what they need – while hoping they won't be judged for doing so – and top of the list are honesty and openness.

Churches must consider the environment they help create. While 'purity plans' (documents drawn up to ensure physical boundaries while single and dating) originated in America, they are increasingly discussed in some UK churches. Not being alone with someone of the opposite sex may still be expected. Such rules can lead to fear and confusion about healthy friendships and interaction (aside from ignoring the prospect of people being attracted to someone of their own sex). This lack of awareness is especially true when it comes to singleness, a much-neglected part of life in the church. Sean Doherty, who was ethics professor at St Melitus theological college when we talked, regularly speaks to church leaders, existing and emerging, and has observed how most churches organise their relationship priorities. He shares the following observation:

'If I'm teaching this, especially to a mixed group of people from different churches, I'll say put your hands up if you're from a church that has a marriage enrichment or marriage preparation course, something that proactively supports marriage, and typically maybe half to three-quarters raise their hands...then I'll say OK now put your hands up if you're in a church that in some way proactively encourages people in healthy singleness, or invests intentionally in that, and in rooms full of hundreds of people, maybe five people put their hands up.'

Church leaders should consider the effect of neglecting investment in single people of all ages, and the dissatisfaction this creates and compounds when marriage is highly visible and valued in the same community.

By giving space for people to talk about the issues in their lives, something can evolve that permeates the culture and encourages openness and mutual support, rather than something an all-knowing leader must own. When asked what advice they wished they'd been given, over 750 people responded in thoughtful detail. These are some of the key themes to emerge:

Invest time in teaching about and developing emotional health - Emotionally healthy churches and people (or those working towards it) will create healthier, more respectful and robust relationships. Church leaders may not feel qualified to facilitate conversations about this, but helpful resources already exist.[6] It can't be superimposed. It can't be modelled by having token 'healthy' people becoming the default ideal – which is unhealthy for the church and for the 'role models' themselves. This is a lifelong journey, and making time to do this might be one of the most important things you do for yourself and all your relationships, whether you're the leader of a megachurch or the last person through the door on a Sunday. Focusing on biblical teaching about the whole person, what personal holiness could encompass, how each of us should relate to God and to others, would benefit everyone whether in romantic relationships or not. Developing emotional literacy matters too. Having the ability to understand and name feelings, for starters, and to experience and show empathy can be life-enhancing. And knowing how to understand your emotional needs and issues sets the scene for an altogether healthier environment in every sense. It can start with small steps.

Take the risk of letting people explore their own boundaries -
Despite an appreciation of spiritual discernment, many
churches enforce a hard-line approach when it comes to romance. Respondents recalled being pushed to be 'intentional'
as soon as coupling became a possibility. Being 'intentional'
focused on not being misleading about where a relationship might go – and often translated into someone panicking
whether they were one day going to marry the person they
had just said hello to at youth group – and being absolutely
clear about this from day one. Every interaction was analysed
for meaning, and motivations questioned in the interest of
staying pure and guarding hearts. Stunted emotional development was often the result. By the time they were older, they
were not necessarily wiser if life choices – or in some cases
lack of choice – were based on advice received as teenagers. Women in their late 30s and 40s found themselves having delayed adolescences when their 'faithful waiting' hadn't
brought them the dream man they'd expected. As they started
actually talking to human males and arranging awkward coffee dates, torrents of repressed hormones surged into action.
Men found themselves stumbling over perceived excesses of
choice, fearful of committing to the 'wrong one', or believing
marriage required them to become spiritually (and potentially
materially) responsible for another adult. What was clear was
that no one 'right way' existed, but often churches were either
vague or silent on relationship matters. Some offered weekly
courses, others offered dogmatic instruction, others nothing
at all. In reality, people wanted a collaborative approach, and
opportunities to talk about their situations and choices. The
more rigid or controlling a church environment, the less likely
this was to happen.

Prioritise learning about building healthy relationships - People are desperate for what will help them flourish. Not to hear what they shouldn't be doing, but what they could do in order to connect with others in a healthy way. From early years onwards, messages are received that impact the rest of life. Teenagers are steered away from inappropriate contact, and adults who are working out how to make contact and develop friendships and relationships with others are often left to flounder. By helping communities recognise and know how to build healthy relationships – and conversely what unhealthy behaviours look like and how they can be avoided, challenged and changed – greater spiritual growth can also occur, as people 'prefer one another', to paraphrase the King James Bible. This doesn't mean adopting 'honour codes' as some ministries have done, with agreed behaviours and patterns of interaction (which are often very gender-specific) but rather to be led by living out the fruit of the Spirit and seeing this in others. Approaching a potential relationship or interaction led by love, joy, peace, patience, kindness and goodness is likely to lead to better outcomes than strictly enforced rules. If people want help to date better, this is a good place to start, alongside demystifying simple things like small talk. It is constantly surprising to me how many people want to meet someone ASAP and get married, thus turning their lives upside down, but balk at the idea of breaking their current routines and social patterns to spend an hour chatting to a stranger in a coffee shop (unless there's a 99% chance it will lead to marriage within three months, which seems both fair and reasonable).

Learn about unhealthy relationships - People need churches that understand emotional manipulation, coercion, domestic violence and abuse. Sometimes they need them urgently. Understanding and being able to respond to the prevalence of unhealthy relationship behaviours that tip into the abusive and dangerous could be a literal life-saver. The church has a chequered history in helping women (usually) who find themselves in relationships with a controlling, violent or abusive partner, and certain theological interpretations have endorsed women staying with men who treat them badly. Where women are seen as 'helpers' to men, part of that help involves enduring this behaviour, praying for them, encouraging them to change, and continuing to 'submit' to them, no matter what risk to them.

This should cease immediately, and instead churches should prioritise training in recognising the signs of abuse, becoming safe places for those being abused to seek help, developing strategies for helping abused people exit their situations, become wise to the control and manipulation involved in keeping them there, and understand the risks of leaving. Heart-breaking stories of women encouraged by their churches to take back a man who seems to have turned over a new leaf only to find the abuse continues in private or escalates should be historical cautionary tales only. Churches need to step up their ability to discern dangerous behaviour and not become unintentionally complicit in it. Examining the subtle messages present in Christian dating language is a good start. A man who 'pursues' a woman while she waits passively to be chosen is a storyline from many real-life tales of control, likewise the quick courtship and marriage hailed as romantic and God's will rather than a red light. Working to understand consent and respect is vital here too. Churches could become a lifeline in this area if they are prepared to prioritise it.

Figure out how to develop a culture of honesty and openness - Many who responded to the Real Life Love survey were clear about what a changed culture could involve. They wanted to be heard, to have opportunities for honest discussion, to not be judged, and to be helped to process and develop their own responses. They wanted to be able to talk to people who would offer private empathetic listening with whom they could be open. They wanted to not be shamed, but rather to be helped to address problems, to identify any underlying issues, and to receive support to change when necessary. They desired someone to talk things over with rather than specific advice, especially between adults. They wanted practical help too. They did not want platitudes or dismissals. If they were struggling with loneliness or isolation, or feeling overwhelmed, they wanted to be able to talk about it but also to find some of the answers through community. Where does a busy leader or leadership team find the time to cultivate this, or even develop the skills? A pertinent question relates to future planning: How could a church work towards this? Are counselling skills or experience valued in staff and members of the community? How does this become something everyone is involved in rather than a niche add-on or the domain of an empathetic few? Are leaders prepared to model this themselves? If a church isn't built on the emotional and spiritual health of its community, what are its foundations?

Do unto others... (and what happens when people don't) - Developing integrity is important in helping churches navigate modern relationship challenges. People have never had more choice, and yet they feel overwhelmed by it. The likelihood of being let down, rejected or not chosen increases as people look beyond the walls of their churches and faith communities for relationships. In addition, women who have felt – or indeed have been – overlooked because of the demographic mix in their church circles may suddenly become noticed outside of them and can be unprepared for the consequences and choices they face. People need help in learning how to deal with being let down, being desired, and how to develop boundaries in their interactions. Teaching responsibility and response is an important factor: How should I act in my dealings with others? Am I responsible for their reactions? Am I 'preferring' the other person? It can be easy for women to assume their role is one of placating, and for men to feel entitled to push boundaries (the 'pursuing' thing again). Knowing how to treat others well but fairly is also a good witness when meeting new people, especially with the new territory of dating sites and apps. Churches must steer away from excusing poor behaviours and encourage integrity as a key value regardless of age, sex, or any other factor.

Get better at the whole singleness thing - For most, being unmarried or without a partner will be a life stage that lasts longer than a few months in early adulthood. For some it may be their lifelong status. And yet, many believe the church doesn't do well at validating this or valuing people regardless of marital status. There is little teaching on what long-term singleness can look like or support in choosing singleness as a way of life. As we've already seen, in one of the lowest scores of the entire survey only 2% of people agreed they felt called to be single, and four-in-ten did not feel called to be single but were. It's a source of great pain and loneliness for people, exacerbated by throwaway comments and poor teaching. Don't tell single people God wants them single, list what they're doing wrong, or suggest they just need to keep waiting (probably don't offer to lend them your treasured copy of *7 Days to Pray the Single Away: Breaking The Chains of Singleness One Day at a Time* either. . .).[7] Do encourage them in their wider life goals, celebrate their achievements and special days, involve them in leading and creating, support them emotionally and practically, and, if they do want to meet a partner, help them learn how to start dating, if that's what they need. Church should be family and community, and many biblical examples show how this relates to our adoption into a wider family; not the elevation of the nuclear family as the goal, with supporting players looking on wistfully.

Valuing life in different shapes, not emphasising one way over another - While some people may prefer a front led be-like-me model, many people are crying out for places they can be themselves and be welcomed home face-to-face. Churches can empower people to know they have choices in whether they marry or not, how their relationships develop, and choices in what their single lives look like too. For those in settled domestic situations, changing relationship norms can feel remote. But, for single people in particular, challenges and opportunities are different. External factors intrude into the life of the church through the people in it, who shouldn't be focused primarily on supporting the structural hierarchy of the church. Instead the church should work on creating spaces where people are supported, brought into positive friendships and relationships, and encouraged in their faith, gifts and vocations.

Single people – especially women – have broader perspectives than in previous eras. Marriages don't all look the same. Families are different shapes. Living arrangements can be transient, fluctuating and challenging for those who don't fit the traditional model. The church may need to go on a steep learning curve to work out how to support and honour this, and offer something stable, honest and loving to wider society rather than be perceived as a place led by rules and specific expectations.

Get better at talking about sex - Much of the awkwardness about Christians and relationships comes back to fear of sexual activity. Centuries of history loom, and the church has played a changing and questionable role in modelling where sex fits into relationships. People's own stories demonstrate there is no one formula for everyone, no matter how much this may be the desired ideal. People need to talk about how to balance out emotions, sexuality and spirituality to work towards wholeness, not just to be told not to have sex. They need to learn about establishing boundaries in all areas of life, so that sexuality is a part of them they understand and manage, rather than something they don't understand, are fearful of, or react to compulsively. Churches need to focus on positives and negatives of sex – honestly – rather than use guilt and shame to control behaviour.

Where people are celibate, there should be sensitivity to the reality of not having sex. Some will be using all their self-control not to even think about it (and probably failing) and others will be wondering if their lack of desire is normal. It would be helpful – though understandably feel risky – not to assume all Christians share the same ideals and sexual ethics. The main difference in this situation is one of openness rather than changed behaviour. It is likely that those who are acting in ways different from their church's teaching will have varying reasons for doing so and are currently doing this in private or even secrecy. Some may have reached their own conclusions about what they feel is permitted, or may have evolving views, and in other cases their behaviour may be the result of reacting against strict teaching, purity messages, shame, community expectations, ingrained views of God and judgement, or even dangerous, compulsive or abusive behaviour. While the appropriate reaction to each person's situation is going to be personal to them (pesky humans with their complex mix of needs), what would help is for honest conversations to be allowed and for genuine explorations of boundaries to take place without resorting to judgement. Ask where God is in the situation. Frame sex in terms focused on developing discernment, understanding the dynamics at play, managing social expectations, sexual health, long-term vs short-term expectations, the impact of desire and action, love and respect for others, what it means to honour God, and acknowledgement that there are many other things to consider than just DON'T DO IT.

These are long overdue conversations for many. People may appreciate advice, guidelines and teaching (they may not), but they always need support, trust, space to talk, and opportunities to change if their behaviour is damaging. Churches need to accept that emphasising virginity has been unhelpful for many, and perspectives that aren't modesty- or purity-related would be appreciated. Many people have sexual pasts (as well as presents). Avoiding sex outside of marriage does not mean they are not facing issues within marriage either. The idea of crossing into a new state once married, where a person is changed and experiencing conjugal bliss, is not helpful and dismisses the humanity involved. While much of this teaching may be ideological, it doesn't mean those exposed to it will agree with it, even if they are nodding along on a Sunday morning, nor that they will act accordingly.

Be prepared to look again at what it means to be men and women - Consider personhood before male or female labels. Sex and relationship teaching based on expectations, formulas, even interpretations of science, about what it means to be a man or a woman can have a significant impact on behaviour. Women reported growing up in a culture that denied they had any sexual desire (while they were painfully aware they did). Men remembered teaching that suggested their sexual desire was an almost uncontrollable force (causing them shame, and leading them to feel they were abnormal if this wasn't the case). The historical context of 'biblical marriage' also plays a part – are people in the present day expected to emulate dramatically different historical models, particularly where women in the original scenarios had no agency? Can churches set people free from these limiting roles, and encourage mutuality and respect between people no matter their age or life stage? Can they be instrumental in creating spaces, cross-generational communities, for people to flourish as themselves, share wisdom, and not expect them to fit into stereotyped roles or behaviours in order to be accepted? Are new conversations possible about what it means to be a man or woman, exploring faith and humanity together?

In Their Own Words

Many Real Life Love participants had good advice to offer, too, thanks to their own hard-won knowledge and experience. While they don't all share the same view (of sex, in particular) each offers something that has helped others already and gives a hint of the kind of compassionate support that exists, often under the radar, in church communities. So, here are some of the things Real Life Love respondents want you to know:

'If this was me talking to my daughter, I would make sure she has a really strong sense of self-worth and positive self-image. That's what I wish I had had earlier on – make lots of friends and not be too keen to find attention/affection from someone. I think that's really key and growing up in the 90s I don't think this was as well recognised as it is now.'

'That abstinence doesn't guarantee plain-sailing when it comes to sex within marriage, and that girls are sexual beings too. Being a "good Christian girl" doesn't mean being void of any sexuality.'

'Relationships are messy and we all make mistakes.'

'It's ok if the first guy you date doesn't end up being the one you marry!'

'We hear that being in a relationship makes you whole. I would have liked to hear that I shouldn't worry – not

237

everything is about being in a relationship and you are not half a person outside of a relationship.'

'Focus on becoming a sensible mature person who can then use God-given discernment to make decisions about dating as you do in other areas of your life.'

'Make sure you maintain your friendships with people as they get married/have children. You'll need them.'

'Learn to be content. Contentment in who you are is vital for healthy relationships. Openness and honesty and sharing with others is healthy. Sex and the sexual drive needs talking about openly and honestly. Trite black and white approaches are recipes for disaster.'

'There's no rush to get married, and you're not immediately and permanently happy and sorted once you get married. You'd still need to work on things.'

'Get your mainstay of life intimacy NOT from your partner but from a broad range of deep and intimate healthy relationships with people of all ages and genders. If you do this you won't be needy in your romantic relationship or need a relationship in the same way.'

'Wish I'd been told that I was a sinner marrying a sinner and should not expect my husband to be my Saviour. It's ok to still need female friends and not everyone's spouse is their best friend.'

'It is often not straightforward, but God understands and is with you in your loneliness, broken-heartedness, and confusions and can guide you through.'

'Use discernment, and don't beat yourself up if you feel you may have misjudged a situation or relationship. Know that your past and upbringing greatly affects your outlook on experiences, but don't need to dictate how they end up.

'If you don't feel able to bring up or talk about difficult stuff you probably shouldn't be together.'

'YOU are enough on your own – don't look for someone to complete you.'

'Value yourself for who you are – you don't have to change to suit someone else's ideals.'

'Be comfortable in your own skin – not fearful of singleness or solitude.'

'It's hard! It's hard being single, in a relationship, and from what I've witnessed, it's hard being married too. No stage fixes the problems with the other, and no person is free from wondering, even if very rarely, if the grass is greener. . .'

'In everything, ask yourself: is this helping or hindering your relationship with God?'

'People still bring their own baggage and brokenness, being a Christian doesn't make everything magically better, it just means we're not alone in the mess.'

Relatable Resources

* * * * *

A Practical Guide to Meeting Another Human

OK, you've read all about why Christians are dating and forming relationships – or not – and now you're wondering about the how. You might be one of the quarter of Real Life Love survey respondents who ticked the 'single and looking' box (or maybe one of the 10% who said they were 'single and not looking') or you may be arriving here for the first time. So, you ask, are there any recommended behaviours for the human dating process? No. It's a free for all, and indulging your terrible animal lusts is long overdue, especially if you're a Christian. However, if you prefer to be more restrained, here are a few simple tips for meeting and dating other people.

Don't forget boundaries - In this age of individualism – some would say mild narcissism – decide before you start where the boundaries will be. Plucking up the courage to put yourself out there means entering unknown territory, often in both the digital and physical worlds. The seemingly endless options can lead to confusion and angst. Those who largely avoided the cut (and especially the thrust) of modern dating rituals can be prone to overstate boundaries, particularly when speaking to women – sentiments echoed in most Christian relationship resources. *He'll come if you wait! A real man will step up and pursue you, and you'll know when he does! He'll be worth holding out for! Until then, just wait,* **OK**? But building defensive walls isn't the same as having good boundaries and doesn't help develop good instincts or relationship building skills. What's needed is balance between existing life and the wider world. Think about what to disclose if you set up a dating profile. How available to be to potential dates. How much time to set aside to go actively looking. And how to manage the expectations of a faith community, family, and friends. Being over-exposed and juggling new activities and interests can lead to emotional burnout – and quickly.

Don't Go It Alone - Who do you currently share your time, emotions, maybe living space, possibly even DNA with? Are they going to be open to new people in your life? If coupled, are they in a positive place emotionally? Are they realistic about relationship dynamics? If they're single do they need encouragement and a sympathetic shoulder too? Good supporters will have experiences and perspectives of their own, and can help keep clear vision when the clouds of infatuation or despair blow in. Helpful interactions need boundaries too; your love life – or theirs – shouldn't become the dominant theme of a friendship. Balance your needs with what's going on in the lives of those around you. How recently have they been through a similar experience, if ever? Will you need to explain how dating works, and why you can't just 'pick one and get on with it' as may have been suggested to one author you know? Compassion may be behind their pained 'Why can't they see what they're missing?' when a potential romance falls flat, or the old 'plenty more fish' clichés, but uttered from the cocoon of a happy marriage, may not be comforting. Even the greatest supporters may have an off day – as well as their own lives to lead – so extend some grace, but don't assume others will adjust smoothly and quickly or understand your new vulnerability.

Not-so-Helpful People - Whether you sign up to dating sites, start a flirtation at work or church, or your eyes meet on the bus (your eyes and someone else's, rather than a sudden medical issue) not everyone in your life will be helpful. It can be tiring, unsettling and exposing to look for a potential partner. Coupled people seem to know this, which may be why the happy ones breathe sighs of relief, sometimes in front of their single friends. 'Rather you than me! *I* couldn't do it', as though you've been selected for a sexy Hunger Games-type scenario. Some can be tempted to live vicariously (vicars are obviously more prone to this which is why it's named after them) through their single friends, demanding forensic details of the latest goings-on. Don't feel obliged to turn your experiences into anecdotes to entertain anyone. Some may even – objective scientific research here – pretend to be you and sign up to a dating site to make selections on your behalf and then tell you you're too fussy because they've found *at least* 20 suitable people if you're only prepared to move to Bedford, or don't mind taking part in puppet evangelism every weekend. 'I'd be straight in there if *I* was single', they say, while their beloved brings them a cup of tea and strokes their hair affectionately. Of course you would. Bedford is lovely at this time of year.

Don't Get Carried Away - Everyone knows of a couple who fell in love on date one in fulfilment of several word-perfect prophesies and married weeks later. It's probably not going to happen. Transforming an awkward 2-minute, post-church chat into the start of a Cinderella story is ill-advised. Analysing emoji deployment to decipher just what is going on in the heart and mind of a potential paramour is another bad idea. Likewise resist the projected desires of friends and family. The potential paramour must live up to roles and stereotypes. Only sparks and butterflies and hearts and flowers will do. Don't let crowdsourced excitement push out clarity. Constant post mortems of stalled situations aren't much fun either. If you don't wish to become a holy gooseberry – spending your free time as an anecdote-spouting entertainer of couples – you'll need a bigger or different support network. You might be single at any age with any sort of romantic history, and may even have been married at some point and extending your social circle, whatever your situation, may not be easy but that's where online interaction can help (some dating sites have message boards to chat about whatever subject you like), and far away friends, clubs, volunteering, work buddies, dates-that-didn't-become-relationships, old friends and new may all become just what's needed.

Only Yoooooooooooouuuuu - Work out how to support yourself well (almost eight-in-ten Real Life Love respondents said working on emotional health was a good idea). Work out who will help you along the way. Launching into an 'everything is awful and I will never meet anyone / I fully expect to die alone / why did they leave me when everything was great?' rant, even one delivered through a smile, will be a learning experience for bad ('I will not be open with that person again') or good (who knew they were a brilliant listener / had been through the same / are going through it right now). If you're an extrovert who needs to *let it out* but there's nobody around, write a journal, pray, go for a run, fictionalise your experiences, distract yourself rather than dwell, have a bath, cry when you need to, be honest when you do see people with whom you feel safe, and give it time. You probably won't explode. Try to avoid coping mechanisms that will ultimately harm you (heavy drinking, repeating poor dating habits, that kind of thing). Figure out how to process. It may be tough if baring your soul goes badly (I still squirm at a conversation that ended after a long silence and stony response to my sad story of 'Well, you only have yourself to blame, don't you?') but you'll survive and know this person can be filed discreetly under Unhelpful Supporters.

Do Some Work on Self-Awareness - You can look, sound, and act however you want – this book won't tell you to get a haircut or join a gym – but please note this will have romantic consequences. For example, there's *some* social pressure to use deodorant, sure, but only you can decide if you will hand your cash to The Man and stifle your enticing musk. Some may decide your *au naturel* approach is bold and irresistible. Others will run far, far away. Being yourself, authentically, can take some work, deconstructing all those social messages about what *should* be attractive, especially in the age of personal branding, selfies and social media. Being aware of the effect you have on others is useful. Talk over people if you wish, and maybe some will find it charming while others will set off the fire alarm and run away. Only you can decide if you're making good choices or if there's some personal growth to be had (kidding, there's always some personal growth to be had).

Stay in every night and watch soaps back-to-back if you desire, but it will reduce your chances of meeting someone in the flesh (social media may be your saving grace). You want to meet someone but you don't really want to change anything in your life to facilitate that? You're limiting your options (and maybe don't really want to meet someone). Don't live in fear. By not taking any risks, effectively removing yourself from the equation and becoming passive, you're expecting God to do all the work. Tempting maybe – but not helpful or healthy. You want to meet someone who wants to be around you, so being authentically yourself rather than developing a persona you hope will be attractive is a winning idea. Expect rejection – it happens to everyone – but see it as a filtering process as you (and they) work out who would be a good match.

Self-Awareness Mk2 - A complaint oft heard echoing through the churches of the land is outnumbered men getting their pick of potential partners, leading to all kinds of undesirable behaviour, people dropped casually or treated disrespectfully, and a lack of self-awareness (or in some cases luminous awareness and continued naughtiness). Weird hierarchies form, and entitlement can blossom. Encouraged to believe the odds are in their favour and all women are looking for a husband, a 'Crown Prince syndrome' develops: men survey women as eager potential prospects, and women are reduced to hopeful wives-in-waiting. I've experienced men avoiding conversation, even eye contact, lest they appear romantically interested and confetti automatically falls from heaven.

30% of survey respondents believed 'Christian men do ask women out', which leaves an awful lot of not asking. Almost as many (and almost half of those who are actively dating) think 'there are more Christian women so Christian men are spoilt for choice'. Hmm . . . I've heard more than one man announce he's 'ready to take a wife' and I've witnessed a truly surreal scene where an eligible man in his 20s visiting a church was offered a parade of single women from whom he could select with a Gladiator-style thumb up or down approval system. It's not surprising women find themselves in competition to be noticed and chosen. Men vie over one woman and ignore others. New male arrivals become targeted fresh meat. Sporting phrases often follow: *she's out of his league, he's punching above his weight.* It's degrading to everyone. There are no leagues. No person is worth more than another. Each person has value and should be treated accordingly. If you find yourself outnumbered by potential dates don't allow yourself to be 'spoilt for choice'. If you feel lost in the crowd, don't lose heart. In the artificial goldfish bowl of a church or other limited communities, unhelpful patterns can grow unchecked, particularly where more traditional roles are accepted. Men fearing commitment can get stuck in a permanent adolescence, afraid of settling. ('I was 30 when I joined my church', said one woman, 'surrounded by men my age looking for the perfect 26 year old. I'm 45 now and a lot of the same men are still looking for the perfect 26 year old.') Christian culture can disempower women who want to find a partner by simultaneously reinforcing female passivity as godly femininity and women's key value in being wives and mothers: 'This is what God wants for you, just don't do anything to bring it to pass . . .' There is a world beyond the doors of your immediate church. It's often easier in bigger towns and cities to extend social options. Do it if you can. Try new things and places. Be open minded. Volunteer. Join teams and groups. Even with a low budget it's possible to explore and you'll inevitably meet new people.

Time Management - Managing your time and resources can transform the dating process. The never-off feeling that dominates much of modern life is even more oppressive when you're entertaining strangers. Boundaries become blurred and intimacy can be forced quickly. Someone with whom you've exchanged a couple of messages might expect your phone number or email address as a matter of course. You're not obliged. Set your own pace. Get a little creative, technically speaking. Can you borrow or resurrect an old phone and get a new SIM especially for dating until you know someone well enough to give them the main one? Leave that second phone at home when you go out or only switch it on at set times. Create another email address for joining things and messaging. Check it at 'dating time' and switch off notifications so you're not being interrupted day and night. Not letting strangers set the pace or tone of contact seems oh-so-dull and unromantic (when of course you're going to meet a perfect person straight away) but will help set a steady course for balancing contact and emotional investment. Identify a couple of nice, public places where you can feel relaxed on a first meeting and there's no awkwardness over the bill.

Most dating sites have advice on how to be safe, and if you meet someone through other routes the same common sense guidelines are helpful. Don't give out your address, or information about yourself without knowing who is going to see it. Tell people where you're going and with whom. Balance dating with the rest of your life, and let things unfold. Find what works for you. Have boundaries that protect your equilibrium so a rush of messages that ceases without warning or a 12-hour wonder-date with no follow-up doesn't floor you.

It's also a handy way to weed out the impatient, presumptuous and unsafe, who won't be respectful of your right to manage your life as you choose.

Pace Yourself - Don't over-invest early on. Interestingly, men are more often the ones who've told me they've done this practically, while women have been more inclined to leap in emotionally before anything has actually happened (though it's not unheard of for men to propose to women they're not actually dating. Giveaway phrase: 'God told me we're going to be married'). It's probably down to men being told they must be 'intentional' and do the pursuing, while women should invest their urges in willing him to choose them, but both have tales of throwing pent up desire for connection at virtual strangers. The fancy restaurant can wait, as can drafting personalised vows. One step at a time. Until you get to know someone, big gestures and runaway feelings are projections. Take the pressure off both of you and breathe (breathe anyway, conversation is even harder without it). It's likely the first person or few you date won't turn into everlasting love and that's OK. Enjoy the conversation, find out about another person, and regardless of outcome you'll know more about yourself too. If you find yourself becoming intense, work out why. The Christian trait of delaying dating can ramp up feelings and expectations where a simple coffee can be all-or-nothing, so dating more casually, and developing friendships can be a huge help in diluting this. Dating can be lonely and exposing so you're likely to meet others who are relieved to encounter a friendly face and relaxed conversation if not the love of their life.

Eternal Flame - Don't dismiss someone out of hand in pursuit of the dreaded 'spark'. Many relationships have grown out of friendship, working together, being in the same church or house group, and few of those began with racing hearts (unless you met in A&E). Just r-e-l-a-x, give it time, see someone more than once unless there's a good reason not to. Sometimes the most intense, 'where have you been all my life?' dates are the ones that should come with a warning, so evaluate the situation based on the person you're getting to know rather than your hypothetical list. Be open to people more generally. As loneliness becomes an increasing social problem, we all need connection and conversation. Don't shut yourself away thinking you'll blossom automatically as soon as you find a partner. You and the world deserve better. Don't put yourself on hold for The One.

What if The One Does Actually Exist Though? - Over 10% of respondents believed their search for love would unfold as follows: 'God would send them to me and make it clear they were The One'. I have encountered a handful of stories where The Theory of The One would explain a marriage. Simultaneous dreams where both were sure God told them they would marry each other, for example, and that is what unfolded. A key factor in each of these stories is the apparent purpose behind them. Not a cosy-but-thrilling Cinderella story, more a high stakes, lifelong shared vision and mission. Heidi and Rolland Baker are a couple who felt drawn together despite barely knowing each other. No awkward small talk for them. They've spent the last few decades running an intense ministry caring for the needs of thousands of parentless children in Mozambique. While processing whether you might be in line for a similar life-quake, ponder what else might be going on. Do you feel called to do something you're not doing because you believe you can't do it without a partner? It may not be the case.

Jackie Pullinger famously jumped on a slow boat to China back in the 1960s to work alone with addicts in Hong Kong, a dangerous choice for a single woman. She later married a man in her community, who was addicted to drugs when they first met, and was widowed a few years later. She commented in 2018 'I just married him because I loved him and, you know, it was better to marry him than sin.'[1] Should God have designated a singular person for you, and nobody else will do, it seems God will make that very apparent, and there will be a good, life-changing reason for it. Regular reality checks are wise. Two women who didn't know each other both confided in friends and their church communities God had told them they were going to marry a particular man – the same man. Several years passed, during which time neither woman had a relationship – with him or anyone else. Well-meaning people (unhelpful supporters . . .) encouraged patience and waiting, and all were shocked when news filtered out he was moving overseas – and getting married. So, both women couldn't have been right – nobody was up for polygamy – and the man in question hadn't expressed an interest in either of them. But what if one of them had been on the right track? Well, everyone had free will and could have said no, even if God was trying to get their attention; there are few modern-day examples of disobedient prophets being swallowed whole by whales for turning down a date. Most Christians choose life paths with some sense of their talents, abilities, timing, calling, and an understanding of faith coming together rather than heavenly decree or angelic visitation, yet some are reluctant to follow similar wisdom when contemplating relationships. Unpacking theology, family experiences, good and bad advice, faith community expectations, and cultural role models are all helpful in deciding whether you might be one of the few God has designated for a specific person. However, most of these 'chosen ones' were already living their lives and going about their business when they were sure God intervened with specifics, so it's a great idea to follow that example and do the same. It's more likely to be This One or That One rather than The One, and after that, the one is who you make it.

Is It Going to Work Out? - Fear of the unknown and rejection are a big deal. What are the signs something is going to go well and may turn into a happy relationship? It used to be as simple as they called or didn't call (remember phone calls? On phones with wires and dials of numbers and ring tones?! You don't? OK, we probably can't be friends). Or maybe there was no second date or no proposal within 2-6 months (if you were Christian). It was clearly not happening, but people knew the score. Now ambiguity rules. It can be hard to tell if something is even a date or not, much less where it might be leading. Contact starts and ends on screens. Tracing someone you like the look of across social media platforms is tempting but creates a false sense of intimacy. You might not meet with someone for years but still see their holiday pictures, family gatherings, nights out and all the meals they eat. There's no way to know if something is going to work out. People who decide to marry after knowing each other for a few weeks may go on to share many happy years, muddle through, or find themselves stuck with someone they can't stand. Happy relationships that last 20 years and end when one partner dies have 'worked out' in one sense, but still bring deep sadness. Meeting someone who may want to spend more and more time with you, and you with them, will only become apparent as time passes. If the only goal is marriage then many encounters probably won't 'work out', but if you're open to meeting new people then anything is possible, and if you and another person find yourselves choosing to move in the same direction a lasting relationship may unfold. You won't know unless you try.

What If Nobody Asks Me/I'm Too Scared to Ask? - Welcome to Dating Trauma 101. It will happen to pretty much everyone at some point. It may feel that's how it's always going to be. More single Christian women than men means there's a strong possibility some women won't be asked out in their own churches or existing circles. For men, it can be overwhelming to be outnumbered or to hear about the Big Imbalance but not to encounter the multitudes of single women you keep hearing about (or to be turned down when you do ask – what's that about? Don't they want husbands after all?) Try not to panic. Life now isn't life forever. You may not be able to start dating if you change nothing about your life, even if you're doing what you've always been told God wants. You may need to be brave, proactive, convention-breaking and make a change. If you feel desperate about being single that's likely to come across and be pretty off-putting, so try to process your current feelings first. There's no heavenly-ordained 'someone for everyone' but if you want to give it a go, while making the most of life along the way, why not try? Prepare yourself, make sure you heal from anything holding you back as you go, and see what happens.

How Will I Know It's a Date? - You might not. It might be a casual cuppa with zero intentions, or one with an agenda. Maybe they really do just want a theatre buddy. Months after a date I hadn't been sure was a date beforehand, I asked the other person what their thoughts had been at the time. Exactly the same, as it turned out. We'd progressed 'How are you?' messaging to 'Would be good to catch up' messaging to 'What are you up to?' messaging to a drink where neither of us had been sure what was afoot (neither of us used the word afoot, and both of us knew what a foot was). Things became clear, then ambiguous, then clearer, and so on. Letting the situation play out was the only option. While neither of us was responsible for the other, knowing what I wanted, what I was prepared to spend my time on and what my boundaries were meant it was enjoyable and overall fun. Assuming the other person's motives is risky – for good or bad – but being aware of the various things that might be going on in someone's life or intentions is wise. For the record, women aren't all looking to be pursued by a potential husband, and men aren't all looking for a wife – or for a quick seduction. Better to give it time, have good conversations, get to know someone (patchy availability is a sign in itself) and decide how you'll act or respond as things go.

What If It's Not a Date? - It may start out as a date and fade into friendly chat. It may start out as a relaxed catch up and turn into potential romance. It may be something defying belief and social convention, like intense interview scenarios involving interrogation about everything from weight to childbearing ability. The re-emergence of more deliberate dating thanks to the internet has resulted in strangers meeting more often and bumbling their way through. Sometimes the best thing to come out of such experiences is more points on a coffee shop loyalty card. In a panic to understate intentions, romance can be so far removed it dies quietly in a corner. The desire to have a big love story can contribute to this, seeing intentional dating as mere warm up for a forthcoming fairy tale, rather than a realistic way to form a relationship. By all means, date people who don't seem like the dream ticket but be open minded rather than decide in advance they're an endurance test or a good way to practice your social skills. If you need to do that, find people who are on the same page. And don't decide not to continue dating but stay friends for the sake of politeness. Friendships arising from dating situations can only really thrive if both parties are happy with the situation. Nobody needs more emotional baggage.

Moving Forward - If things are looking promising, work towards mutuality. Falteringly move along with suggestions of the next thing you might do together, gradually moving in the same direction – maybe, all the time not knowing if the other person is on the same page as you but testing the water and seeing if red flags or bluebirds appear along the way. Gradually you'll figure out if you've met someone who wants to partner with you in life, and will put effort into that, as you will for them. Support – practical, emotional and spiritual – are good things in a relationship, as they are in good friendships, which is what relationships should be based on. If you're a good friend, you'll be on the way to being a good partner. Have healthy boundaries that work for both of you, but choose to be available and grow intimacy. Developing trust is important and risky, but vital if a relationship is going to grow. Awkward conversations may be needed to confront tricky subjects, but anything else sows seeds of uncertainty. Having fun together is a good sign; you don't have to start with the same interests but you may develop some, and introduce each other to new things. Step back if it seems you're being pushed into the role of counsellor or rescuer. Don't be fooled into believing good dating is always smooth and easy, but it should overall be life enhancing, enjoyable, balanced and respectful. Navigating the shifts and boundaries as relationships develop takes skills you can learn as you go, and extend grace to each other as you do so. Shift from independence to working out what good reliance on another person looks like in a timely way. You'll figure it out, even if you realise you need some (professional) counselling and breathers along the way. Modern dating has its challenges but most single westerners have freedom of choice and the chance to have more say over their romantic relationships than ever before. No pressure. So, start a conversation, go for that coffee, and take it from there.

Good Ways to Say Bye - If you've decided someone you've dated isn't going to become your One True Love, how to farewell them so they fare well? Do as you would be done to, in intention if not in action. You've had a nice time but don't see this becoming a big relationship? Kind honesty works: 'I enjoy spending time with you but for me this isn't developing into a big romance' or 'We aren't developing the sort of momentum I'd have hoped for by now.' Try not to refer to sparks or chemistry unless you're a scientist; it's clichéd and unhelpful. You've realised your lives and plans are too different? How about just that: 'I've noticed our lives and plans are very different, and I think that's going to become a bigger issue as time goes on.' The longer you spend with someone or the more intense the relationship, the more likely it is strong feelings will be involved, for at least one party, so it may not be an easy thing to do. It might not be possible to leave someone better than when you met them, but it's a good goal. If you're not sure what you want, try not to make that the other person's issue; it may already be painful for them to hear true love isn't blossoming for you and vague maybes could be false hope. If it's over, try to keep the door closed, so you don't put old relationships or fantasies on a pedestal. If you find yourself being let down – gently or otherwise – take time to recover. Process with helpful supporters and learn lessons where you can. Allow your feelings to air and heal so you don't bring current hurts into future situations.

Back to the Start - If that special someone says no, that's their choice and not your project. Deep breaths, process and move on when you're ready. Daisy was widowed while still a young mother, and eventually struck up a romantic friendship with a potential partner. She and others were sure God was bringing them together. He seemed keen, and then not. Daisy moved on with her life. A year later she travelled overseas to help with a development project. She found herself on a 2-day cross-country truck ride with a man who'd also come from the UK to help, and guess what . . . conversation bumped along a bit like the terrain, they bonded over their experience, and married 2 years later.

Enjoy Your Own Company - What do you enjoy doing? How do you want to spend your time? Do it anyway. Dating won't take up all your time, and nor will a relationship, should it develop.

The idea that life transforms into #couplegoals and everything happens in tandem from then on is erroneous. Putting life on hold until the perfect person finally happens along will not prepare you for the reality of being around another human a lot of the time. Don't put things off and wait. Enjoy yourself. Nobody likes my jokes more than me, and we have the same brilliant taste in art. I like to have quality time with me – good hot chocolate or even go to a restaurant (tip: order for two and pretend to be sad when you eat the second dessert). Whether I've had a partner or not, these things do not change (I might share the dessert. Might). I'm usually the one to drag someone excitedly round a gallery, boring them about modernism and impasto (and this is why it's good to enjoy being with you. If they run away you probably won't even notice).

Romance Isn't Everything - Romance really *isn't* everything, even when you're dating. In a way, it's all play-acting anyway. Someone who would be a really great life partner may be a terrible romantic. The special moments on your relationship bucket list may just not happen. But the whole moonlit walks thing can be as much about the moment, the deep conversations, the adventure, the sneaking away from the everyday, and for me, those have happened with good friends and alone as well as in more romantic situations. Cultivating meaning in all kinds of personal relationships is life enhancing, rather than expecting one other person to sail into view and fulfil every longing for sunset viewing and country walks.

Be Interested – and Be More Interesting - You're probably going to end up in a relationship with just one person at a time. I would say that's what's in the Bible, but hey they went for polygamy, so maybe not. You may be single till your dotage, or meet someone in your teens. You may be happily married and find yourself single again. A lot of life might be spent un-partnered. As you start dating, building a relationship, or working out living as a single person, think about focusing outwards. Everyone you see has an inner life, as well as varied ways of spending their time. Few people feel fully known or even heard. Making space for other people to talk can benefit you and them. If it doesn't come naturally think about what would make you more relaxed when meeting new people, what you'd like to be asked, and take it from there.

Great Expectations - Unpack the difference between 'expect' and 'hope'. Christians are big on hope, but hope adrift from reality is likely to float away. When asked how do you *expect* a relationship to start and develop, many described what they *hoped* would happen. Crestfallen responders expressed sadness that their perfect partner hadn't yet ambled into view, but their expectations seemed unadjusted. For example – if I've understood correctly – developing a relationship without artificial fertilizers was important for some. Unless they meant a different kind of organic. Organic as in, it *just happened*. This is understandable. An effortless falling into love is much more appealing than trawling through profiles online, swiping endless photos, or awkward small talk in coffee shops with strangers, wondering if a shared love of ballroom dancing or camping is enough to sustain a relationship (it definitely is) but don't despair.

In Defence of Effort - Modern dating, with its visual emphasis and questionnaires, requires us to think about what we want, and what would be good for us. It requires us to take responsibility, stretch ourselves, look at ourselves through others' eyes, and ask if we would be a good partner for someone else, and then upload it for others to assess. It asks us to be brave about showing our faces to the world and risk rejection. It requires us to initiate contact. Asks us to be an active participant in finding and building a relationship. A relationship can not be sustained without effort, and nobody is flattered by a lack of it. 'It was so romantic. They'd made so little effort!' Hot stuff! Proportionate effort is a good and healthy thing. Not a discussion of marital non-negotiables while asking out for coffee or inviting someone to a party that turns out to be dinner for two. Just active, respectful, mutual engagement in the present situation and interaction. Effort to get over the awkwardness of asking without knowing the outcome, and effort to spend time with someone to see what happens. Complaints about not being asked out, messages not sent or replied to, being left hanging without contact? Effort would change this. Things rarely become *effortless,* the desired state, without some energy expended somewhere along the way.

Tune In - If you pray, listen to what God might be saying (86% of Real Life Love participants said they found it helpful to pray about relationships). Don't pressure yourself to hit made-up deadlines. Don't fantasise about a person, formula, or process. Don't idealise anyone else's relationship. Any relationship you might have will be unique and made by you. It could just be timing. You definitely can't force anything. Ask yourself: where is God in this situation? Enjoy life as you go, and find the things that make life fun and worthwhile anyway.

Be kind to yourself.

So, You're Dating Someone You Hadn't Expected...

Many Christian women face real dilemmas when looking for a partner. Outnumbering Christian men, the options – as we previously explored – are to stay single if a faith-matched partner doesn't come along or to date further afield. The women interviewed in chapter eight had lots of experiences to share and common themes emerged from their stories, which are helpful for anyone in or contemplating a similar situation. It's worth exploring well what a potential relationship with someone who doesn't share faith – either at the start or later on – could entail, and think through a few questions . . .

What's Their Faith Story?

Everyone has one, even if it's as simple as being visited by an angel at birth and audibly identified by a voice from heaven as a prophet for the end times tribulation. But that's just me. For most people – apparently – the story is less dramatic. Through childhood influences, encounters with Christians, good or bad spiritual experiences, books and media, and many other things, each of us has formed a view of God. For Christians that view of God can vary wildly – kindly benevolent, furiously angry, smiting-not-liking, and so on. You might be the first Christian they've met, the first one they've been able to relate to, or the hundredth one they've crossed paths with that week. Take time to work out where they're coming from, and where they might be going.

What's Your Faith Story?

Yep, you. You figure in this equation too. Calling yourself Christian could mean many things. Has your faith been filled with certainty or have you had your own wandering journey? Perhaps growing up in a Christian family – nominal or devout – and taking a different path as you got older before finding God again? Were you raised in an atheist, agnostic, indifferent or other faith home and discovered Christianity under your own steam later on? Are you decidedly complementarian – men leading in relationships – or egalitarian – roles not determined by sex? Do you buy into a theology that says women can be pastors, or one that prefers they don't even work outside of the home? Are you of a high tradition with incense and time-tested liturgy or do you express your faith through smoke machines and rock-influenced guitar ballads? Before deciding you absolutely, definitely need a Christian partner, work through what that actually means for you. Are you seeking someone who matches your own interpretation, intensity and expression of faith or something more flexible?

What Are Your Faith Non-Negotiables and Why?

The most common lament I've heard from women frustrated by their situation is 'I want a man I can pray with.' Many of these women have spent years single with no praying spouse, yet the idea of one they can't pray with is something they can't contemplate. Too often absolutes can be far removed from anything important in the long term (hairline? Height difference?) yet wrapped up in the 'God gives the desires of the heart' mantra. Wanting a 'man in leadership' often gets a mention. I suspect this has more to do with what's modelled by a lot of churches – a leader's wife gets status and the opportunity to be a decision maker – than anything God has ordained. In some cases, these non-negotiables are valid. In others, they are more about a desire not to step out and do something alone or feeling compromised if not meeting a spiritual twin. If you're considering a relationship with someone who sees faith differently from you, can you be yourself, openly and honestly? Live out your faith as you feel led, and flourish in it? Do you feel your integrity is compromised in any way?

Are They Supportive of Your Faith?

Is a potential partner actively supportive, rather than just tolerant of your faith? Do they want to know more about it? Are they interested in what it is and what it means to you? Will they spend time listening and learning? Discussing what it means to you, and how you've arrived at your current beliefs? These are all positive signs and demonstrate an openness to listen and learn about you and what matters to you. Will they come to church? Meet your Christian friends and community? Be a part of it?

Are They Respectful - of You and Your Faith?

I've heard several tales of men dating Christian women and spending tedious amounts of time mocking their beliefs, or pursuing them with sexual challenges in mind. Fun! One woman described dates with a man intent on 'breaking the nice Christian girl' as she put it. (Amazingly, they're not still together.) Their interest in the women they were dating seemed to be disconnected from the core of who the women were. They had some flirtatious conversations, drinks, walks and dinners, but conversations became hostile or mean when they veered towards the spiritual. With their own bad experiences or negative perceptions, they projected their animosity onto the women they were dating. No relationship works if one partner is the other's straw (wo)man or counsellor. Men also reported feeling pressured to compromise their values when dating or considering women who didn't share their faith, particularly in relation to sex. Knowing what matters and why is important.

Are You Closer to or Further Away from God as a Consequence of Being Involved with Them?

Have you found the shape of your faith changing? Or your priorities? A key question: What do you envisage your future looking like? Will there be an eventual drift as best behaviour on both sides fades into routine? If you end up making or taking care of mini humans, how will you navigate bringing them up? What do you want long term? Are you a traditional Christian woman who has spent years waiting for her prince and believes a man should set the tone? It's likely to be harder to have your own faith with integrity if you feel a man should lead and guide you. Have you prayed about it? How have you felt God has been present in your relationship choices, and are you able to bring your feelings, doubts, questions, confusions and joys into your prayers?

What Advice, Guidance or Support Have You Sought?

Who knows about your life, thoughts, feelings and faith? Who will listen without condemning, and help you work through your situation? Remember, there's no hurry to decide as you get to know someone. Feeling rushed to commit is a red light, regardless of faith, and it's not unheard of for Christians to spiritualise speedy couplings and rush to marriage so there are no outburst of sexiness. Couples forced apart or together through spiritual pressure are not getting good advice, so choose well who helps to set the direction of your life. Don't assume a pastor will have the best – or worst – advice, or take any unhelpful comments to heart. Counselling and spiritual direction can offer good longer-term foundations for decision making and discernment, and experienced friends or acquaintances who have walked similar paths can be invaluable.

Will People in Your Life Support You?

What can you expect of family and friends in particular? Will their response be helpful or damaging? Do you have an open and welcoming church or faith community, however you live out your faith? If not, where will your support come from? Have you felt additional pressure to find a relationship because of how couples seem valued more than singles? How could the people in your life validate you more, no matter what your marital status?

Have You Reflected on How Life and Relationships Change Over Time?

Have you unpacked how society has changed and worked out how you feel about your place in it? Are you able to take a broader perspective in recognising where God is at work and not assuming every story is the same or God agrees with you (whatever you might think)? If you know people navigating these questions, are you able to respect their maturity, journey, and ability to navigate relationships? Faith and life can change over time in many different ways, and there are no guarantees.

It's wise not to see potential challenges as bigger or 'worse' than between couples who both describe themselves as Christian, or assume a couple who seem spiritually well matched will remain in tandem throughout their marriage.

So, before you rush in – or out – give it some time, thought and prayer. And remember, you are loved.

About the Real Life Love Survey

The Real Life Love survey was developed by Vicky Walker (that's me!) and consisted of 62 questions about faith, beliefs and relationship experiences. It was online and anonymous, unless respondents chose to leave an email address (several hundred did). Between June 2016 and January 2017, 1,447 people responded. All but a handful of questions were optional; some respondents completed all (aside from those that were gender-specific and didn't apply to them), others chose the ones that particularly interested or applied to them. Each question therefore has its own data set, some with 1,400+ responders, others with several hundred. Some of the questions were text based – respondents could write freely and say whatever they wanted to say. Others were questions with tick box options. The survey was divided into sections: current relationship situation; faith and relationships; relationships and church; worries and concerns; sex and all the other stuff; dating dynamics; teaching and expectations; and your relationship future.

The survey was not designed as an academic exercise but rather as a story-gathering tool and place for people to share and vent if necessary (it seems to have been necessary). I received hundreds of detailed responses about what had helped or harmed faith and relationship experiences. Questions relating to specific areas of theology were not necessarily formatted as neutral statements but rather to reflect common beliefs about God and relationships that responders were likely to have encountered. For all such questions, responders were able to answer yes/no or true/false, or move on. In terms of theology or denomination, the largest number (40%) described themselves as 'Just Christian', in preference over terms including Evangelical (13.6%), Anglican (10%), Charismatic (8.5%), Pentecostal (3.5%), and Catholic (1.5%). Responders were recruited through word of mouth and the generous assistance of other writers, relationship organisations, and wonderful, long suffering friends. At the time of closing the survey, around 40% of responders were married compared to 60% of all other relational permutations including single, dating, divorced, cohabiting and widowed. In the gender divided questions on non-negotiable qualities in a partner, 26% of survey respondents answered as men and 71% as women, with some opting to skip the question entirely. A small number – fewer than 10 people – identified their gender in the 'other' category.

Respondents ranged in age from teens to over 60, with the majority – over 80% – falling between early 20s and late 40s. Most were UK based – almost 85% – with the rest coming from the USA, Australia, South Africa, Europe, and the Middle and Far East (and one who answered, 'not sure'. Pray for them). The majority – nearly 90% – of respondents were urban, with almost half (48%) living in a big or capital city, and nearly 40% (39.74% to be specific) living in towns. Those who didn't live with a spouse or partner predominantly lived with friends or family – almost three-in-ten respondents – or alone, with 20% of the split. Almost 90% of responders identified themselves as white, though this was a percentage of 900 respondents and not the full number who answered the survey overall.

It's worth mentioning that the book doesn't cover advice or resources aimed specifically at same-sex relationships. Why?

Firstly, there are people far better qualified than me to write about that, and I should not be a go-to for that subject. But primarily it's about this book being focused on what healthy heterosexuality could look like. The majority of Christian relationship advice has been and is still directed at male-female interactions, which also form the majority of relationships within the Christian community. The bulk of this relationship advice falls within a narrow theological range, and it is rarely analysed (though often despaired over). The rapid spread of the internet has increased the range and number of resources available, and many of these have come from very new sources. Despite addressing the most significant relationships people choose to begin, those offering advice are qualified to vastly differing levels (a polite way of saying that while a few may be genuine experts, most definitely are not). My hope is that by looking at these messages, readers will be encouraged to develop their discernment about what best supports their healthy relational choices, and what they might be wiser to reject.

As a post script, it's always a joy to wonder whether a survey respondent intended to write exactly what they submitted. I'm pretty convinced the person who wrote, 'I always enjoy biblical quotes and use them frequently. But I never let the bible interfere with my hedonistic sex life', probably meant it. Likewise the person who described their ideal partner as, 'Own teeth. Not dead.' Also, the one who wrote 'This survey is too long', was likely to have been very sincere. Not so sure about the person who said there was too much teaching about 'sexual immortality' or the poor soul who worried about being 'overly Hornby'. When did intimacy in the afterlife or a fascination with train sets stop being healthy obsessions, I wonder? I just can't keep up.

The Relatable Reading List

You may have reached the end of *Relatable* and want to explore more. Here are some books and resources I found interesting, helpful or informative while writing.

About love, sex and marriage

Marriage, A History – Stephanie Coontz

The Sex Myth – Rachel Hills

Modern Romance: An Investigation – Aziz Ansari & Eric Klinenberg

Committed – Elizabeth Gilbert

Designer Sex – Philip Yancey

Esther Perel's work on couples (including *Mating in Captivity*)

About women and men – language, science, history and more

Delusions of Gender – Cordelia Fine

Inferior – Angela Saini

The Myth of Mars and Venus – Deborah Cameron

About singleness – history, social changes, and lived-out faith stories

Single Minded – Kate Wharton

Going Solo – Eric Klinenberg

All the Single Ladies – Rebecca Traister

Singled Out – Virginia Nicholson

Bella DePaulo's work on singleness is extensive and helpful: http://www.belladepaulo.com/

About Christian relationships
OK, you'll realise by now there isn't a huge list of books I'd be keen to thrust into your hands, but a few good writers to follow up are:

Drs Henry Cloud and John Townsend have been writing about healthy relationships and dating for a long time and they're good. Their *Boundaries* series is time-tested.

Pete Scazzero and Geri Scazzero have written about 'Emotionally Healthy Spirituality' and their resources are well worth looking into.

Natalie Collins' *Out of Control* is a timely book on the church and domestic abuse.

Equals by Jenny Baker is a great starting point for couples wanting to know how to build an egalitarian marriage.

Of the helpful resources named by Real Life Love respondents, I've listed the ones that got at least a handful of mentions that I haven't mentioned above. (Some appeared in the unhelpful list too – which, for the sake of kindness, I'm not including in detail – so it's apparent that what's helpful is clearly subjective! Work out what's useful for you.)

The *Love Languages* books by Gary Chapman

The Relatable Reading List

The Meaning of Marriage by Timothy and Kathy Keller

The HTB marriage prep and marriage courses

Damaged Goods by Dianna Anderson

Happy relating!

The Gratitude Page

Enormous thanks to all those who helped this book into existence.

Firstly, the book is only here because of all of those who shared their stories through the Real Life Love survey, interviews, messages, and in person. Huge and heartfelt thanks to everyone who trusted me with their experiences.

A passing conversation with Malcolm Down early in 2016 led to the development of an idea of a book exploring how faith and relationships, and finally – a mere 3 years later - a book called *Relatable*. Thank you to the MD Publishing team for being willing to bring it to life. Thanks to Ed Cyzewski for making the editing process more entertaining than it should have been, and to Chloe for being an angel of endnotes.

Huge thanks to Madeleine Davies. The book would have fallen over numerous times without her inspiration, advice (both writing and personal) and wise feedback. Likewise, Chine McDonald for helping from the outset with shaping the survey and on-going encouragement and discernment when I couldn't see the pages for the trees. Marian Elizabeth for faithful reading of many, many drafts, sincere and helpful feedback, practical and emotional support, and contagious certainty that I would finish what I started. Natalie Collins for clear-headed advice and expertise, and being a warrior for the causes of women. All the fantastic people who made time in their busy lives to read and respond to various drafts, share ideas from the very start to the final touches, and more, including

Laura Collingridge, Joseph Colliass, Oli Griffiths, Elizabeth Oldfield, Liz Evershed, Sheyi Martins-Allen, Sarah Lothian, Catherine Francis, Lucie Tremblay and Sarah 'Disasters of a Thirtysomething' Clarke. Special thanks to Steve Mawhinney for knowing all about statistics and casting an analytical eye over the survey results, and the eagle eyes of Sheila Siebert.

I'm extremely grateful to the very smart bunch of people in the Real Life Love Project group who took the time to answer questions along the way and give valuable advice on all kinds of practicalities and concepts and stripes. Simon Radford and Casey Mackenzie-Johnson for deploying their title-shaping skills. The Mighty Women crew for being at the end of a WhatsApp message when it mattered. Tim Rawe who believed in what I was trying to do in a money-where-his-mouth-is-as-well-as-being-relentlessly-supportive kinda way. Marijke Hoek for her frankness and clarity. Katie Harrison for directing me to helpful research and Dr David Pullinger for sharing his work on singleness.

A small army of encouraging friends who didn't once roll their eyes when I banged on about The Book yet again (special mention: Sasha Graham), and those who asked regularly about its arrival with an impatience I took as encouragement to keep going.

Special mention for anyone whose name came rushing into my brain at 3am the day after the print deadline. Your contribution was invaluable and my subconscious is sincerely grateful.

And very, very, very importantly DD for walking the journey with me every day, providing every kind of support imaginable, and telling me I could every single time I was convinced I couldn't and is still here. Thank you xx

Notes

Chapter 1:

1. *Marriages in England and Wales: 2013*, Office for National Statistics. Accessed December 15, 2018. https://www.ons.gov.uk/peoplepopulationandcommunity/birthsdeathsandmarriages/marriagecohabitationandcivilpartnerships/bulletins/marriagesinenglandandwalesprovisional/2013.

2. Ibid.

3. "Wedding Vows." *Your Church Wedding*, Church of England, 3 Nov. 2015, https://www.yourchurchwedding.org/article/wedding-vows/.

4. Haines, Nicola. *Marriages in England and Wales: 2014*. Office for National Statistics, 14 Mar. 2017, https://www.ons.gov.uk/peoplepopulationandcommunity/birthsdeathsandmarriages/marriagecohabitationandcivilpartnerships/bulletins/marriagesinenglandandwalesprovisional/2014.

5. Aaron, Charlene. *Growing Number of Americans Ditching Church Weddings*. CBN News, 1 Aug. 2017, https://www1.cbn.com/cbnnews/us/2017/august/growing-number-of-americans-ditching-church-weddings.

6. "Domain Name." *Wikipedia*, Wikimedia Foundation, 17 Dec. 2018, https://en.wikipedia.org/wiki/Domain_name.

7. "Dotcom Domains." *The History of Domain Names*, 19 Nov. 2016, http://www.historyofdomainnames.com/dotcom-domains/.

8. "Timeline of online dating services." *Wikipedia*, Wikimedia Foundation, 3 Jan. 2019, https://en.wikipedia. org/wiki/Timeline_of_online_dating_services.

9. Zwilling, Martin. "How Many More Online Dating Sites Do We Need?" *Forbes*, 2 Mar. 2013, https://www.forbes. com/sites/martinzwilling/2013/03/01/how-many-more-online-dating-sites-do-we-need/#475be46d7882.

10. Ansari, Aziz, and Eric Klinenberg. *Modern Romance* (London: Penguin, 2015), 80-81.

11. Shermer, Michael. "The Number of Americans with No Religious Affiliation Is Rising." *Scientific American*, Springer Nature America, 1 Apr. 2018, https://www.scientificamerican. com/article/the-number-of-americans-with-no-religious-affiliation-is-rising/.

12. "More than Half in UK Are Non-Religious, Suggests Survey." *BBC News*, BBC, 4 Sept. 2017, https://www.bbc. co.uk/news/uk-41150792.

13. Ansari, Aziz, and Eric Klinenberg. *Modern Romance*. 80-1.

14. "Gender." *Admission Statistics*, University of Oxford, May 2018, https://www.ox.ac.uk/about/facts-and-figures/admissions-statistics/undergraduate-students/current/gender?wssl=1.

15. "King's College London." *The Complete University Guide*, Mayfield University Consultants, 23 Apr. 2018, https:// www.thecompleteuniversityguide.co.uk/kings-college-london/.

16. McLaren, Elizabeth. *Marriages in England and Wales: 2013*. Office for National Statistics, 27 Apr. 2016, https://www.ons.gov.uk/ peoplepopulationandcommunity/birthsdeathsandmarriages/ marriagecohabitationandcivilpartnerships/bulletins/ marriagesinenglandandwalesprovisional/2013.

17. "Historical Marital Status Tables." *Census Bureau*, United

States Census Bureau, 14 Nov. 2018, https://www.census. gov/data/tables/time-series/demo/families/marital.html.

18. Thompson, Gavin, et al. "Population." *Olympic Britain*, House of Commons Library, UK Parliament, 2012, https:// www.parliament.uk/documents/commons/lib/research/ olympic-britain/olympicbritain.pdf#page=23.

19. Grueninger, Natalie. "Death in Tudor England." *On The Tudor Trail*, 31 Oct. 2010, http://onthetudortrail.com/ Blog/resources/life-in-tudor-england/death-in-tudor-england/.

20. Chen, Sandie Angulo. "Six Unbelievable, But True, Facts About Colonial Life." *Blogs*, Ancestry.com, 8 Jan. 2015, https://blogs.ancestry.com/cm/six-unbelievable-but-true-facts-about-colonial-life/.

21. Haines, Nicola. *Marriages in England and Wales: 2014*. Office for National Statistics, 14 Mar. 2017, https:// www.ons.gov.uk/peoplepopulationandcommunity/ birthsdeathsandmarriages/divorce/bulletins/ divorcesinenglandandwales/2014.

22. "A Brief History of Divorce." *Cambridge Family Law Practice*, 18 Apr. 2012, http://www.cflp.co.uk/a-brief-history-of-divorce/.

23. Bingham, John, and Ashley Kirk. "Divorce Rate at Lowest Level in 40 Years after Cohabitation Revolution." *The Telegraph*, 23 Nov. 2015, https://www.telegraph.co.uk/ news/uknews/12011714/Divorce-rate-at-lowest-level-in-40-years-after-cohabitation-revolution.html.

24. Thackray, Jemima. "Why Do More Women Flock to the Church?" *The Telegraph*, 3 May 2013, https://www.telegraph. co.uk/women/womens-life/10035155/Why-do-more-women-flock-to-the-Church.html.

25. Arnold, Damian. "Baptists Go Full Immersion on Troubled Youth." *The Times*, 8 Apr. 2017, https://www.thetimes.co.uk/article/baptists-go-full-immersion-on-troubled-youth-gc2nshtp3.

26. Bloxham, Andy, and Martin Beckford. "Average Age of Churchgoers Now 61, Church of England Report Finds." *The Telegraph*, 22 Jan. 2010, https://www.telegraph.co.uk/news/religion/7054097/Average-age-of-churchgoers-now-61-Church-of-England-report-finds.html.

27. "Research co-funded by Single Christians Confirms that the Church is Not Attracting Enough Single Men into Its Pews." *Single Friendly Church,* 2014, https://www.singlefriendlychurch.com/research/yougov.

28. "Meet Those Who 'Love Jesus but Not the Church.'" *The Barna Group*, 30 Mar. 2017, https://www.barna.com/research/meet-love-jesus-not-church/.

29. Coontz, Stephanie. "In Search of A Golden Age: A Look at Families throughout U.S. History Reveals There Has Never Been an 'Ideal Form.'" *Caring for Families*, no. 21, Spring 1989, p. 18, https://www.context.org/iclib/ic21/coontz/.

30. "Silver Ring Secrets." *The Mirror*, 21 Jul. 2017, https://www.mirror.co.uk/news/uk-news/silver-ring-secrets-492619.

31. Augustine. *Confessions*, Book II.

32. Augustine. *City of God*, Chapter 26, Book 14.

33. Clement of Alexandria. *Paedagogus III*.

34. Jerome. *Against Jovinianus*. Book 1, Section 20.

35. Coontz, Stephanie. *Marriage, A History* (London: Penguin, 2005), 7.

36. Ansari, Aziz, and Eric Klinenberg. *Modern Romance*, 23.

37. Rutter, Virginia. "CCF Press Advisory: Gender and

Millennials Online Symposium." *Council on Contemporary Families*, 30 Mar. 2017, https://contemporaryfamilies.org/ccf-gender-and-millennials-online-symposium/.

38. Coontz, Stephanie. *Marriage, A History*. 20.

39. Ibid., 23.

40. Ibid., 30.

41. Shultz, Valerie. "Thoughts on the 'Vena Amoris." *America*, 30 September 2013, https://www.americamagazine.org/content/all-things/thoughts-vena-amoris.

42. "Marriage Was & Is a Civil, Not Religious, Relationship." from *National Celebrants e-Magazine*, Civil Celebrations Network, 21 Nov. 2015, https://www.celebrations.org.au/celebrants/2085-marriage-was-is-a-civil-relationship.

43. "Tying the Knot: Handfasting through the Ages." *BBC Scotland History*, BBC, 26 Apr. 2011, http://www.bbc.co.uk/scotland/history/tying_the_knot_handfasting_through_the_ages.shtml.

44. Macnab, Scott. "Humanist Weddings Overtake Church of Scotland Ceremonies." *The Scotsman*, 1 Aug. 2018, https://www.scotsman.com/news/politics/humanist-weddings-overtake-church-of-scotland-ceremonies-1-4777088.

45. "Marriage and Virginity." *Coptic Orthodox Church Network*, St. Mark Coptic Church, 2014, www.copticchurch.net/topics/patrology/schoolofalex2/chapter19.html.

46. May, Simon. *Love, A History* (New Haven: Yale UP, 2011).

47. Coontz, Stephanie. *Marriage, A History*, 21

48. Ibid., 126-7.

49. Nicholson, Virginia. *Singled Out: How Two Million Women Survived Without Men After the First World War* (London: Penguin, 2007). 'Surplus women' are discussed throughout.

50. Coontz, Stephanie. *Marriage, A History*. 166-167.

51. Ibid., 169

52. Ibid., 173.

53. Schaff, Philip, and C. L. Cornish. "Of the Good of Marriage." *Nicene and Post-Nicene Fathers*, vol. 3, ser. 1, 1887. *New Advent*, www.newadvent.org/fathers/1309.htm.

54. "Polygamy in the Christian Church." *Wikipedia*, Wikimedia Group, 23 Jan. 2019, https://en.wikipedia.org/wiki/Polygamy_ in_Christianity.

Chapter 2:

1. "The Danvers Statement." *The Council on Biblical Manhood and Womanhood*, 26 Jun. 2007, cbmw.org/uncategorized/ the-danvers-statement/.

2. Bunce, Robin and Lucy Dallas. "Complementarianism at Thirty." *Christian Feminist Network*, 2017, https:// christianfeministnetwork.com/2018/07/16/grappling- with-the-history-of-complementarianism/.

Chapter 3:

1. "Christian Marriage." Search on *Amazon.com Books*, 2018.

2. "Christian Singleness." Search on *Amazon.com Books*, 2018.

3. Driscoll Mark, Driscoll Grace. *Real Marriage: The Truth About Sex, Friendship, and Life Together*. Thomas Nelson 2012. Author bio.

4. Prince, Derek. *The Marriage Covenant: The Biblical Secret for a Love that Lasts*. Whitaker House,U.S. 2006 (First published 1978). Foreword by Ruth Prince.

5. Blue, Miranda. "Here's How Focus on The Family Convinced The IRS To Call It a Church." *Right Wing Watch*, 17 Apr. 2018, http://www.rightwingwatch.org/post/heres-how-focus-on- the-family-convinced-the-irs-to-call-it-a-church/.

6. Dobson, James. *Bringing Up Boys* (Carol Stream, IL: Tyndale, 2001), 2.

7. Dobson, James. *Bringing Up Girls* (Carol Stream, IL:Tyndale Momentum, 1 Oct. 2010), 3.

8. "No More Boys and Girls: Can Our Kids Go Gender Free?" *BBC Two*, BBC, 25 Aug. 2017, http://www.bbc.co.uk/programmes/p05d9kmg.

9. "Gender Specific Toys: Do You Stereotype Children?" *BBC News*, BBC, 16 Aug. 2017, http://www.bbc.co.uk/news/av/magazine-40936719/gender-specific-toys-do-you-stereotype-children.

10. *Let Clothes Be Clothes*, letclothesbeclothes.co.uk/, Accessed February 22, 2019.

11. Marks & Spencer, https://www.marksandspencer.com/c/kids, Accessed February 2018.

12. Saewyc, Elizabeth, ed. "The Global Early Adolescent Study: An Exploration of the Factors That Shape Adolescence." *Journal of Adolescent Health*, vol. 61, no. 4, Oct. 2017, www.jahonline.org/issue/S1054-139X(17)X0014-1.

13. "Girls Attitudes Survey 2017." *Girlguiding*, 2017, https://www.girlguiding.org.uk/globalassets/docs-and-resources/research-and-campaigns/girls-attitudes-survey-2017.pdf.

14. CWR, http://www.cwr.org.uk/store/c-58-for-youth.aspx, Accessed February 22, 2019.

15. Wright, Emma. *Homicide*. Office for National Statistics, 9 Feb. 2017, https://www.ons.gov.uk/peoplepopulationandcommunity/crimeandjustice/compendium/focusonviolentcrimeandsexualoffences/yearendingmarch2016/homicide.

16. Flatley, John. *Homicide in England and Wales: Year Ending March 2017*. Office for National Statistics, 8 Feb. 2018, https://www.ons.gov.uk/peoplepopulationandcommunity/crimeandjustice/articles/homicideinenglandandwales/yearendingmarch2017.

17. Whipp, Lindsay. "Made-Up Men Reflect Changing $50bn Male Grooming Industry." *Financial Times*, 3 Feb. 2017, https://www.ft.com/content/825e520c-c798-11e6-8f29-9445cac8966f.

18. "Use of Anabolic Steroids in the UK." *Freedom of Information*, Office for National Statistics, 12 May 2017, https://www.ons.gov.uk/aboutus/transparencyandgovernance/freedomofinformationfoi/useofanabolicsteroidsintheuk.

19. Jorgenson, Jon. "Who You Are: A Message to All Women." *YouTube*, 18 Jul. 2013, https://www.youtube.com/watch?v=uWi5iXnguTU.

20. Jorgenson, Jon. "Who You Are: A Message to All Men." *YouTube*, 26 Jul. 2013, https://www.youtube.com/watch?v=aTAntk2pDA.

21. "Afternoon Seminar Sex Talk Hosted by Ben & Vikki Rowe." Newday Seminar 2015 Day 5, *New Day Generation*, https://newdaygeneration.org/audio-video/afternoon-seminar-sex-talk-hosted-by-ben-vikki-rowe.

22. Tsui, Anjali, et al. "Child Marriage in America: By the Numbers." *Frontline*, PBS, 6 Jul. 2017, http://apps.frontline.org/child-marriage-by-the-numbers/.

23. Tobias, Suzanne Perez. "Christian Group Seeks 'Early Marriage' Retreat in Wichita." *The Wichita Eagle*, 5 May 2016, https://www.kansas.com/news/local/article75983632.html.

24. Richardson, Hannah. "'Girls Outperform Boys at School' Despite Inequality." *BBC News Education & Family*, BBC, 22 Jan. 2015, https://www.bbc.co.uk/news/education-30933493.

25. Fine, Cordelia. *Delusions of Gender: How Our Minds, Society and Neurosexism Create Difference.* (London: W. W. Norton, 2010), 48.

26. Saini, Angela. *Inferior: How Science Got Women Wrong and the New Research That's Rewriting the Story* (Boston: Beacon Press, 2017), 41.

27. Ibid., 43.

28. Long, Tony. "Jan. 23, 1911: Science Academy Tells Marie Curie, 'Non.'" *Wired*, 23 Jan. 2012, https://www.wired.com/2012/01/jan-23-1911-marie-curie/.

29. Darwin Correspondence Project. "Letter no. 13607." http://www.darwinproject.ac.uk/letter/?docId=letters/DCP-LETT-13607.xml.

30. Gray, John. *Men Are from Mars, Women Are from Venus: A Practical Guide for Improving Communication and Getting What You Want in Your Relationships* (New York: HarperCollins, 1992).

31. Farrel, Billy, and Pam Farrel. "Why Are Men Like Waffles? Why Are Women Like Spaghetti?" *Focus on The Family*, 10 Nov. 2015, https://www.focusonthefamily.com/marriage/gods-design-for-marriage/why-are-men-like-waffles-why-are-women-like-spaghetti/why-are-men-like-waffles-why-are-women-like-spaghetti.

32. Sutton, Jon. "The Battle of the Sex Differences." *The Psychologist*, BPS, 1 Nov. 2010, https://thepsychologist.bps.org.uk/volume-23/edition-11/battle-sex-differences.

33. Morgan, James. "Women 'Better at Multitasking' than Men, Study Finds." *BBC News Science & Environment*, BBC, 24 Oct. 2013, http://www.bbc.co.uk/news/science-environment-24645100.

34. Bian, Lin, et al. "Gender Stereotypes about Intellectual Ability Emerge Early and Influence Children's Interests." *Science Magazine*, Vol. 355, no. 6323, 27 Jan. 2017, pp. 389–391., http://science.sciencemag.org/content/355/6323/389.

35. Turner, Camilla. "Girls Do Better than Boys at School,

Despite Inequality." *The Telegraph*, 22 Jan. 2015, https://www.telegraph.co.uk/education/11364130/Girls-do-better-than-boys-at-school-despite-inequality.html.

36. Saxon, Jamie. "Women Seen as Lacking Natural 'Brilliance' May Explain Underrepresentation in Academia." *Office of Communications*, Princeton University, 15 Jan. 2015, https://www.princeton.edu/news/2015/01/15/women-seen-lacking-natural-brilliance-may-explain-underrepresentation-academia.

37. "Research Suggests Students Are Biased Against Female Lecturers." *The Economist*, 21 Sept. 2017, https://www.economist.com/news/science-and-technology/21729426-how-long-does-prejudice-last-research-suggests-students-are-biased-against.

38. Flaherty, Colleen. "Same Course, Different Ratings." *Inside Higher Ed*, 14 Mar. 2018, https://www.insidehighered.com/news/2018/03/14/study-says-students-rate-men-more-highly-women-even-when-theyre-teaching-identical.

39. Carroll, Sean. "Scientists, Your Gender Bias Is Showing." *Discover Magazine*, 19 Sept. 2012, http://blogs.discovermagazine.com/cosmicvariance/2012/09/19/scientists-your-gender-bias-is-showing/#.W61rtWhKhPY.

40. Piper, John. "Should Women Be Police Officers?" *Desiring God*, 13 Aug. 2015, https://www.desiringgod.org/interviews/should-women-be-police-officers.

41. Piper, John. "Is There a Place for Female Professors at Seminary?" *Desiring God*, 22 Jan. 2018, https://www.desiringgod.org/interviews/is-there-a-place-for-female-professors-at-seminary.

42. Traister, Rebecca. *All the Single Ladies: Unmarried Women*

and the Rise of an Independent Nation (London: Simon & Schuster, 2016).

43. Farley, Harry. "Suffrage: The Church's Rocky Relationship with Rebellion." *Christian Today*, 12 Oct. 2015, https://www.christiantoday.com/article/suffrage-the-churchs-rocky-relationship-with-rebellion/67361.htm.

44. Peterson, Jordan B. *12 Rules for Life: An Antidote to Chaos* (London: Penguin, 2018).

45. VICE News. "Jordan Peterson Is Canada's Most Famous Intellectual | VICE News Full Interview (HBO)." *YouTube*, 7 Feb. 2018, https://www.youtube.com/watch?v=blTglME9rvQ.

46. Penny, Gemma, et al. "Why Are Women More Religious than Men? Testing the Explanatory Power of Personality Theory Among Undergraduate Students in Wales." *Mental Health, Religion & Culture*, 18 (6). pp. 492-502, 2015, http://wrap.warwick.ac.uk/81722.

47. Davis, Shannon N. "Bem Sex-Role Inventory." *Encyclopædia Britannica*, Encyclopædia Britannica inc., 1 May. 2017, https://www.britannica.com/science/Bem-Sex-Role-Inventory.

48. Saini, Angela. *Inferior: How Science Got Women Wrong and the New Research That's Rewriting the Story* (New York: HarperCollins, 2017).

48. "Captivating." Ransomed Heart, 28 Jul. 2014, https://www.ransomedheart.com/events/captivating.

50. Fine, Cordelia. *Delusions of Gender: How Our Minds, Society and Neurosexism Create Difference.* 41.

51. James River Church. "Stronger Men's Conference 2018 | July Promo | James River Church." *YouTube*, 31 Jul. 2017, https://www.youtube.com/watch?v=dijGlaH9jbk.

52. "Baptist Churches Giving Away Guns to Attract New

Members." *Fox News*, 16 Mar. 2014, http://www.foxnews. com/us/2014/03/16/baptist-churches-raffle-off-guns-to-attract-new-members.html.

53. Tellefson, Shea, and Daniel Hopkins. "Broverbs." *Gateway People*, Gateway Church, 22 Mar. 2016, http://gatewaypeople. com/ministries/life/story/2016/03/22/broverbs.

54. "Become a Defender." *Shared Hope International*, 16 Dec. 2012, https://sharedhope.org/join-the-cause/become-a-defender/.

55. Thebarge, Sarah. "Enlisting Men in the Sex Trafficking Fight." *Christianity Today*, 20 Oct. 2011, https://www.christianitytoday.com/thisisourcity/portland/traffickingfight.html.

Chapter 4:

1. O'Connor, Ema. "In Closed-Door UN Meetings, Trump Administration Official Pushed Abstinence for International Women's Health Programs." *Buzzfeed News*, Buzzfeed, 17 Apr. 2018, https://www.buzzfeed. com/emaoconnor/un-meeting-trump-administration-abstinence.

2. McCammon, Sarah. "Abstinence Only Education Is Ineffective and Unethical, Report Argues." NPR, 23 Aug. 2017, https://www.npr.org/sections/health-shots/2017/08/23/545289168/abstinence-education-is-ineffective-and-unethical-report-argues.

3. *Worth the Wait*. Scott & White Wellness & Sexual Health, Temple, TX, https://www-secure.sw.org/resources/docs/sexual-health-wellness/sexual-health-wellness-curriculum-preview.pdf.

4. *No Shame Movement*, 4 Dec. 2018, http://noshame movement.com.

5. Union, Gabrielle. "Tarana Burke." *TIME 100: The Most Influential People of 2018*, TIME Magazine, 19 Apr. 2018, http://time.com/collection/most-influential-people-2018/5217577/tarana-burke/.

6. Klein, Linda Kay. *Pure: Inside the Evangelical Movement That Shamed a Generation of Young Women and How I Broke Free* (London: Touchstone Books, 2018).

7. Feldhahn, Shaunti. *For Men Only* (Colorado Springs: Multnomah Books, 2006).

8. Feldhahn, Shaunti. *For Women Only, Revised and Updated Edition: What You Need to Know About the Inner Lives of Men* (Colorado Springs: Multnomah Books, 2013).

9. Cameron, Deborah. *The Myth of Mars and Venus* (Oxford: Oxford UP, 2008).

10. Eggerich, Emerson. *Love and Respect* (Nashville: Thomas Nelson, 2004).

11. Chapman, Gary. *The 5 Love Languages for Men* (Chicago: Moody Press, 2015).

12. Jaynes, Sharon. *Becoming the Woman of His Dreams: Seven Qualities Every Man Longs For.* Harvest House, 2005

13. Prinz, Jesse J. *Beyond Human Nature: How Culture and Experience Shape the Human Mind* (London: Penguin Books, 2014), 342.

14. Tracy, Kate. "Mars Hill Defends How Mark Driscoll's 'Real Marriage' Became a Bestseller." *Christianity Today*, 7 Mar. 2014, https://www.christianitytoday.com/news/2014/march/did-mark-driscoll-real-marriage-earn-nyt-bestseller-status-.html.

15. Bueno, Antoinette. "Josh Duggar Addresses Ashley Madison Accounts: I'm Addicted to Porn, Have Been Unfaithful to My Wife." ET Online. August 20, 2015

https://www.etonline.com/news/170350_josh_duggar_
addresses_ashley_madison_accounts_and_says_he_
addicted_to_porn

16. Ohlheiser, Abby. "Christian vlogger Sam Rader on his
Ashley Madison account: My wife – and God – have
forgiven me" The Washington Post. August 22, 2015
https://www.washingtonpost.com/news/acts-of-faith/
wp/2015/08/22/christian-vlogger-sam-rader-says-his-
wife-and-god-have-forgiven-him-about-his-ashley-
madison-account/

17. "Religious Experience and Journal of Mrs. Jarena Lee."
Resource Bank: Africans In America, PBS, http://www.pbs.
org/wgbh/aia/part3/3h1638.html.

18. Dudzinska, Paulina Natalia. *The Consequences of Eating
with Men: Hawaiian Women and the Challenges of
Cultural Transformation*. UiO DUO Research Archive,
2007, http://urn.nb.no/URN:NBN:no-17690.

19. "Marriage: Property and Children." *Living Heritage*, UK
Parliament, 2 Jul. 2009, https://www.parliament.uk/
about/living-heritage/transformingsociety/private-lives/
relationships/overview/propertychildren/.

20. The Dohnavur Fellowship, 10 Mar. 2018, http://dohna
vurfellowship.org.

21. Crosby, Kevin. "How Women Finally Got the Right to
Jury Service." *Blogs*, The British Academy, 8 Feb. 2018,
https://www.britac.ac.uk/blog/how-women-finally-got-
right-jury-service.

Chapter 5:

1. Fiegerman, Seth. "Facebook is Closing in on 2 Billion
Users." *CNN Business*, CNN, 1 Feb. 2017, http://money.cnn.

com/2017/02/01/technology/facebook-earnings/index.html.

2. Solon, Olivia. "Ex-Facebook President Sean Parker: Site Made to Exploit Human 'Vulnerability.'" *The Guardian*, 9 Nov. 2017, https://www.theguardian.com/technology/2017/nov/09/facebook-sean-parker-vulnerability-brain-psychology.

3. Wong, Julia Carrie. "Former Facebook Executive: Social Media Is Ripping Society Apart." *The Guardian*, 12 Dec. 2017, https://www.theguardian.com/technology/2017/dec/11/facebook-former-executive-ripping-society-apart.

4. Smith, Aaron, and Monica Anderson. "Social Media Use in 2018." *Pew Research Center*, 1 Mar. 2018, http://www.pewinternet.org/2018/03/01/social-media-use-in-2018/.

5. Matsakis, Louise. "Facebook Dating Looks a Whole Lot Like Hinge." *Wired*, 3 May 2018, https://www.wired.com/story/facebook-dating-hinge-app/.

6. "From Breadcrumbing to Stashing: How Well Do You Know Your Dating Language?" *BBC Radio 4*, BBC, 5 Aug. 2018, https://www.bbc.co.uk/programmes/articles/tZLnqfKxj0DKnGWGpvWqSc/from-breadcrumbing-to-stashing-how-well-do-you-know-your-dating-language.

7. Prescott, Cecil. *Internet Users in the UK: 2017*. Office of National Statistics, 19 May 2017, https://www.ons.gov.uk/businessindustryandtrade/itandinternetindustry/bulletins/internetusers/2017.

8. Anderson, Monica, et al. "11% of Americans Don't Use the Internet. Who Are They?" *Pew Research Center*, 5 Mar. 2018, http://www.pewresearch.org/fact-tank/2018/03/05/some-americans-dont-use-the-internet-who-are-they/.

Chapter 6:

1. Vallotton, Kris, and Jason Vallotton. *Moral Revolution:*

The Naked Truth About Sexual Purity (Bloomington, MN: Chosen Books, 2012).

2. Fileta, Debra. "Premarital Sex: 3 Simple Reasons You Should Wait for Sex." *True Love Dates*, 4 Jun. 2018, http://truelovedates.com/talkaboutsex/.

3. "Medieval Sex and Sexuality." Interview with Dr Juanita Feros Ruys, *History Channel Australia*, 20 Aug. 2013, https://www.historychannel.com.au/articles/medieval-sex-and-sexuality/.

4. Gilbert, Elizabeth. *Committed: A Love Story* (Bloomsbury, 2011) 262

5. "Medieval Sex and Sexuality." Interview with Dr Juanita Feros Ruys, *History Channel Australia*, 20 Aug. 2013, https://www.historychannel.com.au/articles/medieval-sex-and-sexuality/.

6. "Pope Leo XII." *Wikipedia*, Wikimedia Group, 23 Jan. 2019, https://en.wikipedia.org/wiki/Pope_Leo_XII.

7. Lister, Kate. "The Bishop's Profitable Sex Workers." *The Rules of Sex*, The Wellcome Collection, 5 Jun. 2018, https://wellcomecollection.org/articles/WxEniCQAACQAvmUE.

8. Levine, Joshua. *The Secret History of the Blitz* (London: Simon & Schuster, 2015).

9. Ibid.

10. Turner, Natasha. "10 Things That American Women Could Not Do Before the 1970s." *Ms. Magazine*, 28 May 2013, http://msmagazine.com/blog/2013/05/28/10-things-that-american-women-could-not-do-before-the-1970s/.

11. Molloy, Mark, et al. "1918 vs 2018: 13 Things Women Couldn't Do 100 Years Ago." *The Telegraph*, 6 Feb. 2018, https://www.telegraph.co.uk/women/life/1918-vs-2018-13-things-women-couldnt-do-100-years-ago/.

12. Buck, Stephanie. "In 1970s Ireland, Women Weren't Allowed to Order Pints of Beer. But This One Did." *Timeline*, 17 May 2015, https://timeline.com/nell-mccafferty-ireland-b9b972ca2696.

13. *The Statutory Maternity Pay (General) Regulations 1986.* UK Government Legislation, http://www.legislation.gov.uk/uksi/1986/1960/contents/made.

14. *Regina Respondent and R. Appellant.* The Incorporated Council of Law Reporting for England & Wales, http://www.bailii.org/uk/cases/UKHL/1991/12.html.

15. Turner, Natasha. "10 Things That American Women Could Not Do Before the 1970s." *Ms. Magazine*, 28 May 2013, http://msmagazine.com/blog/2013/05/28/10-things-that-american-women-could-not-do-before-the-1970s/.

16. "Historical Report: Diversity of Sexual Orientation." *Kinsey Institute*, Indiana University, https://kinseyinstitute.org/research/publications/historical-report-diversity-of-sexual-orientation.php.

17. "Masters & Johnson Collection." *Kinsey Institute*, Indiana University, https://kinseyinstitute.org/collections/archival/masters-and-johnson.php.

18. Moeller, Robert L. "The Sex Life of America's Christians." *Christianity Today*, 1 Jul. 1995, https://www.christianitytoday.com/pastors/1995/summer/5l3030.html.

19. Ibid.

20. *Peggy Orenstein*, 27 Feb. 2018, https://www.peggyorenstein.com/.

21. Wallis, Lucy. "Is 25 the New Cut-Off Point for Adulthood?" *BBC News Magazine*, BBC, 23 Sept. 2013, https://www.bbc.co.uk/news/magazine-24173194.

22. Lusko, Levi. "Introduction." *Swipe Right: Life, Death, Sex, and Romance* (Nashville TN: Thomas Nelson, 2017) xxi.

23. QIdeas.org. "Donna Freitas: Hookup Culture." *YouTube*, 8 Feb. 2015, https://www.youtube.com/watch?v=02kenYkx3F4.

24. Banks, Adelle M. "With High Premarital Sex and Abortions Rates, Evangelicals Say It's Time to Talk About Sex." *Huffington Post*, 34 Apr. 2012, https://www.huffingtonpost.com/2012/04/23/evangelicals-sex-frank-talk_n_1443062.html.

25. Burns, Janet. "Millennials Are Having Less Sex Than Other Gens, But Experts Say It's (Probably) Fine." *Forbes*, 16 Aug. 2016, https://www.forbes.com/sites/janetwburns/2016/08/16/millennials-are-having-less-sex-than-other-gens-but-experts-say-its-probably-fine/#44b0da23d958.

26. Armstrong, Elizabeth A., et al. "Is Hooking Up Bad for Young Women?" *Contexts*, vol. 9, no. 3, 1 Aug. 2010, pp. 22–27., doi:https://doi.org/10.1525/ctx.2010.9.3.22.

27. Cornell University. "Donna Freitas: Sex and the Soul." *YouTube*, 5 Aug. 2009, https://www.youtube.com/watch?v=J5xDPp0oV5I.

28. "What Americans Believe About Sex." *Barna*, 14 Jan. 2016, http://barna.org/research/what-americans-believe-about-sex/#.V5DKGFf6fNW.

29. McMinn, Lisa Graham. *Sexuality and Holy Longing: Embracing Intimacy in a Broken World* (San Francisco: Jossey-Bass, 2004), 18.

30. "What Americans Believe About Sex." *Barna*, 14 Jan. 2016, http://barna.org/research/what-americans-believe-about-sex/#.V5DKGFf6fNW.

31. "What Everyone Should Know About the Female Orgasm and Hooking Up (INFOGRAPHIC)." *Huffington Post*, 6 Dec. 2017, https://www.huffingtonpost.com/2014/03/14/female-orgasm-_n_4966621.html.

32. Yancey, Philip. *Designer Sex* (Downers Grove, IL: InterVarsity Press, 2005).

33. Nagoski, Emily. *Come as You Are: The Surprising New Science that Will Transform Your Sex Life* (London: Simon & Schuster, 2015).

34. Quoted in Yancey, Philip. *Designer Sex*, 2.

35. Miley, Jessica. "Sex Robot Samantha Gets an Update to Say 'No' If She Feels Disrespected or Bored." *Interesting Engineering*, 28 Jun. 2018, https://interestingengineering.com/sex-robot-samantha-gets-an-update-to-say-no-if-she-feels-disrespected-or-bored.

36. "Houston Mayor Pushes Back Against Proposed 'Robot Brothel.'" *The Guardian*, 27 Sept. 2018, https://www.theguardian.com/us-news/2018/sep/27/houston-robot-brothel-kinky-s-dolls-opposition.

37. Vincent, James. "Pretending to Give a Robot Citizenship Helps No One." *The Verge*, 30 Oct. 2017, https://www.theverge.com/2017/10/30/16552006/robot-rights-citizenship-saudi-arabia-sophia.

38. France-Presse, Agence. "Saudi Arabia: Women's Rights Activists Arrested Before Lifting of Driving Ban." *The Guardian*, 18 May 2018, https://www.theguardian.com/world/2018/may/19/saudi-arabia-womens-rights-activists-arrested-before-lifting-of-driving-ban.

39. "Experts Predict When Artificial Intelligence Will Exceed Human Performance." *Technology Review*, 31 May 2017, https://www.technologyreview.com/s/607970/experts-

predict-when-artificial-intelligence-will-exceed-human-performance/.

Chapter 7:

1. "America's Changing Religious Landscape." *Pew Research Center*, 12 May 2015, http://www.pewforum.org/2015/05/12/americas-changing-religious-landscape/.

2. Cox, Kiana, and Jeff Diamant. "Black men are less religious than black women, but more religious than white women and men." *Pew Research Center*, 26 Sept. 2018, http://www.pewresearch.org/fact-tank/2018/09/26/black-men-are-less-religious-than-black-women-but-more-religious-than-white-women-and-men/.

3. "The Gender Gap in Religion Around the World." *Pew Research Center*, 22 Mar. 2016, http://www.pewforum.org/2016/03/22/the-gender-gap-in-religion-around-the-world/.

4. Murphy, Caryle. "Q&A: Why are women generally more religious than men?" Interview with David Voas. *Pew Research Center*, 23 Mar. 2016, http://www.pewresearch.org/fact-tank/2016/03/23/qa-why-are-women-generally-more-religious-than-men/.

5. Murphy, Caryle. "Q&A: Why Are Women Generally More Religious Than Men?" Interview with David Voas. *Pew Research Center*, 23 Mar. 2016, http://www.pewresearch.org/fact-tank/2016/03/23/qa-why-are-women-generally-more-religious-than-men/.

6. McKay, Brett. "Podcast #253: Why Men Hate Going to Church." Interview with David Murrow. *Art of Manliness*, 17 Nov. 2016, https://www.artofmanliness.com/articles/podcast-253-men-hate-going-church/.

7. Birger, Jon. "Dateonomics." *TIME Magazine*, 24 Aug. 2015, http://time.com/dateonomics/.

8. "Why Women Are More Religious Than Men." The Economist Explains, *The Economist*, 13 Apr. 2016, https://www.economist.com/the-economist-explains/2016/04/13/why-women-are-more-religious-than-men.

9. Shellnut, Kate. "Willow Creek Investigation: Allegations Against Bill Hybels Are Credible" Christianity Today. February 20th 2019. https://www.christianitytoday.com/news/2019/february/willow-creek-bill-hybels-investigation-iag-report.html

10. Engelkemier, Joe. "A Church that Draws Thousands." *Ministry*, May 1991, https://www.ministrymagazine.org/archive/1991/05/a-church-that-draws-thousands.

11. Warren, Rick. *The Purpose Driven Church* (Grand Rapids MI: Zondervan, 1995), 170.

12. "Inside Sarah's Circle: 5. Meet David Murrow." *Texans For Sarah Palin*, 10 Jun. 2009, http://texansforsarahpalin.blogspot.com/2009/06/who-is-david-murrow.html.

13. "About David Murrow." *Church for Men*, http://www.patheos.com/blogs/churchformen/author/dmurrow/.

14. *Church for Men*, 24 Jan. 2019, http://churchformen.com/.

15. Beck, Richard. "Thoughts on Mark Driscoll … While I'm Knitting." *Experimental Theology*, 14 Feb. 2009, http://experimentaltheology.blogspot.com/2009/02/thoughts-on-mark-driscoll-while-im.html.

16. Murashko, Alex. "John Piper: God Gave Christianity a 'Masculine Feel.'" *The Christian Post*, 1 Feb. 2012, https://www.christianpost.com/news/john-piper-god-gave-christianity-a-masculine-feel-68385/.

17. Bruenig, Elizabeth. "The Failure of Macho Christianity." *The New Republic*, 24 Feb. 2015, https://newrepublic.com/article/121138/mark-driscoll-and-macho-christianity.

18. Grove, Sarah. "He Makes It Manly to Worship Jesus." *News24*, 6 Mar. 2010, https://www.news24.com/Archives/Witness/He-makes-it-manly-to-worship-Jesus-20150430.

19. McKay, Brett. "Podcast #253: Why Men Hate Going to Church." Interview with David Murrow. *Art of Manliness*, 17 Nov. 2016, https://www.artofmanliness.com/articles/podcast-253-men-hate-going-church/.

Chapter 8:

1. https://www.singlefriendlychurch.com/research/research

2. Gledhill, Ruth. "The Choice for Many Christian Women: Singleness or Marry a Non-Christian." *Christian Today*, 5 Feb. 2015, https://www.christiantoday.com/article/the-choice-for-many-christian-women-singleness-or-marry-a-non-christian/47496.htm.

3. Gledhill, Ruth. "The Choice for Many Christian Women: Singleness or Marry a Non-Christian." *Christian Today*, 5 Feb. 2015, https://www.christiantoday.com/article/the-choice-for-many-christian-women-singleness-or-marry-a-non-christian/47496.htm.

4. Sherwood, Harriet. "More Than Half UK Population Has No Religion, Finds Survey." *The Guardian*, 4 Sept. 2017, https://www.theguardian.com/world/2017/sep/04/half-uk-population-has-no-religion-british-social-attitudes-survey.

5. Ashworth, Jacinta, et al. "Churchgoing in the UK." *Tearfund*, Christian Vision for Men, April 2007, https://cvm.org.uk/downloads/03_04_07_tearfundchurch.pdf

6. "2015 Research." *Talking Jesus*, 2015, https://talkingjesus. org/2015-research/.

Chapter 9:

1. "Research co-funded by Single Christians confirms that the church is not attracting enough single men into its pews." *Single Friendly Church,* 2014, https://www. singlefriendlychurch.com/research/yougov.
2. "The Trends Redefining Romance Today." *Barna*, 9 Feb. 2017, https://www.barna.com/research/trends-redefining-romance-today/.
3. "Women shoulder the responsibility of 'unpaid work." Office for National Statistics, 10 Nov. 2016, https://www.ons.gov .uk/employmentandlabourmarket/peopleinwork/ earningsandworkinghours/articles/womenshoulderthe responsibilityofunpaidwork/2016-11-10.
4. Frymorgen, Tomasz. "Women really are stronger than men, according to study." *BBC Three*, BBC, 10 Jan. 2018, https://www.bbc.co.uk/bbcthree/article/7b6484fb-3b00-46d6-a557-ac2a0b6f8591.
5. "The Willful Submission of a Christian Wife." *Sermons,* Grace to You, 19 Feb. 2012, https://www.gty.org/library/sermons-library/80-382/the-willful-submission-of-a-christian-wife.
6. "Bridebook Wedding Report 2018." *Bridebook*, 19 Mar. 2018, https://bridebook.co.uk/article/bridebook-wedding-report-2018.
7. "Average Wedding Cost Rises." Telegraph Financial Solutions, *The Telegraph*, 28 Nov. 2017, https:// www.telegraph.co.uk/financial-services/currency-exchange/international-money-transfers/average-cost-wedding/.

8. Jacobs, Sarah. "The Average Wedding Cost in America Is Over $30,000 — but Here's Where Couples Spend Way More Than That." *Business Insider*, 2 Apr. 2018, https://www.businessinsider.com/average-wedding-cost-in-america-most-expensive-2018-3?r=UK.

9. Frost, Katie. "The Average Cost of a UK Wedding Has Risen Again." *Harper's Bazaar*, 19 Mar. 2018, https://www.harpersbazaar.com/uk/bazaar-brides/a19478376/average-cost-of-uk-wedding/.

10. Doughty, Steve. "Millennials Still Value Marriage: Three Quarters of 18 to 35-Year-Olds Still Dream of Getting Wed." *The Daily Mail*, 12 Apr. 2018, https://www.dailymail.co.uk/news/article-5610323/Millennials-value-marriage-Three-quarters-18-35-year-olds-dream-getting-wed.html.

11. Bennett, Jessica. "The Beta Marriage: How Millennials Approach 'I Do.'" *TIME Magazine*, 25 Jul. 2014, http://time.com/3024606/millennials-marriage-sex-relationships-hook-ups/.

12. Khazan, Olga. "The Divorce-Proof Marriage." *The Atlantic*, 14 Oct. 2014, https://www.theatlantic.com/health/archive/2014/10/the-divorce-proof-marriage/381401/.

13. Hurley, Dan. "Divorce Rate: It's Not as High as You Think." *The New York Times*, 19 Apr. 2005, https://www.nytimes.com/2005/04/19/health/divorce-rate-its-not-as-high-as-you-think.html.

14. "The Trends Redefining Romance Today." *Barna*, 9 Feb. 2017, https://www.barna.com/research/trends-redefining-romance-today/.

15. "Cohabiting Couples Warned of 'Common Law Marriage'

Myths." *BBC News UK*, BBC, 27 Nov. 2017, https://www.bbc.com/news/uk-42134722.

16. Chan, Francis, and Lisa Chan. *You and Me Forever: Marriage in Light of Eternity* (San Francisco: Claire Love Publishing, 2014).

17. Thomas, Gary L. *Sacred Marriage: What If God Designed Marriage to Make Us Holy More Than to Make Us Happy?* (Grand Rapids MI: Zondervan, 2015).

18. Keller, Timothy, and Kathy Keller. *The Meaning of Marriage: Facing the Complexities of Commitment with the Wisdom of God* (London: Hodder & Stoughton, 2011).

19. Perel, Esther. "The Secret to Desire in a Long-Term Relationship." *TED*, February 2013, https://www.ted.com/talks/esther_perel_the_secret_to_desire_in_a_long_term_relationship.

Chapter 10:

1. "Tattoo Statistics – How Many People Have Tattoos?" *History of Tattoos*, 15 Sept. 2015, http://www.historyoftattoos.net/tattoo-facts/tattoo-statistics/.

2   Rajanala, Susruthi, et al. "Selfies – Living in the Era of Filtered Photographs." *JAMA Network*, Nov/Dec 2018, https://jamanetwork.com/journals/jamafacialplasticsurgery/article-abstract/2688763.

3. Davies, Anna. "People Are Getting Surgery to Look Like Their Snapchat Selfies." *BBC Three*, BBC, 19 Apr. 2018, https://www.bbc.co.uk/bbcthree/article/9ca4f7c6-d2c3-4e25-862c-03aed9ec1082.

4. "Protecting Children from Female Genital Mutilation (FGM)." *NSPCC,* 31 Aug. 2018, https://learning.nspcc.org.uk/child-abuse-and-neglect/fgm/.

5. "'Unprotected Texts': The Bible on Sex And Marriage." *Fresh Air*, NPR, 10 Mar. 2011, https://www.npr.org/2011/03/10/133245874/unprotected-texts-the-bible-on-sex-and-marriage?t=1538089040302.

6. Ibid.

7. Hills, Rachel. *The Sex Myth* (London: Simon & Schuster, 2015), 2.

8. O'Haver, Hanson. "What Swearing Off Sex Does to Your Brain." Broadly. February 13th 2017. https://broadly.vice.com/en_us/article/j5epex/what-abstinence-does-to-your-brain

9. Bowerman, Mary. "Survey: Sleeping Together Before a First Date Is A-OK, but Cracked Phones Are a Put Off." *USA Today*, 6 Feb. 2017, https://www.usatoday.com/story/news/nation-now/2017/02/06/sex-before-first-date-intimacy-online-app-dating-sites-match-singles-america-dating-taboos/97341904/.

10. Ro, Christine. "What Sex Guides Say About Our Changing Ideas on Sex." *Broadly*, 13 Feb. 2017, https://broadly.vice.com/en_us/article/d3gpza/alternative-inclusive-sex-guides.

11. Ibid.

12. Marston, C., and R. Lewis. "Anal Heterosex Among Young People and Implications for Health Promotion: A Qualitative Study in the UK." *BMJ Open*, 2014, doi: 10.1136/bmjopen-2014-004996.

13. McCleneghan, Bromleigh. *Good Christian Sex: Why Chastity Isn't the Only Option and Other Things the Bible Says About Sex* (New York: HarperOne, 2016).

14. TEDx Talks. "The Great Porn Experiment | Gary Wilson | TEDxGlasgow." *YouTube*, 16 May 2012, https://www.youtube.com/watch?v=wSF82AwSDiU.

15. "The Christian Porn Conversation." *Sophia Network*, 18 Aug. 2015, http://blog.sophianetwork.org.uk/2015/08/the-christian-porn-conversation.html.

16. 'Teen' Why Has This Porn Category Topped The Charts For 6+ Years?" *Fight The New Drug*, 3 Jan. 2019, https://fightthenewdrug.org/this-years-most-popular-genre-of-porn-is-pretty-messed-up/.

17. Illing, Sean. "Proof that Americans Are Lying About Their Sexual Desires." *Vox*, 30 Sept. 2018, https://www.vox.com/conversations/2017/6/27/15873072/google-porn-addiction-america-everybody-lies.

18. Ley, David J. "Science Stopped Believing in Porn Addiction, You Should Too." *Psychology Today*, 21 Aug. 2018, https://www.psychologytoday.com/us/blog/women-who-stray/201808/science-stopped-believing-in-porn-addiction-you-should-too.

19. Van Der Werff, Todd. "Why So Many Christians Blame Pornography for Other Sins Like Adultery." *Vox*, 26 Aug. 2015, https://www.vox.com/2015/8/26/9211127/christians-pornography-hate-why.

20. EbonBoy. "Pornhub 2017 year in review." *Imgur*, 11 Jan. 2018, https://imgur.com/gallery/0m4MT.

21. Park, Brian Y et al. "Is Internet Pornography Causing Sexual Dysfunctions? A Review with Clinical Reports." *Behavioural Sciences (Basel, Switzerland)* vol. 6,3 17. 5 Aug. 2016, doi:10.3390/bs6030017.

22. "The Christian Porn Conversation." *Sophia Network*, 18 Aug. 2015, http://blog.sophianetwork.org.uk/2015/08/the-christian-porn-conversation.html.

23. @BethMooreLPM. "Make It a Safer World to Report It and You'll Make a Safer World." *Twitter*, 22 Sept. 2018,

https://twitter.com/BethMooreLPM/status/10434
73012987695104.

24. Nagoski, Emily. *Come as You Are: The Surprising New Science that Will Transform Your Sex Life* (London: Simon & Schuster, 2015).

25. "Mental health statistics: UK and Worldwide." Mental Health Foundation, 5 Oct. 2016, https://www. mentalhealth.org.uk/statistics/mental-health-statistics-uk-and-worldwide.

26. Bronner, Ethan. "Adultery, an Ancient Crime Still on Many Books." *The New York Times*, 14 Nov. 2012, https:// www.nytimes.com/2012/11/15/us/adultery-an-ancient-crime-still-on-many-books.html?_r=0.

27. "Attachment Style May Predict Infidelity." *GoodTherapy*, 19 Dec. 2011, https://www.goodtherapy.org/blog/attachment-style-predicts-infidelity-1219113/

Chapter 11:

1. Constable, John. "Crossbones: History." http://crossbones. org.uk/history/

2. "Christmas Cake." *Urban Dictionary*, 13 Jun. 2013, https://www.urbandictionary.com/define.php?term= Christmas%20Cake.

3. Lister, Kate. "The Bishop's Profitable Sex Workers." *The Rules of Sex*, The Wellcome Collection. https://well comecollection.org/articles/WxEniCQAACQAvmUE.

4. Bolick, Kate. "Linguistics Shows that Being a Single Guy Has Gotten Better and Being a Single Woman Has Gotten Worse." *Business Insider*, 27 Apr. 2015, http:// uk.businessinsider.com/words-for-single-men-vs-single-women-2015-4?r=US&IR=T.

5. Coontz, Stephanie. *Marriage, A History*. 230.

6. "Research Co-Funded by Single Christians Confirms that the Church Is Not Attracting Enough Single Men into Its Pews." *Single Friendly Church*, 2014, https://www.singlefriendlychurch.com/research/yougov.

7. "Who Is Most Readily Identified as Single." *Single Friendly Church*, https://www.singlefriendlychurch.com/research/who-is-most-readily-identified-as-single.

8. "About Bella DePaulo." *Bella DePaulo*, 29 Sept. 2015, http://www.belladepaulo.com/about-bella-depaulo/.

9. DePaulo, Bella. "Debunking Every Myth about Marriage, All in One Place." *Psychology Today*, 14 Jan. 2014, https://www.psychologytoday.com/gb/blog/living-single/201401/debunking-every-myth-about-marriage-all-in-one-place.

10. Bolick, Kate. "All the Single Ladies." *The Atlantic*, November 2011, https://www.theatlantic.com/magazine/archive/2011/11/all-the-single-ladies/308654/.

11. Coontz, Stephanie. "For a Better Marriage, Act Like a Single Person." *The New York Times,* 10 Feb. 2018, https://www.nytimes.com/2018/02/10/opinion/sunday/for-a-better-marriage-act-like-a-single-person.html.

12. Klinenberg, Eric. *Going Solo: The Extraordinary Rise and Surprising Appeal of Living Alone*. (New York: Penguin, 2013), 5.

13. Knipe, Emily. *Families and Households: 2017*. Office for National Statistics, 8 Nov. 2017, https://www.ons.gov.uk/peoplepopulationandcommunity/births deathsandmarriages/families/bulletins/familiesand households/2017.

14. Klinenberg, Eric. *Going Solo: The Extraordinary Rise and Surprising Appeal of Living Alone*. 10.

15. Traister, Rebecca. *All the Single Ladies: Unmarried Women*

and the Rise of an Independent Nation (London: Simon & Schuster, 2016), 14.

16. Abbott, Elizabeth. A History Of Marriage: From Same Sex Unions to Private Vows and Common Law, the Surprising Diversity of a Tradition (Seven Stories Press, 2011)

17. McCulley, Carolyn. *Did I Kiss Marriage Goodbye? Trusting God with a Hope Deferred* (Wheaton, IL: Crossway, 2004) Foreword by Joshua Harris, Pp.11

18. *Saltwater and Honey*, 3 Jan. 2019, http://saltwaterandhoney. org/.

19. Wharton, Kate. "Beloved Ceremony pt 2." *Single Minded: The Life of a Single Female Vicar in Liverpool*, 23 Nov. 2017, http://katewharton.blogspot.com/2017/11/beloved-ceremony-pt-2.html.

20. Fry, Richard. "For First Time in Modern Era, Living with Parents Edges Out Other Living Arrangements for 18- to 34-Year-Olds." *Pew Research Center*, 24 May 2016, http:// www.pewsocialtrends.org/2016/05/24/for-first-time-in-modern-era-living-with-parents-edges-out-other-living-arrangements-for-18-to-34-year-olds/.

21. Broadway, Anna. *Sexless in the City: A Memoir of Reluctant Chastity* (Colorado Springs: WaterBrook, 2008).

22. *Rule of Life. The Community of St Anselm*, July 2016, http:// stanselm.org.uk/rule-of-life/

23. "Begijnhof (Beguinage)." *Amsterdam Sights*, 4 Aug. 2011, http://www.amsterdamsights.com/attractions/begijnhof. html.

24. DePaulo, Bella. "Is It True that Cities Are for Singles, and Suburbs and Rural Areas for Married Couples?" *Psych Central*, 23 Jul. 2018, https://blogs.psychcentral. com/single-at-heart/2018/07/is-it-true-that-cities-are-

for-singles-and-suburbs-and-rural-areas-for-married-couples/.

25. British Medical Journal. "Wide Circle of Friends Key to Mid-Life Wellbeing for Both Sexes." *Science Daily*, 22 Aug. 2012, www.sciencedaily.com/releases/2012/08/120822222649.htm.

26. Coontz, Stephanie. "For a Better Marriage, Act Like a Single Person." *The New York Times*.

27. "The Trouble with Averages: The Impact of Major Life Events and Acute Stress May Not Be What You Think." Council on Contemporary Families, 29 May 2013, https://contemporaryfamilies.org/trouble-with-averages-briefing/.

28. Davis, Nicola. "Is It True that Eating Alone Is Bad for You?" *The Guardian*, 6 Jul. 2018, https://www.theguardian.com/science/2018/jul/06/is-it-true-that-eating-alone-is-bad-for-you.

29. "Threat to Health." *Campaign to End Loneliness*, 18 Dec. 2018, https://www.campaigntoendloneliness.org/threat-to-health/.

30. Wilkinson, Richard, and Kate Pickett. *The Inner Level: How More Equal Societies Reduce Stress, Restore Sanity and Improve Everyone's Well-Being.* (New York: Penguin, 2018).

31. Spencer, Nick and Katherine Ajibade. "'They Are Dying of Hopelessness': How Inequality Affects Our Mental Health." Interview with Richard Wilkinson and Kate Pickett. *Theos Think Tank*, 13 Jun. 2018, https://www.theosthinktank.co.uk/comment/2018/06/13/they-are-dying-of-hopelessness-how-inequality-affects-our-mental-health.

32. "Personal Brand." *Girlguiding*, 22 Jul. 2018, https://www.girlguiding.org.uk/what-we-do/our-badges-and-activities/badge-finder/personal-brand/.

33. "Religion in Everyday Life." *Pew Research Center*, 12 Apr. 2016, http://www.pewforum.org/2016/04/12/religion-in-everyday-life/.

34. "Religion and Belief: Some Surveys and Statistics." *Humanists UK*, 30 Oct. 2014, https://humanism.org.uk/campaigns/religion-and-belief-some-surveys-and-statistics/.

Chapter 12:

1. "5 Reasons Millennials Stay Connected to Church." *Barna*, 17 Sept. 2013, https://www.barna.com/research/5-reasons-millennials-stay-connected-to-church/.

2. "When Americans Become Christians." *National Association of Evangelicals*, Spring 2015, https://www.nae.net/when-americans-become-christians/.

3. "Founding Fathers: Father's Day Pack." *Christian Vision for Men*, 2017, https://www.cvm.org.uk/downloads/founding-fathers-fathers-day-pack-2017.pdf.

4. "Meet Those Who 'Love Jesus but Not the Church.'" *Barna*, 30 Mar. 2017, https://www.barna.com/research/meet-love-jesus-not-church/.

5. Birger, John. *Date-onomics: How Dating Became a Lopsided Numbers Game*. (New York: Workman Publishing Company, 2015).

6. Cloud, Henry, and Townsend, John, https://www.cloudtownsend.com. Accessed February 26, 2019. Emotionally Healthy Spirituality, https://www.emotionallyhealthy.org/, (Accessed February 26, 2019).

7. Shannon, Nakilah S. *7 Days to Pray the Single Away: Breaking the Chains of Singleness One Day at a Time.* (Indianapolis, IN: Judah House Press, 2013).

Relatable Resources:

1. Hailes, Sam. "Jackie Pullinger: 'We're Going to Feel Stupid for Eternity if We Waste This Life.'" Interview with Jackie Pullinger. *Premier Christianity*, 15 Jan. 2019, https://www.premierchristianity.com/Past-Issues/2019/January-2019/Jackie-Pullinger-We-re-going-to-feel-stupid-for-eternity-if-we-waste-this-life.